Leaving the Grove

Also published by The Graduate School Press of Syracuse University

On the Borders of the Academy
Challenges and Strategies for First-Generation Graduate Students and Faculty

The Mentoring Continuum
From Graduate School through Tenure

Collaborative Futures
Critical Reflections on Publicly Active Graduate Education

Building Community
Stories and Strategies for Future Learning Community Faculty and Professionals

Pedagogy, not Policing
Positive Approaches to Academic Integrity at the University

Interrupting Heteronormativity
Lesbian, Gay, Bisexual and Transgender Pedagogy and Responsible Teaching at Syracuse University

Building Pedagogical Curb Cuts
Incorporating Disability in the University Classroom and Curriculum

Using Writing to Teach

LEAVING THE GROVE

A Quit Lit Reader

Edited by
Christopher Flanagan and Glenn Wright

Syracuse University
The Graduate School Press

Contributions to this volume originally appeared in *The Chronicle of Higher Education*, *The Guardian*, *Inside Higher Ed*, *Al Jazeera*, the *London Review of Books*, and *Times Higher Education*, as well as in blogs and other online venues. Reused with permission.

Library of Congress Cataloging-in-Publication Data

Names: Flanagan, Christopher J., 1987- editor. | Wright, Glenn, 1968- editor.
Title: Leaving the grove : a Quit Lit reader / edited by Christopher J. Flanagan, Glenn D. Wright.
Description: Syracuse : The Graduate School Press of Syracuse University, [2022] | Includes bibliographical references and index. | Summary: "Leaving the Grove is the first book-length work devoted to the phenomenon of "quit lit"-farewells to academia by those at all levels (graduate student through tenured professor) who have elected to resign their posts or stop looking for one. Part I anthologizes classics of the genre along with some original contributions, while Part II comprises secondary essays exploring quit lit from various critical and historical perspectives. The volume as a whole uses quit lit as a lens through which to examine the academic labor system, precarity, graduate education, and the future of the professoriate. Among the contributors are Rebecca Schuman, Karen Kelsky, Alexandra Lord, Kelly J. Baker, Melissa Dalgleish, Erin Bartram, Katie Rose Guest Pryal, L. Maren Wood, and Leonard Cassuto"-- Provided by publisher.
Identifiers: LCCN 2021050894 | ISBN 9780977784790 (Paperback)
Subjects: LCSH: Career changes. | Underemployment. | College teachers.
Classification: LCC HF5384 .L43 2022 | DDC 331.702--dc23/eng/20211208
LC record available at https://lccn.loc.gov/2021050894

For more information about this publication, please contact:

The Graduate School Press
304 Lyman Hall
Syracuse University
Syracuse, NY 13244

https://graduateschool.syr.edu/student-resources/graduate-school-press

Manufactured in the United States of America

CONTENTS

EDITORIAL NOTE

Most of the pieces in this anthology initially saw light of day online, as blog posts or contributions to web-based publications. Converting these to print format has proved more art than science. Typos and obvious inaccuracies have been silently corrected. Text has been lightly edited to avoid ambiguity and maintain consistent usage throughout the volume. Bracketed emendations are used to clarify chronology (for instance, "last month" = September 2018) and, rarely, to expand abbreviations or for other purposes.

Hyperlinks in the originals have been converted to source notes where appropriate, and to substantive notes if warranted. Bad links have been updated where possible, otherwise deleted from notes and references. An exception applies for the many pieces published in *Chronicle Vitae* and the Chronicle Community web space. *The Chronicle of Higher Education* brought these to an end in July 2021, as this volume was in production. Since removing URLs for these sites would have necessitated resetting type for the entire volume, these now-defunct references have been retained.

ACKNOWLEDGMENTS

The editors would like to extend our deepest appreciation to all of the contributing authors who shared their stories and their wisdom: Kelly J. Baker, Erin Bartram, Leonard Cassuto, Jessica Collier, Joseph Conley, Melissa Dalgleish, Sydni Dunn, Susan Ferber, Joe Fruscione, Kristen Galvin, Howard Gardner, Malcolm Gaskill, Pepita Hesselberth, Constantina Katsari, Christine Kelly, Karen Kelsky, Sarah Kendzior, Terran (Heather) Lane, Oliver Lee Bateman, Alexandra Lord, Josh Marshall, Liz Morrish, Katie Rose Guest Pryal, Ian Saxine, Grant Shreve, Rebecca Schuman, Jennifer Vannette, Matt Welsh, L. Maren Wood, James Van Wyck, and the anonymous contributor to *The Guardian*.

Thanks likewise to *The Chronicle of Higher Education, The Guardian, Inside Higher Ed, Al Jazeera*, the *London Review of Books*, and *Times Higher Education* for permission to reprint material originally appearing in their publications.

Special thanks to Emily Bruder for the illustrations, based on our cover image — Gustave Doré's wood engraving, "Adam and Eve Driven Out of Eden," from 1866 — that wittily grace the book's interior.

Finally, we offer our sincere gratitude to the National Endowment for the Humanities, whose award of a Next-Generation Humanities PhD planning grant to Syracuse University provided an opportunity to pursue this project: a book exploring the real careers, the career challenges, and the wider career possibilities for current academics — and also helped to fund one of the editors during their two-year position at Syracuse.

Foreword: The Art of the Academic Heart Perforation

Rebecca Schuman

BEFORE THE ADVENT of those bleep-bloop machines you always see on hospital TV shows (and, I suppose, in real hospitals), the medical act of adjudicating relative levels of human demise necessitated a measure of human creativity. I think, for example, of the bell-equipped "safety coffins" that allowed the unexpectedly awakened to ring for a last-minute exhumation. Yes, while death itself was as much a certainty in, say, the nineteenth century as it is now, certainty of death was another thing entirely.

Enter, then, the heart perforation, a procedure with whose erstwhile utilization I have been preoccupied for a number of years both because I am morbid and because I happen to enjoy the literary stylings of Rainer Maria Rilke, who detailed it in his novel *The Notebooks of Malte Laurids Brigge*, when the titular character recounts the *Herzstich* of his own father:

> Who, for example, could have imagined the resistance. No sooner had the wide, high breast been laid bare before the hurried little man located the spot in question. But the quickly applied instrument did not penetrate. I had the feeling that all time had suddenly left the room. As if we were all in a picture. But then time crashed back down in, with a small sliding noise, and there was more of it than was used up. Suddenly there was a knock somewhere. I'd never heard a knock

> like that: a warm, reserved double tap. My hearing transmitted it and at the same time I saw that the doctor had reached the bottom. But it took a while before both impressions came together in me. So, so, I thought, now it's through. As far as the tempo was concerned, the knocking was almost gloating. (my translation)

Malte's father might not have been *actually dead* — I mean, he probably was, but it was not outside the realm of possibility that he could have been technically alive and comatose, a heartbeat so faint nobody could detect it. But from all conceivable angles, death was imminent, and to be honest any more dilly-dallying about it wasn't going to do anyone any good.

And so, the doctor at hand did the only reasonable thing: He made sure Malte's father was dead by killing him just in case he wasn't.

In the Spring of 2013, I had been unable to detect the heartbeat of my academic career for many months. I was haggard and ashamed, incandescent with a rage I was only allowed to express in private to a select few others (lest my angst somehow reach the ears of someone who might be on a search committee someday), all of whom now wished to tap needles through their own hearts so as not to have to listen to my disconsolate jawing for another solitary minute.

It was my fourth year on the job market, in search of a tenure-track or similarly stable teaching position in the discipline of German studies. To be fair, each successive annual attempt had brought me a paradoxical Zeno's skosh closer to that goal. My first year, I'd netted zero interviews of any sort but managed to eke my way into a manageable adjuncting gig. My second, I'd made the shortlist for a renewable three-year position and been awarded a two-year postdoctoral fellowship that placed me at Ohio State. My third, I'd interviewed for one tenure-track job ... and biffed it spectacularly; my fourth, I'd received *two* tenure-track interviews and only biffed *one* spectacularly, thus resulting in a single campus invitation.

However, while I'd managed not to eat shit during my initial meet with this well-regarded public institution, I was ill-suited to the pressure of that single campus visit — *one chance* to "make it" in the field: that is, onto the tenure track at a nationally ranked university, the only acceptable outcome of doctoral study in my discipline. And so, yet again, failure impaled me like so many icicles on a single-digit day, which it indeed was as I tottered across that aggressively manicured campus, shivering in my ill-fitting Banana Republic interview suit.

To be fair, my one chance was no chance. My teaching demo was an ambush, a 9 AM class on Friday full of hungover dudebros who not only hadn't been apprised of my impending substitution, but who also had an essay due and had not even begun to *think* about the homework assigned on the clearly abandoned syllabus from which I had so diligently planned. A few hours later, I gave a flaccid job talk whose only worthwhile outcome was when the woman knitting in the front row completed about two good inches of a scarf. The university hired their inside candidate.

I'd promised my partner at the time that this was it. *Four years*, I'd negotiated, *I'll go on the market for four years and then cut bait.* That was as long as we could handle the uncertainty, and the waiting, and the hundreds of hours of emotional labor that always, somehow, ended in rejection anyway and threw an inky pall over the relationship and the household and my soul. So it was over. I was going to do the thing that when people did it, their names ricocheted through the hallowed halls in shame-whispers: *Oh, she Left the Field.* Left. The. Field. The emotional cadence of those ludicrous words was about two degrees more intense than death. Because even when you're dead, theoretically someone can still cite your books.

Yep, I was Audi 5000 – and I *still* couldn't tell anyone. Or rather, I was *very much* not supposed to (imaginary search committees everywhere), but this was 2013 so people Facebooked, and so sometime around March, I, too, Facebooked: *I regret getting a PhD with every possible part of me. It has broken me beyond measure and given me nothing.* Actually I'm not sure what I wrote, because I deleted it, after I was pummeled with comments about how it couldn't have been all bad because I *got to spend all that time doing what I loved*, didn't I?

Anyone who thinks someone is still "in love" with their research after four unsuccessful years of trying to impress search committees with it is incorrect.

If you're reading this volume, then you don't need *me* to tell you why it was so wrenching to Leave The Field: that's literally the point! Read on! Other people have done this work, much better than I! You might also not need me to tell you why, when an editor from *Slate* magazine on my Friends list (who'd glimpsed that deleted status) thought my brand of bile was the perfect #SlatePitch, my colleagues in The Field were horrified. I spent an entire night emailing with one who, in his defense, had spent the last two years attempting to mentor me and likely viewed my cratering as a personal failure:

> *You can't publish this, Rebecca, a search committee might see it!*
>
> *That's just it. I don't have to give a solitary flying fuck what a search committee thinks of me, ever again.*
>
> *Oh god, Rebecca, what if a search committee heard you say that?*

My colleague, bless his Teutonic soul, refused to believe what was dead was dead. *Nobody* believed me, in fact. Not my dissertation committee, not my colleagues, not what few friends I had left after spending the past decade transforming into a monstrous mirth-sucking vampire, and definitely not my parents. It hurts to write "parents" now, by the way, because in the intervening years I've lost one of them, and it reminds me that when I was blessed with an inerrantly kind and supportive father, I wasted my time, and his, bitching about *academe*.

At any rate, speaking of dead fathers and, thus, Rilke: I knew what I had to do. Part of the reason that nobody believed me was that I was, indeed, still beholden to the academic code of secrecy about how dehumanizing the job-search process is. And so it was time to *make* them believe me. I told Dan, my *Slate* editor friend, that I'd do it. (And then, consummate academic I still was, I worried over those 1,250 words for an entire month.)

And so I didn't just quit. I quit as publicly as I was humanly able. And that, friends, brings me to the genre I joined by doing that – now known, for better or worse, as Quit Lit. As you're about to see, every public confessional quitter quits differently, for a host of different reasons. But the quitters here basically boil down to four categories.

You've got your Private Sector Quitters, such as Matt Welsh and Terran Lane, who bemoan academia's slow turnaround for peer-reviewed work and even slower pace for real-world adoption of their discoveries. (And, let's be honest, the money. Call me gauche, but I'm guessing even Harvard doesn't pay Google money.) Then you've got your Fed-Up Tenureds, such as Karen Kelsky and Lexi Lord, who succeeded on the ultra-competitive tenure track but still left because they found the life of a scholar in a strange town to be alienating and, in the end, untenable. Then there are the Never Starters, such as Jessica Collier, who sometimes leave their programs and sometimes finish them, but *always* decide to opt out of the job market pretty much entirely, and thus never give it a chance to turn them into detritus.

And then, finally, there's the detritus. The Shut-Outers. The job-market casualties who, after four, or eight, or ten, or even fifteen years of temporary positions and interviews and waiting and rejection (so, so, so much rejection), finally just can't take it anymore. Kelly Baker. Joe Fruscione. Erin Bartram. And, yes, me.

It is possible that I'm biased in the way only neurotic people can be, but I maintain that of the Shut-Outers, my work was (and remains) the most ... let's just say *untethered*. I don't have the word-limit necessary to enumerate the, well, *outré* aspects of my own expletive-laced contribution to the genre, my needle-pierce, the reason your intrepid editors asked me to write this foreword in the first place: "Thesis Hatement," which was first published in

Slate on May 5, 2013, definitely a date I always wanted to remember for the staggering amount of emails from strangers I received, and not because it was, indeed, the day of my sister-in-law's wedding, in which I was a bridesmaid.

"Thesis Hatement" was my truth at the time. It was. Every bile-filled word. And I don't want to negate that or try to self-excoriate it away. But I did want to take a small amount of the space I'm afforded in reflection to say that I deeply regret using in it (more than once!) the intellectually lazy and ableist term "stupid," which 2021-me would never think of doing. I would also like to acknowledge the level of privilege and entitlement that I, as a white woman with no financial insecurity growing up, had not examined in any meaningful way when I wrote it, so engulfed was I in the shame of failure and insecurity about my future. And I also now feel some legitimate regret for trivializing the worth of my own academic research, which, like most academic research, was perfectly good. In demeaning my work – I used the term "bat-shit" at a time *Slate* still forbade curse words except under truly special circumstances; *you're welcome* – I hurt the feelings of not only anyone *else* who's ever done academic research, but of my PhD advisor, whom I loved and still love like a young curmudgeonly uncle, and the other patient and unfailingly supportive mentors who helped shepherd my dissertation through.

Now that I'm older (*so* much older), and have, to be blunt, lived through something resembling hardship – a miscarriage; the breakup of my marriage followed almost immediately by the sudden death of my father in a horrific accident; the coronavirus pandemic and the near-constant pall of the Trump presidency – I recognize that by lashing out at the "bat-shit" nature of academic research, I was simply writing out my worst possible fear at the time, which was that other people would think my work was a joke. "Thesis Hatement" is also hard for me to read now because it hurts to relive that kind of raw anguish, anguish at such a total rejection of the life and identity to which I'd dedicated my whole self, to remember how gutted I was that academia didn't want me. Truly, I began to forget that feeling almost immediately after "Thesis Hatement" posted, and now it really is gone.

But here's part I don't regret. In embarrassing myself so thoroughly, I also made myself immune to further embarrassment. In perforating my own heart with such efficiency, I accidentally made myself immortal. Well, sort of. As I suspect also happened with more than one of my cohort here, owning my exit, and centering it in a discourse of academia's systemic issues, brought control to my destiny (or felt like it did), and recentered The Field as just another job, rather than an all-inclusive identity. Finding my voice through my failure helped, in a way, to diminish that failure – to help me realize I was never a failure in the first place. And though I don't pretend to know the hearts of everyone in this volume, I can confidently say that *nobody* here is a failure by any measure, both because most have excelled in their new careers, but also because simply by writing whatever their own equivalent of a heart perforation is, they've succeeded in owning *their* exits and recentering *their* identities.

As clearly self-absorbed as my own contributions to quit lit are, I am fully aware that this book is not about me, but I'd be denying you the whole story if I didn't Where-Are-They-Now myself for just a second. I'm not dead. And neither, I guess, is my academic career? I actually ended up going back on the job market in 2018 – with "Thesis Hatement" on my CV. And I got a tenure-track interview, conducted over video conference, as is now the norm thanks in no small part to the fearless nature of quit lit to call academia out on the unnecessary bullshit of, among other indignities, the conference interview. (The university hired their inside candidate.) In 2019, I did it again – and though I kept forgetting about my applications entirely, I was reminded when I got not only an interview (Zoom, again) but a campus visit, which was once again terrifying, but primarily because it was the first night I had ever spent away from my little daughter. On *this* visit, I had fun. The campus was stunning, the conversations were lively – and, despite not having set foot in a German classroom for six years, I absolutely murdered my teaching demonstration beyond any possible hope of coffin-bell reincarnation, because it was a classroom full of volunteers who were eager to meet me and earn some extra credit. (The university hired their inside candidate – and I thought: *Mazel tov for him!*)

That was the end of that little experiment – but even as I write this, I'm balancing part-time gigs (adjuncting *actually adjunct* to other employ!) at the University of Oregon, the Stanford Continuing Studies creative writing program, and even my alma mater, Vassar. (Remote teaching does have this one advantage, but I still never want to do it again.)

It is now beyond my ability to comprehend that self-evident truths such as *conference interviews are unnecessary*, or *academia is not a meritocracy*, or *structurally, the university is still set up like a 1950s suburb where every professor was a white dude with a stay-at-home wife*, were once verboten in mixed imaginary-search-committee company. If you finished (or didn't finish!) your own doctorate after around 2014, you may take for granted that you can say things like that in public now – but I assure you, you can, and that's due, in part, to the bravery of the people who wrote the essays here.

The book you're about to read is a series of heart perforations, people from all rungs on and off the tenure ladder, murdering their own academic careers to keep themselves alive. The reasons they offer for leaving are as unique as they are, and yet every one of those reasons should ring true to someone who's thinking of quitting or has already done so. I hope that you're inspired by the honesty here, and the intimacy of bringing an audience along as each author jumped out of the ivory tower and hoped they'd land softly. It is my sincere hope that their wise words – and possibly even my embarrassing ones – might help keep you alive, too.

Introduction

Christopher Flanagan

LEAVING THE GROVE

In this volume, we have brought together a variety of voices of individuals who chose to leave academia. By academia, we specifically mean the traditional path of scholarly advancement from graduate student through to tenured professor. There are of course many other aspects to academic institutions, from the undergraduates and terminal Master's students who make up the majority of most campuses' populations, to the administrative, fundraising and student support staff who fill the university's offices and keep campuses running on a daily basis. Yet the tenured professor remains in many ways the archetypal image when we think of academia: indeed, that is part of the problem this book hopes to address. It is to become a professor that so many scholars sign up for multi-year graduate programs, learning the tools of the trade in the hope of one day achieving the distinguished position themselves.

Yet the lived reality of this branch of academia has long been out of sync with the popular imagination. The vast majority of graduate students who receive a PhD do not go on to be tenured professors. Many struggle with exactly what career direction they will pursue, upon discovering the unhappy reality that a long-desired tenure-track job may be forever out of reach. And for those who make it to the promised land of a tenure-track position — or of tenure itself, as with some of our authors — they can find that the job is far from the career they imagined. Different enough, disappointing or alienating enough, that they decided to leave the "dream job" and take their career in a different direction.

This brings us to Quit Lit.

Coined as a term by Rebecca Schuman in 2013 (as "I Quit Lit"), the genre encompasses a wide variety of authors, ranging from graduate students through to tenured professors, bidding farewell to their vocation, as they resign their academic posts, or choose to stop looking for one. So varied are the writers' circumstances, their attitudes, and their future careers after academia, that little may seem to unite them. But at the heart of all the pieces of this genre is a single thought:

"This isn't what I signed up for."

All the essays contained here, and many more that we didn't have space to include, echo that unavoidable dissonance. A dissonance that perhaps explains why so many academics choose to write about their reasons for leaving, at the moment of departure. And why this phenomenon, "quit lit," is uniquely centered upon academia and academics. It speaks to the power of that archetypal image of the professor, of the myths that our society still clings to about the nature of academia and of academic careers. Your average professor, so this vision of academia goes, lives a cushy professional life, far removed from the nine-to-five rat race of their nonacademic peers. Sitting in their book-lined office or study, they work at their own pace, with the academic freedom to read, research, and philosophize on whichever big issues in their discipline have taken their intellectual fancy. At intervals, they leave this private space to share their current research, lecturing to a classroom of eager students. And while they may not receive the highest salary for all of this, they have the recompense of unrivaled job security, through their tenured position. Even if not sporting the tweed, elbow patches, and bow tie of popular caricature, the archetypal professor is still a middle-aged white male, an identity adding several extra layers of privilege to their already desirable situation.

Missing from this image is the intensity of teaching work at all but the most elite institutions; the many demands of departmental, institutional, and disciplinary service; undergraduate advisement; and the demands to chase external research funding or to develop prestigious collaborations. And while the job security and academic freedom of tenure exist for a shrinking number of the most fortunate and most visible scholars, for the vast and mostly unseen majority, the reality is one of short-term employment contracts, often on a per-course basis and lacking even basic benefits such as subsidized health insurance.

Still, the durable myth of the professorial lifeway both motivates and haunts junior members of the academy, graduate students and newly minted assistant professors striving to make their way to the top of the profession. Coming face-to-face with evidence that challenges such deeply held assumptions is a jolting experience. For many writers, the "quit-lit moment" has been one of disillusionment, sadness, or anger – a chance to vent at an unfair or ineffective system. For others, it has been a call to educate their peers, to warn them away from those same misconceptions, from making major personal and career choices based on woefully incomplete information, or from the exceptionalist mode of thinking that insists, despite all evidence, that "*I'll* be one of the select few who make it...."

Quit lit didn't appear from whole cloth in the years immediately preceding Schuman's 2013 article. In fact, as our contributor Grant Shreve records, there was an earlier batch of "proto-quit lit" in the 1970s, when tough economic times brought an earlier generation to the realization that not every PhD candidate would become a professor. Yet the years after 2008 and the Great Recession brought a particular set of circumstances that makes the current crop of quit lit so affecting, and so wide-ranging in its critique of academia. As several of our authors detail, the institution of the university is under pressure on several fronts. Cultural and political shifts in how the American (and to a lesser extent, the British and Canadian) public sees the university have undermined its formerly privileged place in society. At the same time, university governors across the US, UK, and Canada, with their eyes on the budgetary bottom line, have come to favor a consumer model for how the institution will operate, focusing their resources on the "student experience" (undergraduate accommodations, sports and recreation facilities, luxurious study-abroad options, and the like) over their research and teaching staff. In the face of this, the academic job market – the annual gateway for hopeful scholars to gain tenure track employment – has contracted, and for decades the number of academic job seekers has significantly outpaced the number of academic jobs available. After the briefest moment of optimism in the late 2000s came the sharp, short-term system shock that was the collapse of the world financial markets in 2008, and the deep recession that followed. The academic job market, already in a multi-generational funk, collapsed even further and has never recovered. At this point we can assert that the tenured professorial role has been effectively supplanted by contingent academic labor – "visiting" professorships, "teaching postdocs," and, of course, adjunct appointments: short-term, low-paid teaching positions, usually without benefits and with minimal chance of advancement within the profession.

This toxic blend – of fewer jobs, less meaningful and less valued jobs, and pay lower than even the most reasonable job entrant might expect –

explains the scale of the exodus from academia at this moment in history, and the powerful need to write about that exit that drove the authors included here to take up the pen.

A Quit Lit Reader

What then, you might ask, is the value of compiling a selection of these "I Quit" testimonials in one place – beyond sheer aggregation, or contributor Sarah Kendzior's wry suggestion that there ought to be "a Norton Anthology of Academics Declaring They Quit"?[1]

This volume will, we hope, be of value to its readers on a number of fronts.

First, the volume aims to serve as a wake-up call to the many scholars applying for, or working their way through graduate education, believing that a professorial career beckons at the end of their labors. As so many of our contributors lay out, the unvarnished truth is that this career is becoming almost impossible to achieve for the vast majority of scholars-in-training. Graduate education, and the university itself, usually does a poor job of explaining this until it is far too late. Despite recent leaps forward on many campuses, where various forms of professional development and career diversity are being built into curricula, academia still strives to replicate academia, professors training younger versions of themselves to one day (... eventually ...) replace them, and little more.

Second, the volume aims to speak to all those scholars who are already in the midst of, or who've already gone through this process: of frustrated job searches, low-paying adjunct work, or desperate exploration of other career paths – those whom Rebecca Schuman refers to, quite appropriately, as "the Shut-Outers." For this group the label "quit lit" is least appropriate, it being more accurate to say that the academy quit on them. As the essays that follow reveal, discovering that the career path you have invested so much time, energy, and self-identity into has resulted in *nothing* can, unsurprisingly, lead to emotional, financial, and professional turmoil. Too many talented, hard-working scholars are left feeling lost, isolated, and let down – angry at themselves, angry at the system that let them get to this place, and unsure in what direction they can go next. This volume, and the personal testimonials herein, tell those people that they're not alone. But more than that, we hope their stories can give the reader hope. The authors in this volume have gone on to do awe-inspiring things after leaving academia, personally and profession-

1. Sarah Kendzior (@sarahkendzior), "There needs to be a Norton Anthology of Academics Announcing They Quit," Twitter, October 20, 2013, https://twitter.com/sarahkendzior/status/392095346907557888

ally. Their stories of career transitions and new paths in life, while not all plain sailing, remind readers that they are talented, capable people too, and give them hope that there are many different places and careers where they can utilize their skills, experiences, and interests.

Third, the volume aims to speak to those still committed to pursuing the elusive tenure-track career. Many of them, like many of the contributors here, may have very little idea what tenured academic scholarship is really like as a "day job." And once again, the old myths of the well-heeled professor give little guidance for what to expect. More troublingly, *neither does graduate school*, which all too often fails to prepare trainee scholars for the teaching loads, the departmental service, the demands of tenure review, the departmental politics, and the day-to-day lifestyle and work-life balance issues faced by a tenure-track or tenured professor. By sharing the authors' experiences at various stages of this process, we hope to shine a light on the lived experience of academics in the modern university, so that aspiring professors can glimpse what the career really entails.

Fourth, we hope that through the writings of the quitting authors, and through the series of broader reflections and analyses of quit lit as a genre, this volume can cast a critical eye on the institutions of the academy itself. These reflections use quit lit as a lens through which to examine the academic labor system, precarity, graduate education, and the future of the professoriate. In the humanities and social sciences – and increasingly in STEM fields – PhDs granted far outstrip jobs advertised year on year. In all subjects, an ever-increasing proportion of academic jobs are contingent. And many of our authors repeat the same lament, that again and again in recent years, universities have chosen to invest their resources on administrative staff and student amenities, leaving the scholars supposedly at the heart of the academic venture a mere appendix to the modern university. These are all daunting challenges, but the writers in this volume can at least begin to suggest an agenda for confronting them.

Finally, although this volume was conceived in the final days of 2019, before any of us knew what the years 2020 and 2021 would mean for the world, the coronavirus pandemic has highlighted and worsened some of the deep structural challenges facing academia. Job adverts have dried up, even some contingent jobs have ceased to exist, and some institutions totter on the brink of financial collapse due to the mass withdrawal of students from their campuses. The voices gathered here remind us of the longer-term origins of some of these issues, and of the human toll already taken on the people who chose to pursue a career in this profession. If there is any hope of building a better academia in the wake of recent events, these voices need to be heard.

Part One of the book presents an anthology of original quit-lit pieces.

The essays appeared in a range of locations, from the pages of *The Guardian* and *The Chronicle of Higher Education*, to a great many that were simply published on the author's personal blog or website. Many are what could be called classics in the field – such as Rebecca Schuman's infamous "Thesis Hatement," published in *Slate* in 2013, or Erin Bartram's poignant blog post, "The Sublimated Grief of the Left Behind," which went viral in 2018 – and two are published for the first time in this volume. Yet they all bring powerful, personal stories of the challenges and tribulations within academia that drove the authors to leave it behind.

Since quit lit is a highly self-referential genre in which predecessors are routinely invoked, we have ordered the selections chronologically, by date of initial publication. Nonetheless, readers will quickly observe that the essays fall into three broad categories, connected to the academic career stage at which the quitter quit. First are the scholars who realized in graduate school that academia was a poor fit for them. As Joseph Conley points out in "Just Another Piece of Quit Lit," graduate training is something high achievers can drift into after succeeding as undergraduates, seeing further study and research as an escape from the "real world" of nine-to-five jobs. Absent better systems at the undergraduate level of conveying what graduate school, and an academic career, actually entails, budding scholars can soon discover that their skills and interests diverge from the expectations of the profession. Susan Ferber reveals how she found the individualistic culture of academia off-putting, and the focus on a scholar's own research and on showing off intellectual prowess in seminars inconducive to humility or intellectual collaboration. Similarly, Jessica Collier and Josh Marshall both found that academia would not reward their flair for concise, communicable writing. The constant demands of heavy teaching loads and academic service threatened to take Collier away from the writing that she loved most about her work; Marshall bridled at the hyper-specialized content and intended audience of academic writing, founding the current affairs blog Talking Points Memo to bring his expertise to a wider audience.

Second are the individuals who completed their degree, entered the academic job market, and experienced the frustrations, injustices, and disappointments of the annual lottery by which tenure-track positions are awarded. Some, like Melissa Dalgleish, walked away from this broken system within a single hiring cycle, whereas others held on in hope of better days to come, like Joe Fruscione, who taught as an adjunct for eight years before throwing in the towel. All the authors in this category share the same criticisms: there are painfully few jobs in any and every field; scholars have no control over the physical location in which their lives unfold; and, above all, adjunct lecturers are overworked, underpaid, and undervalued throughout academia. As mentioned previously, these are the authors for whom the term "quit" is least accurate – they worked hard to remain in a system that ultimately had no place for them. Yet some of the most memorable pieces of quit lit are found in this category. Notably, both Schuman's and Bartram's viral pieces are in this camp: something about the rawness of the deal handed to these individuals, and the big issues that they pass such incisive indictments of, have obviously struck a nerve in wider academia. And experiencing such frustrations themselves, many of these authors now work to help the next generation of junior academics. Rebecca Schuman writes essays of advice and criticism on the state of academia for *Slate* and *The Chronicle of Higher Ed*; Joe Fruscione and Erin Bartram are editors of the book series Rethinking Careers, Rethinking Academia with the University Press of Kansas, publishers of Fruscione and Kelly Baker's coedited book, *Succeeding Outside the Academy*;[2] Maren Wood runs Beyond the Professoriate, an organization helping graduate students find careers that match their skills; and Melissa Dalgleish is the president of Canada's Graduate and Professional Development Network, an association for professionals who advise and support graduates in their career choices.

Finally, are the lucky few who made it to the summit of the academic career: the tenure-track or tenured professorship. Yet as the essays here indicate, even those who "won" the career lottery often found the academic career unfulfilling, stifling, or even alienating. Some found the job impossible to sustain on a personal level. Alexandra Lord protests the demand that scholars permanently leave behind the people and places they know and love for whichever city, state, or region the unicorn "perfect job" appears in; and Karen Kelsky criticizes the cold, isolating, career-above-everything environment fostered at the United States' leading research institutions. Others came to feel that their professional aspirations could not be met within the confines of the academy. Matt Welsh and Terran Lane, both STEM scholars, left academia for Google, lamenting the difficulty of doing big projects and making a major impact within academia, while spending all of their time chasing grants; Constantina Katsari quit her lectureship in history to go full time as an entrepreneur, citing a growingly inflexible academic environment that stifles innovation.

Notably, the majority of the UK writers featured in this volume, including Katsari, appear in this section, and speak of an academia that has become overly bureaucratic, forcing scholars to jump through endless hoops of service and administrative oversight. Liz Morrish and Malcolm Gaskill both

2. Joseph Fruscione and Kelly J. Baker, eds., *Succeeding Outside the Academy: Career Paths beyond the Humanities, Social Sciences, and STEM* (Lawrence: University of Kansas Press, 2018).

suggest that systems of accountability have made it almost impossible for them to deliver high-quality teaching or research. Yet this UK trend connects to a larger critique seen in US academia, too. As both Gaskill and US author Oliver Lee Bateman argue, universities have taken on consumer-centric business models, putting the student at the (supposed) center of the university experience at the expense of the scholars and teachers who provide the actual education. Bateman suggests that in the US, the bloat of university administration has become its own end, existing to make money off of student enrollments – exploiting underpaid employees while charging students tens of thousands of dollars a year and giving only a mediocre education in return.

Several of the authors of the original quit-lit pieces have also offered short postscripts for their essays in this volume. Along with Rebecca Schuman's wry and percipient thoughts in the volume's foreword, Matt Welsh, Alexandra Lord, and Liz Morrish all reflect on the response to and afterlife of their essays, and share a bit of their subsequent careers in light of their now-immortalized decisions to part ways with tenure-track academia.

Part Two comprises a series of essays that step back and explore quit lit as a genre, from a variety of critical and historical perspectives. The authors in this section investigate where quit lit came from and what quit-lit authors are trying to do, and wrestle with what the genre says about the current state of academia. Three broad trends emerge from these pieces.

First are the foundational pieces that drew attention to the exodus from academia, that labeled quit lit as a particularly academic phenomenon, and that showed how the current situation was long in the making. Sarah Kendzior, writing before there even was a genre called quit lit, argued that the mix of low pay and high costs to entering the profession would price a generation of scholars out of the academy. Then came Rebecca Schuman (with her second entry in this volume) giving the genre its name, and bringing attention to how quit lit encompassed more than frustrated, shut-out job-seekers. Even tenured professors were quitting, and using the opportunity to criticize the broken system. As the genre became better known, Sydni Dunn proposed an early taxonomy of quit lit, exploring three broad types of quitters – the explainers, the statement makers, and the destigmatizers – and their motivations for writing. And taking a historical perspective, Grant Shreve and Jennifer Vannette explore how the structural problems of academic employment were decades in the making, coalescing out a succession of adverse economic and political developments.

A second, unavoidable trend within discussions of quit lit is engagement with Erin Bartram and "The Sublimated Grief of the Left Behind." Arguably the most famous entry in the quit-lit canon, Bartam's piece has been deconstructed to show tensions both within the concept of quit lit, and in the pervasive myths surrounding academia that fuel the genre. Ian Saxine challenges the very terminology of quit lit, insofar as scholars like Bartram aren't "quitting" but being forced out of the profession they've been trained in by a broken system that can't provide stable employment. Katie Rose Guest Pryal and Grant Shreve both discuss how the emotional farewell to an academic good life, encapsulated in Bartram's piece, fails to critique this unjust, central element of the predicament. They suggest that, rather than calling out the broken system, Bartram unintentionally reinforces the myths surrounding academia that lead so many would-be scholars to pursue a mirage of a career. In a trenchant essay that situates quit lit within the "politics of withdrawal," Pepita Hesselberth ties the particularly emotive qualities of the genre to the fact that for many authors, including Bartram, leaving academia represents a *second* moment of withdrawal. Having already withdrawn to the false, idealized image of the ivory tower university as a place where they can challenge and critique the problems of capitalism and power in the modern world, the writers find themselves caught up in those same systems *within* academia, and are forced to retreat yet again.

A final common characteristic of these essays is the analysis of how quit lit approaches the question of next steps – of "where do we go from here?" – and its continued ability to affect conversations about reform within academia. Leonard Cassuto and Howard Gardner both assert that the profusion of quit lit demands fundamental reform in graduate education, but the authors approach the problem from different directions. Gardner suggests a major reduction in the number of doctoral candidates being trained, in return for a guarantee that those who gain a PhD will receive an academic job. In contrast, Cassuto argues that graduate training needs to prepare students for a more diverse range of careers, so that professorial positions become just one of a number of career paths a PhD holder can choose to pursue. Christine Kelly praises the work that quit lit has done to raise awareness of previously hidden challenges in academic careers and of possibilities beyond academe. In this way quit lit wards against the damage to emotional and mental welfare a frustrated academic career can bring. Kristen Galvin also highlights the important role quit lit has played in promoting career diversity and helping scholars and public intellectuals mobilize for change. Suggesting that the aggregation of each individual writer's criticism forms a sort of online megaphone, Galvin portrays quit lit as a vehicle for holding academia accountable for its most exploitative practices.

Within the bounds of this single volume, there are inevitable absences and silences. Running beside and informing the genre of quit lit is what can be called "Just Don't Go Lit." Emblematic is William Pannapacker's *Chronicle* column from 2009 (under the pseudonym Thomas H. Benton), "Graduate School in the Humanities: Just Don't Go," referenced numerous times by subsequent quit-lit authors.[3] Schuman's famous "Thesis Hatement" piece blends the "just don't go" genre with quit lit, as she reflects on why she quit while advising her readers to learn from her experience and avoid graduate school entirely. These and other jeremiads against the academy drew responses. Katie Roiphe defended the value of graduate education for its own sake, and Tressie McMillan Cottom introduced the vital qualifier that blanket "just don't go" advice ignores and threatens to entrench existing racial disparities within graduate education and the professoriate.[4] While this strain of writing certainly informs the quit-lit genre and wider discussions surrounding the state of academia, to include such pieces here would have fundamentally reoriented the collection in a way that obscures the specific features and contributions of quit lit per se.

However, the debates within the "just don't go" genre, foregrounded most notably in McMillan Cottom's piece, shed some light on another inescapable feature of the present volume: its whiteness. Academia remains a disproportionately white space, and academic environments have historically been, and too often remain, hostile to non-white students and scholars. Thus, the makeup of this volume's authors may in part simply reflect this historical bias. There may also be a degree of entitlement at work. White scholars, particularly those from middle-class and upper-class backgrounds, are much less likely to have experienced such a structurally unfair system, and so more likely to raise their voices in response to this particular one. However, McMillan Cottom's piece hints at more complex tensions that may explain why the genre is so dominated by white voices. Her argument is underpinned by the idea that academia needs more students and professors from diverse backgrounds, to bring more voices to the table of academic teaching, research, and governance. Yet McMillan Cottom recognizes that such a commitment will entail extra burdens for non-white scholars in comparison with their white counterparts, in the form of enhanced mentorship for underrepresented students, service on numerous committees and other

3. Thomas H. Benton [William Pannapacker], "Graduate School in the Humanities: Just Don't Go," *Chronicle of Higher Education*, January 30, 2009, https://www.chronicle.com/article/graduate-school-in-the-humanities-just-dont-go/; and "Just Don't Go, Part 2," *Chronicle of Higher Education*, March 13, 2009, https://www.chronicle.com/article/just-dont-go-part-2/.

4. Katie Roiphe, "Thesis Defense," *Slate*, April 8, 2013, https://slate.com/human-interest/2013/04/a-literature-ph-d-is-not-a-waste-of-time.html; Tressie McMillan Cottom, "Blanket 'Don't Go to Graduate School!' Advice Ignores Race and Reality?" *Tressie McMillan Cottom* (personal blog), April 6, 2013, https://tressiemc.com/uncategorized/blanket-dont-go-to-graduate-school-advice-ignores-race-and-reality/

institutional functions requiring minority representation, and the multitude of microaggressions that can occur in any predominantly white space. These observations suggest at alternate view of academia less saddled with idealizing myths, either about the university as a "safe" countercultural refuge or as a practically desirable site of day-to-day employment. If a big part of quit lit involves puncturing the myths of academia, then for non-white scholars there may simply be fewer myths to be punctured.

The editors of this volume were surprised to find that the response to an international call for quit-lit pieces arose overwhelmingly from the United States. The exception to this, as noted already, is the series of essays that portray the United Kingdom as ground zero for a very specific model of bureaucratic hyper-management, in which it is predominantly experienced academics who are driven from the profession by a system undermining their creativity. Beyond that, the pieces in this volume focus overwhelmingly on the ever-more-visible structural flaws of the corporatized American university. Is quit lit, then, primarily a response to disillusionment with long-standing myths about academia, as the academy is seen specifically in Anglo-American culture? Consider Germany, where graduate training has adapted to better reflect the needs of the academic job market, and holding a PhD retains significant social prestige, particularly in the realm of politics. Or countries such as India, Pakistan, or China, where academic expansion has been driven by regimes with particular ideological or utilitarian demands, minimizing the scope for academic freedom and leaving much less to be disillusioned about from the start. Alternatively, is quit lit better seen as an economically focused response to ever-declining labor conditions, and a growing call to confront an exploitative institution? Many regions lack the extensive and well-endowed higher education system in place in the US, with its consequent lure towards maximizing profit. So, if the vagaries of late capitalism have a central role in the genre, we may still see quit lit replicated internationally in the future, if and when the corporatized American model of the university is exported to the rest of the world.

Looking to the Future

The question then remains, where do we go from here?

As several authors of the previously unpublished pieces reflect on, this volume was put together in the midst of the 2020-21 COVID-19 pandemic. The virus's effects on the way academia operates, as with so much else, has been significant. Yet, while initial fears that it would lead to the wholesale collapse of traditional academia now seem unwarranted, we still don't know what, if any, large structural changes might emerge from this disruptive period. One tempting assumption is that, having discovered cheaper ways to deliver instruction to their students through mass videoconferencing, institutions will find more ways to squeeze spending on their teaching staff. But given the parlous pre-pandemic circumstances for adjunct instructors documented within these pages, it might be worth asking if future changes can make things much worse than they already were. Searching for silver linings, perhaps the transition toward more remote instruction may provide some relief for those scholars forced to work and teach between multiple locations to piece together a living wage.

Looking further down the road, what does quit lit suggest about the state of academia, and its future? As Kristen Galvin points out in her essay, major changes have already begun in recent years. The National Endowment for the Humanities, the American Historical Association, and the Modern Language Association have all undertaken high-profile initiatives to address the chronic problem of careers in academia for students in the humanities. And in the current landscape of PhDs looking for diverse careers, some of the key authors and commentators of the quit-lit genre are now helming projects of their own to help scholars better understand and navigate the worlds of academic and non-academic jobs. In addition to the work of Wood, Baker, Dalgleish, Fruscione, and Bartram noted above, Karen Kelsky gives her readers the unvarnished truths about the workings of academia in her long-time blog and consultancy The Professor Is In. And as Christine Kelly explores, the movement of quit lit from the blog to the vlog has allowed for a new wealth of accessible solidarity and support for scholars facing their own decisions over whether and when to quit the profession.

However, for all the hopeful change, there remains important continuity. Both Galvin and Pepita Hesselberth refer to theorist Lauren Berlant and her concept of "cruel optimism," which "names a relation of attachment to compromised conditions of possibility" maintained "because whatever the *content* of the attachment, the continuity of the form of it provides something of the continuity of the subject's sense of what it means to keep on living on and to look forward to being in the world."[5] The concept speaks well to one unchanging element behind quit lit: the exceptionalist thinking of academics who convince themselves that the fraught economic circumstances of academia do not have to apply to them. Whether this involves seeing academia as a career of a very different sort, immune to the pressures of capitalism and competition; the conviction that making enough sacrifices — in work hours, low pay, geographic movement, or sacrificed relationships — *will* land the dream academic job; or the hope that with tenure and academic seniority, the tensions and compromises will resolve themselves, leading to an academic

5. Lauren Berlant, "Cruel Optimism," *Differences* 17.3 (2006): 21.

"good life," too many scholars damage their well-being and their career prospects by leading themselves down a professional blind alley. Knowledge about the state of academia, and support for those who wish to transition their careers away from it, exist, but it is for academics themselves to learn about and take these opportunities, and consider as fully as possible what life and career choices will be best for them.

In the end, only a minority of scholars will ever write quit lit. Despite the challenges and frustrations described in this volume, many persevere through the various stages of the academic career: to completion of their degree, and through numerous years of the hiring cycle, potentially including one or more short-term, underpaid, or geographically undesirable positions. Some scholars do get on the tenure track, get tenure, and go on to have long academic careers. Academia can undoubtedly bring many joys in teaching, research, and intellectual exchange, and for some people sticking out this long and winding path may be the right and rewarding choice. But committing to academia in its current form should be a considered, rational decision made on the basis of evidence and a clear view of probabilities. Scholars can no longer afford to surrender to cruel optimism. Remaining in academia should mean wanting the sort of job that actually exists there. It should involve careful, ongoing contingency planning – or rather, preparation to give oneself the best chance of landing the most rewarding and self-affirming job that beckons, whether that is a faculty position or a role in a different job sector entirely.

This is where quit lit can help, tearing away the rose-tinted spectacles that remain firmly before many of our eyes when viewing academia, and providing models for how other people in similar situations grappled with the realities of, and their investment in, the academic system. Although quit lit cannot lay out any one definitive path forward, we hope this volume helps some of its readers take the first steps to think critically, plan proactively, and consider new possibilities.

References

Benton, Thomas H. [William Pannapacker]. "Graduate School in the Humanities: Just Don't Go." *Chronicle of Higher Education*, January 30, 2009. https://www.chronicle.com/article/graduate-school-in-the-humanities-just-dont-go/

———. "Just Don't Go, Part 2." *Chronicle of Higher Education*, March 13, 2009. https://www.chronicle.com/article/just-dont-go-part-2/

Berlant, Lauren. "Cruel Optimism." *Differences* 17.3 (2006), 20-36.

Fruscione, Joseph, and Kelly J. Baker, eds. *Succeeding Outside the Academy: Career Paths beyond the Humanities, Social Sciences, and STEM.* Lawrence: University of Kansas Press, 2018.

Kendzior, Sarah (@sarahkendzior). "There needs to be a Norton Anthology of Academics Announcing They Quit." Twitter, October 20, 2013. https://twitter.com/sarahkendzior/status/392095346907557888

McMillan Cottom, Tressie. "Blanket 'Don't Go To Graduate School!' Advice Ignores Race and Reality?" *Tressie McMillan Cottom* (personal blog). April 6, 2013. https://tressiemc.com/uncategorized/blanket-dont-go-to-graduate-school-advice-ignores-race-and-reality/

Roiphe, Katie. "Thesis Defense." *Slate*, April 8, 2013. https://slate.com/human-interest/2013/04/a-literature-ph-d-is-not-a-waste-of-time.html

Part One

Original Pieces

Why I'm Leaving Harvard

Matt Welsh

Originally published in *Matt Welsh*, personal blog, November 15, 2010

http://matt-welsh.blogspot.com/2010/11/why-im-leaving-harvard.html

THE WORD IS OUT that I have decided to resign my tenured faculty job at Harvard to remain at Google. Obviously, this will be a big change in my career, and one that I have spent a tremendous amount of time mulling over the last few months.

Rather than let rumors spread about the reasons for my move, I think I should be pretty direct in explaining my thinking here.

I should say first of all that I'm not leaving because of any problems with Harvard. On the contrary, I love Harvard, and will miss it a lot. The computer science faculty are absolutely top-notch, and the students are the best a professor could ever hope to work with. It is a fantastic environment, very supportive, and full of great people. They were crazy enough to give me tenure, and I feel no small pang of guilt for leaving now. I joined Harvard because it offered the opportunity to make a big impact on a great department at an important school, and I have no regrets about my decision to go there eight years ago. But my own priorities in life have changed, and I feel that it's time to move on.

There is one simple reason that I'm leaving academia: I simply love work I'm doing at Google. I get to hack all day, working on problems that are orders of magnitude larger and more interesting than I can work on at any university. That is really hard to beat, and is worth more to me than having

"Prof." in front of my name, or a big office, or even permanent employment. In many ways, working at Google is realizing the dream I've had of building big systems my entire career.

As I've blogged about before, being a professor is not the job I thought it would be.[1] There's a lot of overhead involved, and (at least for me) getting funding is a lot harder than it should be. Also, it's increasingly hard to do "big systems" work in an academic setting. Arguably the problems in industry are so much larger than what most academics can tackle. It would be nice if that would change, but you know the saying – if you can't beat 'em, join 'em.

The cynical view is that as an academic systems researcher, the *very best* possible outcome for your research is that someone at Google or Microsoft or Facebook reads one of your papers, gets inspired by it, and implements something like it internally. Chances are they will have to change your idea drastically to get it to actually work, and you'll never hear about it. And, of course, the amount of overhead and red tape (grant proposals, teaching, committee work, etc.) you have to do apart from the interesting technical work severely limits your ability to actually get to that point. At Google, I have a much more direct route from idea to execution to impact. I can just sit down and write the code and deploy the system, on more machines than I will ever have access to at a university. I personally find this far more satisfying than the elaborate academic process.

Of course, academic research is incredibly important, and forms the basis for much of what happens in industry. The question for me is simply which side of the innovation pipeline I want to work on. Academics have a lot of freedom, but this comes at the cost of high overhead and a longer path from idea to application. I really admire the academics who have had major impact outside of the ivory tower, like David Patterson at Berkeley. I also admire the professors who flourish in an academic setting, writing books, giving talks, mentoring students, sitting on government advisory boards, all that. I never found most of those things very satisfying, and all of that extra work only takes away from time spent building systems, which is what I really want to be doing.

We'll be moving to Seattle in the spring, where Google has a sizable office. (Why Seattle and not California? Mainly my wife also has a great job lined up there, but Seattle's also a lot more affordable, and we can live in the city without a long commute to work.) I'm really excited about the move and the new opportunities. At the same time, I'm sad about leaving my colleagues and family at Harvard. I owe them so much for their support and encourage-

1. "The Secret Lives of Professors," *Matt Welsh* (personal blog), May 24, 2010, http://matt-welsh.blogspot.com/2010/05/secret-lives-of-professors.html

ment over the years. Hopefully, they can understand my reasons for leaving and that this is the hardest thing I've ever had to do.

References

Welsh, Matt. "The Secret Lives of Professors." *Matt Welsh*, personal blog. http://matt-welsh.blogspot.com/2010/05/secret-lives-of-professors.html

Postscript
February 2021

It's been more than a decade since I jumped ship from academia to join industry. It's been a wild ride: I spent more than eight years at Google, built a large team there, launched products used by billions of people, and learned a ton about technology, leadership, product development, and more. As I transitioned from being an individual contributor to a manager to an engineering director, my job became less about hands-on coding and much more about growing and supporting teams. Not surprisingly, I found myself spending most of my days in meetings – endless meetings! – but also juggling a wide range of responsibilities including hiring, mentoring, and both technical and product work. I loved it.

Yet, I decided about two years ago to leave Google and join a tiny startup called Xnor.ai, which was founded – by academics, no less! – from the nearby University of Washington. Xnor developed technology to make AI run fast on edge devices – a beautiful confluence of two of my technical interests. I also wanted to challenge myself by working in a startup, and I fell in love with the fast-paced, high-energy lifestyle. The shift from academia to big company was similar to the shift from big company to startup – a major change of pace with many new things to learn.

I use the past tense in referring to Xnor, because about a year after I joined, Xnor was acquired by Apple, and I found myself back in the Big Tech setting. Apple is a great place to work, but not for me at that time. I pined for the startup life again, and left Apple shortly after the acquisition to join another small company, OctoML – also founded by academics from UW!

I am often asked whether I miss academia, and whether I would ever consider going back.

There are, to be sure, things I miss about being a professor – mostly teaching and the opportunity to work with such brilliant students. (These days, I try to scratch that itch by hiring smart students as interns.) If I were to ever be a professor again, I would approach the job very differently than I did back at Harvard. I have learned so much about building and managing teams, running projects, and maintaining focus, all of which would be invaluable in a university setting. But I've also learned that the most important thing about academia isn't the funding, the talks, the awards, the papers – it's the students. It's unfortunate that so much of the academic process distracts from that simple fact.

Death of a Soul (on Campus)

Karen Kelsky

Originally published in *Tech in Translation*, July 18, 2011; reposted at The Professor Is In (blog), July 3, 2012

https://theprofessorisin.com/ 2012/07/03/death-of-a-soul-on-campus/

THIS PAST YEAR [2011] I left my tenured professor position and administrative role as a Department Head at a Big Ten Research University. I was making close to six figures and was in my sabbatical year.

Why would I do something like that? Why would anyone? I am obviously out of my mind.

A little background: I got my Bachelor's in Japanese Literature from the University of Michigan in 1985. I completed a PhD in Cultural Anthropology, specialization in Japan, from the University of Hawai'i in 1996. I was offered a tenure-track position at the University of Oregon that same year, received tenure at the UO, and was recruited to a tenured joint position at the University of Illinois at Urbana-Champaign in 2003. In 2004 I was made Head of one of my departments. I was Head for the term of 5 years. In 2010 I took sabbatical. During that year my family and I accomplished our long-awaited goal of moving back to Oregon. I submitted my final resignation to the U of I in early 2011.

As a Department Head of a small foreign language and literature department at a major research institution in the Midwest I made, as I said, an excellent salary. I had graduate students, generous summer research funding, and few obligations beyond the ones for which I was paid: holding faculty meetings, balancing the department budget, running searches, meeting staffing needs, handling tenure cases, filing faculty paperwork, and calculating faculty raises, on the occasions there were any. Don't get me wrong, this was a great deal of work. I was busy, stressed, and I worked hard. But I was not nearly as busy and stressed as I had been as a new assistant professor. And I had far more to show for it at the end of the day. I enjoyed administration.

So why would I leave?

This is a hard question to answer in a single blog post, because obviously, my reasons were many, and unique. But in the end they revolved around two fundamental problems: 1) I needed to remove my children from a bad custody situation; and 2) my soul was dying at the University of Illinois.

These two problems intertwined over time – the difficulties I faced in caring for my children became so all consuming that they forced a major life decision: focus all my non-work energies on my children, and give up research, or continue doing research, and put my children's well-being at possible risk. I made the decision without a second thought, but the outcome of making my children my first priority, while remaining in an administrative position, was an end to my writing and research. When the time came to address my second problem – my unhappiness at the University of Illinois – I did not have a publication record that would allow me to move to another faculty position.

And so, my partner and I made a joint decision. If she found a job back in our beloved Pacific Northwest good enough to support the family, I would leave behind academic work entirely.

This was not a completely wrenching decision for me to make. I was ready to leave academia. I had created a jewelry business and was enjoying building that. And I was desperately unhappy at the University. I had reached the unfortunate point where just being on the UIUC campus reduced me to tears.

And this brings me to the crux of the issue: the whole dying soul thing. Why was my soul dying in Illinois? Why was I so miserable? Why was it so bad that I was willing to chuck a highly successful twenty-year career to get away?

People instantly assume it is because Illinois is "conservative" or "homophobic." It is neither. It is a blue state. It is Obama's state. It is politically moderate to slightly left of center in much of its northern half. The college town I lived in was of course an even more liberal-ish sort of place, with more than its share of progressives and the occasional radical.

And as far as homophobia goes – that was a non-starter. From the university to our neighborhood to the kids' teachers to the plumber who came to fix the toilet – people pretty much took us in stride. Even the court system, when custody was at its most contested, categorically refused to countenance any hint of a homophobia, or to consider us as in any way less than or different from a heterosexual family. I won custody. It was heartening.

No, life in Illinois was bad mostly because of the University itself. It was a dreadful place.

When I was at the University of Oregon, even as a harassed assistant professor, it was kind of fun. The students were curious. My colleagues were funny and irreverent. The staff was capable and opinionated. The administrators were down to earth. Nobody took themselves too seriously. We weren't paid for shit. It was actually humiliating how badly paid we were – from administration on down. But people had their unassuming little houses and sweet gardens, and spent their weekends rafting or hiking or biking or driving about visiting wineries. Nearly everyone had a vibrant life outside of work. Dinner invitations flew back and forth, and when someone was facing a life crisis, people pitched in. We organized dinner brigades for new parents, helped out with yardwork for ailing friends. When I had my kids, delicious home-cooked dinners were delivered to our door every night for three weeks.

I assumed that that's how campuses are. I thought they were communities. In fact, being young, and ambitious, I spent much more time focusing on what I didn't have at the UO – a decent salary, adequate research funding, status.

So, when the offer came from the University of Illinois, I jumped at it. I was sure I had made the right decision. Money, status, research funding ... all these things beckoned.

And then I found out. Found out what it's like to be at a place where most everyone is convinced, beyond the shadow of a doubt, that they are very, very important people. Where most everyone is convinced, beyond the shadow of a doubt, that they are doing very, very important work. Where most everyone is convinced, beyond the shadow of a doubt, they are very, very smart. That they are, indeed, the smartest boys and girls in the whole world.

I discovered the unbridgeable, heartbreaking chasm between a place where no one takes themselves very seriously, and a place where pretty much everyone takes themselves very (very) seriously.

A few encounters set the tone quickly: In the first week when I had my music playing as I unpacked boxes in my office, a colleague came by within minutes to say, "please turn that off; it's very distracting." In the first month or so, when one colleague and I drove out into the country for a secretary's housewarming party, and discovered, awkwardly, that we were the only 2 of the 20 or so faculty members invited, who actually had bothered to show up. In the first semester, when, while teaching a seminar in the department seminar room, the Head burst in to berate me in front of the students for not getting his authorization first. In the first year, when I entertained colleagues at dinner parties only to have them act as if they had never met me when next I saw them. When, with painful regularity, the averted eyes and contact avoidance in the hallways made me wonder if Asperger's Syndrome was epidemic on the campus.

Human connection was virtually impossible. Early in my first summer I asked a colleague in English if she'd be free for lunch one day. "I'm sorry, I'm on a strict writing schedule. I only have the nanny from 8 to 5 four days a week over the summer, so those days are out. I could schedule you in one of my off days I suppose."

Of course at first I assumed these encounters were exceptions, and that soon I would find the fun colleagues, the ones with a sense of humor, the ones willing to take time for a human connection. But as the years passed by, I was forced to admit, there really weren't any. At least among the regular humanities and social science faculty members with whom I mostly interacted. I found a few friends in the professional schools, and heard rumors of dinners and parties among colleagues in the sciences "North of Green." And I found one good friend who was non-tenure line. Even the Jews and the queers, far from being the people with the loudest laughs and the raunchiest jokes, were, with but a couple of exceptions, stiff and self-important. Self-important queers? I couldn't even wrap my mind around that one.

The only thing that people "did," outside of work, was leave town. Leave town, that is, to work. I said we invited people for dinner, but really we didn't often succeed in that, because most invitations were met with, "Sorry, I'm at a conference that weekend."

In desperation we started attending a church. It was better. Mostly because no university people were there. But of course, that felt odd too. My family is half-Jewish. And we were, after all, university "types." I like that whole academic schtick, with the sarcasm and the irony and the obscure references. The people at church were mostly lovely, but it never really stuck.

The few times I met others on campus also sadly trolling for human connection, they were on their way out. Nobody who cared about community stayed long at the UI, at least that I could see. I certainly would have exited within a year or two at the most, had I not been tied down by truly inextricable personal circumstances.

As it was, I stayed and kept trying to make it my home, for far, far longer than I expected. But in the end, I failed. Ultimately, I too gave up and stopped trying, and became exactly like the others – insular and unavailable.

I, who have lived and thrived in countless parts of the globe, could not thrive in East Central Illinois.

Sure the weather sucked. But truth be told, I didn't care that much. Sure it was flat and ugly. But in reality, I could live with that.

No, it was the people. The people on campus. I couldn't make it at the UI because of the culture of the UI. It was a culture organized around ego, self-importance, defensiveness, and pretension. Nobody trusted each other. There were no alliances.

At Oregon, the battles around the recruitment and representation of Native American students and faculty had been intense. I had been called on the carpet by Native American students in my classes, and had learned, through hard, earnest dialogue, to be a better, more aware, far less race-blind teacher.

At the UI, such dialogue was impossible. One of my departments fractured the year I arrived when the Latina/o students and faculty finally lost patience with the institutionalized racism and exclusion of the campus. Supported by the wonderful then-Chancellor Nancy Cantor (who was hounded out shortly after by the Good Ol' Boys), they spoke out. But they were not heard. There was no way to hear them. There was no trust or good will. The black students, the Asian students, the white students, the faculty as an appallingly defensive collective – the department splintered into racialized factions, and never recovered, as far as I could see.

Not all faculty members were politically passive during my years there. Some worked to confront the racist Chief Illiniwek mascot, just as some worked to unionize. As I said, it is not a conservative place. No, in the end, it was something worse, for me. It was a cold place. It was an empty place. It was a place where nothing, not any damn thing, was more important than the next publication, the next grant, the next conference.

And I couldn't do it. I could not make it work. Ashamed of myself, lonely beyond belief, alienated in ways I had never imagined possible for someone as energetic and passionate as I am, I stepped away. Faced with the choice between money and status there, and no money and no status in the place I'd known before and loved, I chose the latter. And I have not looked back.

I'm not bitter. I don't hate academia. I know what it means to enjoy an academic job, and I hope that a few lucky individuals still have the opportunity to do that. To that end, I've created a business, *The Professor Is In*, offering my institutional and practical knowledge to graduate students and junior faculty who need it.

For myself, I feel spectacularly lucky to be back in Oregon, raising my kids, building a business, hiking the trails, and working half-time at the

University, this time as an advisor in the McNair Scholars program, which prepares exceptional first-generation, low-income, and underrepresented undergraduate students to apply to and succeed in PhD programs. I am in the right place. I made the right choice, and I'm happy.

On Leaving Academe

Terran Lane

Originally published in *The Chronicle of Higher Education*, August 19, 2012

https://www.chronicle.com/article/on-Leaving-Academe/133717

EARLIER THIS YEAR [2012], I resigned from my position as an associate professor of computer science at the University of New Mexico; in July, I started as a software engineer at Google. Countless people, from my friends to my (former) dean, have asked, Why? Why give up an excellent – some say "cushy" – tenured faculty position for the grind of corporate life?

It's a good question. Tenure represents the ultimate in intellectual freedom; my colleagues in my department were talented, friendly, and incredibly innovative; and I was privileged to work with some excellent students, a number of whom would have fit in just fine at powerhouse institutions like the Massachusetts Institute of Technology or Purdue University.

Honestly, the reasons are myriad and complex, and some of them are purely personal. But I wanted to lay out the ones that speak to larger trends at the university, in New Mexico, in academe, and in the United States in general. I haven't made this move lightly, and I think it's an important cautionary note to sound: The factors that have made academe less appealing to me will also affect other professors. I'm concerned that the United States – one of the innovation powerhouses of the world – will hurt its own future considerably if we continue to make educational professions unappealing.

Making a difference. Ultimately, I got into academic science to make a positive contribution in the world. My goal hasn't changed, but, for some of the reasons I outline below, it has become harder to achieve over time. Google is a strong example of an organization that actually is using advanced computer science to make a real, positive difference in the world. While it's also difficult to make an impact working at an immense company like Google, in the current climate it seems I have a better chance here than in academe.

Work-life imbalance. Immense amounts have been written about the imbalance issue, and I won't try to reprise the arguments here. Suffice it to say that the professorial life can be grueling, if you try to do the job well, and being post-tenure doesn't make it easier.[1] This is a widespread problem in academe, and my university was no different. As of my departure, the University of New Mexico had still not approved a unified parental or family-leave policy for faculty, let alone established consistent policies and support for work-life balance.

Centralization of authority and decrease of autonomy. In my time at the university, I served under four presidents, three provosts, and two deans. The consistent pattern of management changes was centralization of control and resources, and increased pressure on departments and faculty members. Those trends gradually, but quite noticeably, produced implicit and explicit attacks on faculty autonomy (less money under faculty control and more uncertainty). In turn, I (and many others) feel that those attacks subvert both teaching and research missions of the university.

Budget climate. A near-decade of two simultaneous foreign wars, topped off by the most brutal recession in two generations, has left federal and state budgets reeling. A poisonous political climate and a Congressional meltdown has destroyed any chance of coherent, reasoned budget planning.

In the face of such pressures, we have seen at least seven years of flat or declining support for federal science programs while state legislatures have slashed educational spending across the country. Together, those forces are crunching universities, which has led to additional pressure on faculty members. Professors are being pushed ever harder to win ever higher levels of federal research money precisely at a time when that money is ever tougher to come by.

Such trends hurt the university by putting the teaching mission at odds with the research mission and subjugating both to the quest for the elusive dollar. A recent policy change in my old university's engineering school, for example, uses teaching load as a punishment to goad professors into chasing grant money. (Indeed, the policy measures research success *only* as a func-

1. Robin Wilson, "Why Are Associate Professors So Unhappy?" *Chronicle of Higher Education*, June 3, 2012, https://www.chronicle.com/article/why-are-associate-professors-so-unhappy/

tion of dollars brought in. Strangely, research productivity doesn't enter the picture, let alone creativity.)

Hyperspecialization, insularity, and narrowness of vision. The economic pressures have also turned into intellectual pressures. When humans feel panicked, we tend to become more conservative and risk-averse — we go with the sure thing, rather than the gamble.

The problem is that creativity is all about exploratory risk. The goal is to find new things — to go beyond state-of-the-art and to discover or create things that the world has never seen. It's a contradiction to simultaneously forge into the unknown and to insist on a sure bet. Traditionally, US universities have provided a safe home for that kind of exploration, and federal, state, and corporate dollars have supported it (incidentally, buying advanced research far cheaper than it would cost in either industry or government, and insulating those entities from the risk). The combination has yielded amazing dividends, paying off at many, many times the level of investment.

In the current climate, however, all of those entities, as well as scientists themselves, are leaning away from exploratory research and insisting on sure bets. Most of the money goes to ideas and techniques (and researchers) that have proven profitable in the past, while it's harder and harder to get ideas outside of the mainstream to be accepted by peer review, supported by the university, or financed by grant agencies. The result is increasingly narrow vision in a variety of scientific fields and an intolerance of creative exploration. (My colleague Kiri Wagstaff, of NASA's Jet Propulsion Laboratory, has written an excellent analysis of one facet of this problem within our own field of machine learning.)[2]

Poor incentives. The "publish or perish" and "procure funding or perish" pressures discourage exploration outside one's own specialty. It's hard to do exploratory or interdisciplinary research when it is unlikely to yield either novel publications or new grant money (let alone, say, help students complete their degrees) in your own field.

But many things that are socially important to do don't necessarily require novel research in all of the participating fields, so there's a strong disincentive to work on those projects. As just one example from my own experience: My research team was asked to help on a medical-school project that would actually help save babies' lives. But the statistical techniques needed for the project were already established, so there was nothing precisely publishable for my graduate students working on it and no good basis for new grant proposals from the work. Any time spent on it would delay students' progress toward their PhD with nothing to show for it on

2. Kiri L. Wagstaff, "Machine Learning that Matters," 29th International Conference of Machine Learning, Edinburgh, UK, June-July 2012, https://icml.cc/2012/papers/298.pdf

their CV's. When you can't get credit for helping to save babies' lives, then you know there's something seriously wrong in the incentive system.

Mass production of education. There's been a lot of excitement in the media about Stanford University's 100,000-student courses in computer science, MIT's open-sourced classes, and other efforts at mass distance education.[3] In some ways, those efforts really are thrilling – they offer the first truly deep structural change in how we do education in perhaps a thousand years. They offer democratization – opening up access to world-class education to people from all over the globe of diverse economic and social backgrounds. How many Srinivasa Ramanujans might we enable, if only we could get high-quality education to more people? But I have to sound three notes of caution.

First, I worry that mass production in this case will have the same effect that it has had on manufacturing for over two centuries: Administrators and regents, eager to save money, will push for ever larger remote classes and fewer faculty members to teach them.[4] Are we approaching a day in which there is only one professor of computer science for the whole country?

Second, I suspect that the "winners win" cycle will distort academe the same way that it has industry and society. When freed of constraints of distance and tuition, why wouldn't every student choose a Stanford or MIT education over, say, the University of New Mexico? How long before we see the AT&T, Microsoft, or Google of academe? How long before 1% of the universities and professors garner 99% of the students and money?

Third, and finally, this trend threatens to kill some of what is most valuable about the academic experience – to both students and teachers. At the most fundamental level, education happens between individuals – a personal connection, however long or short, between mentor and student.

Whether it's answering a question raised in class, taking 20 minutes to work through a tricky idea during office hours, or spending years of close collaboration in a PhD-mentorship relationship, the human connection matters to both sides. It resonates at levels far deeper than the mere conveyance of information – it teaches us how to be social together and sets role models of what it is to perform in a field, to think rigorously, to be professional, and to be intellectually mature. I am terribly afraid that our efforts to democratize the process will kill the human connection and sterilize one of the most joyful facets of this thousand-year-old institution.

3. Thomas L. Friedman, "Come the Revolution," *New York Times,* May 15, 2012, https://www.nytimes.com/2012/05/16/opinion/friedman-come-the-revolution.html

4. Marcus Wohlsen, "Silicon Valley Creating Jobs, But Not for Everyone," *Wired,* August 3, 2012, https://www.wired.com/2012/08/silicon-valley-creates-jobs-but-not-for-everyone/

Salaries. It has always been the case that academics are paid less – substantially so – than their comparable colleagues in industry. (That is especially true in highly competitive fields, such as science, technology, engineering, and math as well as various health fields, law, and certain other disciplines.)

Traditionally, universities compensate for the disparity with broad intellectual freedom, a flexible schedule, and the joy of mentoring new generations of students. But all of the trends I have outlined above have cut into those compensations, leaving faculty members underpaid, but with little to show for it. As one of my colleagues remarked when I announced my departure, "We're being paid partly in cool. If you take away the cool parts of the job, you might as well go make more money elsewhere."

Anti-intellectualism, anti-education, and attacks on science and academe. There is a terrifying trend in this country right now of attacking academe, specifically, and free thought and intellectualism, generally. Free thought is painted as subversive, dangerous, elitist, and (strangely) conspiratorial. ("That word. I do not think it means what you think it means.")

Universities are accused of inefficiency and professors of becoming deadwood after tenure or of somehow "subverting the youth." (Socrates's accusers made a similar claim before they poisoned one of the great thinkers of the human race.) Politicians attack science to score points with angry voters, religious fundamentalists, and corporate sponsors. Some elements of those feelings have always floated through the United States psyche, but in recent years they have risen to the level of a festering wound in the zeitgeist of the country.

Perhaps those who sling accusations at education have forgotten that the United States helped reshape millennia of social and economic inequity by spreading public education in the nineteenth century? Or that education has underlaid the majority of the things that have made this country great fields in which we have led the world? Art, music, literature, political philosophy, architecture, engineering, science, mathematics, medicine, and many others? That the largest economy in the world rests on (educated) innovation, and that the most powerful military in human history is enabled by technological and engineering fruits of the educational system? That the very bones of the United States – the Constitution we claim to hold so dear – were crafted by highly educated political idealists of the Enlightenment, who firmly believed that freedom and a more just society are possible only through the actions of an enlightened and educated population of voters?

Frankly, it's sickening, not to mention dangerous. If the haters, fearers, and political opportunists have their way, they will gut one of the greatest institutions in human history and, in the process, will cut the throat of this country, draining its lifeblood of future creativity. Other countries will be happy to fill the gap, I'm sure.[5]

There are other factors behind my decision, of course. Any life change is too complex to express in a short essay. Those are the major ones, though.

Nor am I necessarily done with academe forever. I'm going to give the industry track a try for a while, but I could well find myself back in higher education in the future. There are certainly many things I still find beautiful and joyful about faculty work. In the interim, I will look for other ways to contribute to society, other ways to help educate the future, and other ways to change the world.

References

Friedman, Thomas L. "Come the Revolution." *New York Times*, May 15, 2012. https://www.nytimes.com/2012/05/16/opinion/friedman-come-the-revolution.html

Osnos, Evan. "Science Superpowers." *New Yorker*, January 5, 2010. https://www.newyorker.com/news/evan-osnos/science-superpowers

Wagstaff, Kiri L. "Machine Learning that Matters." 29th International Conference of Machine Learning, Edinburgh, UK, June-July 2012. https://icml.cc/2012/papers/ 298.pdf

Wilson, Robin. "Why Are Associate Professors So Unhappy?" *Chronicle of Higher Education*, June 3, 2012. https://www.chronicle.com/article/why-are-associate-professors-so-unhappy/

Wohlsen, Marcus. "Silicon Valley Creating Jobs, But Not for Everyone." *Wired*, August 3, 2012. https://www.wired.com/2012/08/silicon-valley-creates-jobs-but-not-for-everyone/

5. Evan Osnos, "Science Superpowers," *New Yorker*, January 5, 2010, https://www.newyorker.com/news/evan-osnos/science-superpowers

Location, Location, Location

Alexandra Lord

Originally published in *The Chronicle of Higher Education*, September 12, 2012
https://www.chronicle.com/article/Location-Location-Location/134264/

I STILL REMEMBER the post office where I made the biggest mistake of my life. In the fall of 1996, I stood in its outer room holding a manila envelope in my hand, shifting it from hand to hand. To mail or not to mail? That was the question.

It was my second year on the academic job market, and although I had been fortunate enough to obtain a postdoctoral fellowship my first year out, I knew how rare it was to find a job ad that fit you. But this one clearly described me: It was seeking a PhD in British history who could also teach the history of science, with a preference for a medical historian who specialized in women's history. What were the odds of my ever seeing a job ad like that again in my lifetime?

The problem was that the job was located in a region of the country where I did not want to live. I was 30 years old, and I knew myself, my likes, my dislikes, and my needs clearly. This job, for all that I was a "perfect" fit, did not fit me. As I stared at the envelope containing my application materials, I remembered everything I had been told in graduate school and as a postdoc. "You can always trade up." "You may wind up liking the region." "Have an open mind!" And most powerful of all: "Don't be prejudiced, you snobby East Coast urban elitist."

I closed my eyes and dropped the envelope in the slot.

I got the job. Even as I accepted it, I knew that I was making a terrible mistake. The job might have fit someone else perfectly, but I grew up in the Northeast and I had spent six years living a peripatetic life. I'd gone to graduate school in the Midwest, done research in London and Edinburgh, and held a postdoctoral fellowship in the Bay Area. While I had enjoyed living in London and Edinburgh, and while I had begun my 20s believing that I could live anywhere, each move clarified how very much I wanted to return home to the Northeastern United States.

I am the fourth child of a close-knit family. I wanted to live near my widowed mom. I was also eager to be close to my siblings and my very new niece and nephew. Having grown up in a racially diverse area, I wanted to live and work in racially diverse places. As a historian, I loved living where the landscape clearly reflected centuries of dense occupation. Most worrisome of all, as a single woman who wanted to marry, I knew that opportunities to meet a potential spouse would be limited in a small town in the rural Northwest. But who wants to be accused of being an elitist? So I buried my concerns and took the holy grail, the tenure-track job with a 2-2 teaching load.

The next two years were hell – not because my colleagues were unpleasant and not because the job was difficult (they were not and it was not) but rather because I had compromised everything I valued to take the position.

Living in a small town, I was hesitant to see a therapist for fear that my colleagues would know. I had already learned the hard way that indicating that I was unhappy there was unacceptable. Single, I had no one in whom I could confide my unhappiness. I became severely and clinically depressed. Even as I struggled with my depression, I reminded myself that I had it all. The tenure-track job! Affordable living! Low crime! Good schools ... for the children I didn't have! I could barely get out of bed.

Desperate, I applied for all sorts of jobs – ones with higher teaching loads, visiting professorships. Anything, provided it was in the Northeast. After two years, I took a visiting professorship at a less prestigious university in another small town but one that was only 40 miles from my mother. The job had an expiration date, but so did I.

When that date came, I changed careers, left academe, and moved to Washington, DC, to live in an area I had always wanted to live. I met my husband there. Yes, we live in a city where affordable housing is rare, but frankly, despite being mugged twice in our gentrifying neighborhood, I love where I live. Other people might absolutely hate our neighborhood, but that is irrelevant; it suits me perfectly.

This all came back to me when I read David D. Perlmutter's column,

"Embrace Your Inner North Dakotan."[1] He advised new PhDs on the market to persuade "yourself to appreciate different – not 'lower' – standards for your first job. If you are seeking employment, not martyrdom, then a shift in how you view your potential employers is crucial."

But contrary to what Perlmutter and many academics may believe, the reasons that some people do not apply for jobs in, say, North Dakota, rarely have to do with elitism. In speaking to PhDs, both of my generation and those who have recently completed or are in the process of completing their degrees, what I have heard is that their concerns about certain geographic locations are more complicated and personal than just an aversion to a particular region.

Their spouse cannot find a job in a specific region, and they do not want a commuter marriage. They have a child with a disability, and they need a job in a place where the schools can handle the child's specific needs. They feel strongly about being Jewish, keeping kosher, and want to expose their children to a Jewish environment, which makes living in some isolated small towns impossible. Their family is racially mixed, and they want their children to be raised in a place where they will not be alone. They have an aging parent and need to be within a quick direct flight back to their hometown. They are gay and want to live in a place with a significant gay community.

The concerns I have heard over eight years of running *Beyond Academe* – a website that provides job advice for PhDs about leaving higher education – are too numerous to list here as they reflect the complex lives of real people. To anyone struggling with such concerns, they are not trivial, incorrect, or "snobby" – however much they be viewed that way by outsiders.

Critics often say: Shouldn't doctoral students have been aware of the realities of an academic job market in which you don't get to choose where you want to live? In fact, most people enter graduate school in their 20s, a period of intense change in which it's difficult, if not impossible, to predict what your needs and desires will be eight years down the road.

Academic culture can be unforgiving. The message I heard in graduate school, over and over, was that a true scholar sacrificed for her career. My worries about my personal or family life were misplaced, especially as I did not yet have my own family. I listened to people who told me in subtle and not-so-subtle ways that I was wrong to feel as I did and that my concerns stemmed from elitism. And I bought into a culture that told me that leaving

1. David D. Perlmutter, "Embrace Your Inner North Dakotan," *Chronicle of Higher Education*, August 12, 2012, https://www.chronicle.com/article/embrace-your-inner-north-dakotan/

academe indicated that I was not a serious scholar or teacher and that I just did not love history enough.

Academe is, as a faculty friend once put it, incredibly infantilizing. It is one of the only places where faculty members feel no qualms in telling adults in their late 20s and early 30s how to approach the most important decisions of their lives. It is also a culture in which those who leave are often treated with disdain. Although I was an adult and although the people telling me to "try it!" did not know me, I was persuaded to ignore my heart.

Which is why it rankles now when I hear people urge graduate students to "try the academic job in the place they never dreamed of living" or when I read a piece telling PhDs to "embrace their inner North Dakotan." That is poor advice for most people, especially when it comes couched in an assumption that the failure to be "open-minded" in one's job search is a professional or even moral failing.

Recently a new PhD told me that he had just turned down a "good" job as he recognized that taking the position would be a mistake in terms of his personal life. He struggled greatly with the decision and worried that his advisers and colleagues would view his choice as a lack of commitment to his scholarship. What does it say about the power of academic culture that this adult almost made a life-changing decision against his better judgment?

We need to shift the conversation. Don't push people into the choice that worked for you. Instead, speak candidly and without judgment to graduate students about all of their options, in and outside of academe, so that PhDs can make the very real and very complex decisions they need to make about their futures – just as lawyers, doctors, therapists, and other professionals do.

We also need to recognize that if academe genuinely values diversity of opinions, it should be OK that some of us like cities – or rural areas – and that some of us do not and never will.

References

Perlmutter, David D. "Embrace Your Inner Dakotan." *Chronicle of Higher Education*, August 12, 2012. https://www.chronicle.com/article/embrace-your-inner-north-dakotan/

Postscript

October 25, 2020

When I came into the office on September 12, 2012, I idly opened my Internet browser and checked the website of *The Chronicle of Higher Edu-*

cation to see if my piece, "Location, Location, Location," had been published. I then made a mistake – I checked the comments section and felt the blood drain from my face. I was stunned by the vitriol which the piece had provoked.

At the time I wrote the piece, I was the Branch Chief for the National Historic Landmarks Program, the National Park Service's premier preservation program. In my day-to-day work, I worked with people to save the communities in which they lived. It did not matter to me where those communities were or why people loved them. What was important was that *they* loved their communities.

The job was a good fit for me because I am one of those people who, on a spectrum, falls very strongly to the side of seeing place as incredibly important. Obviously, there are some people who feel incredibly strongly about this issue, others for whom location is irrelevant, and lots of people who fall at different points on the spectrum in between.

While in academia, I found the quickness to condemn those for whom place was important deeply disturbing. It was especially odd to see academics push other adults to make decisions that ran counter to their needs and desires. That advisors, faculty, and fellow graduate students made this push under the guise of persuading others to be "open-minded" had a disturbing element of bullying. This, combined with the simple fact that no one possesses the knowledge to make judgments about others' life choices, shaped my decision to write the article.

In critiquing "Location, Location, Location," commentators repeatedly insisted that those for whom place was important should simply not go to graduate school. But this critique missed an important point: people typically enter graduate school in their early 20s, a time of intense change. By the time most PhDs receive their degrees, they are radically different people from the people they were when they began their graduate programs.

Additionally, because academic life is by its very nature peripatetic, many people go on the job market with not just a knowledge of diverse regions but also experience living in many different places.

When I headed off to a job in a very rural region of the country, I was 30. I knew what I liked and I knew, too, what was important to me. This was not a case of a bias against certain areas. Rather it was about being an adult and knowing myself. That I allowed myself to be dissuaded against what I knew to be right for me speaks volumes about the power of academic culture.

In the 20 years since I made the decision to leave academia, I have met many people who made the choice I made to leave academe when it did not fit with their lives. I know, like me, those who leave academe have complicated lives that shape their career choices in ways no one else can possibly understand or judge. None have expressed regret about their decisions and all of them are happy with their personal and professional choices.

After all, it's all about choice. And having a choice is a starting point for happiness.

Thesis Hatement

Rebecca Schuman

Originally published in *Slate*, April 5, 2013
http://www.slate.com/articles/life/culturebox/2013/04/there_are_no_academic_jobs_and_getting_a_ph_d_will_make_you_into_a_horrible.html

WHO WOULDN'T WANT a job where you only have to work five hours a week, you get summers off, your whole job is reading and talking about books, and you can never be fired? Such is the enviable life of the tenured college literature professor, and all you have to do to get it is earn a PhD. So perhaps you, literature lover, are considering pursuing this path.

Well, what if I told you that by "five hours" I mean "80 hours," and by "summers off" I mean "two months of unpaid research sequestration and curriculum planning"? What if you'll never have time to read books, and when you talk about them, you'll mostly be using made-up words like "deterritorialization" and "Othering" – because, as Ron Rosenbaum pointed out recently, the "dusty seminar rooms" of academia have the chief aim of theorizing every great book to death?[1] And I can't even tell you what kind of ass you have to kiss these days to get tenure – largely because, like most professors, I'm not on the tenure track, so I don't know.

Don't do it. Just don't. I deeply regret going to graduate school, but not, Ron Rosenbaum, because my doctorate ruined books and made me

1. Ron Rosenbaum, "Should You Go To Grad School?" *Slate*, December 27, 2012, https://slate.com/human-interest/2012/12/should-i-go-to-grad-school-ron-rosenbaum-explains.html

obnoxious. (Granted, maybe it did: My dissertation involved subjecting the work of Franz Kafka to first-order logic.) No, I now realize graduate school was a terrible idea because the full-time, tenure-track literature professorship is extinct. After four years of trying, I've finally gotten it through my thick head that I will not get a job – and if you go to graduate school, neither will you.

You might think your circumstances will be different. So did I. There's a little fable from Kafka, appropriately called "A Little Fable," that speaks to why this was very stupid:

> "Alas," said the mouse, "the world gets smaller every day. At first it was so wide that I ran along and was happy to see walls appearing to my right and left, but these high walls converged so quickly that I'm already in the last room, and there in the corner is the trap into which I must run."
>
> "But you've only got to run the other way," said the cat, and ate it.

The mouse wasn't going in the wrong direction so much as it was walking cat food the entire time. A graduate career is just like this, only worse, because "A Little Fable" lasts three sentences and is made up, while graduate school lasts at least six years and will ruin your life in a very real way. But, as in the fable, this ruin is predestined, and completely unrelated to how "right" you do things.

Other well-meaning academics have already attempted to warn you, the best-known screed in this subgenre being William Pannapacker's "Graduate School in the Humanities: Just Don't Go."[2] But this convinced no one. It certainly didn't convince me! Why? Because Pannapacker is a tenured professor. He pulled it off, so why can't you? After all, someone has to get these jobs.

Well, someone also has to not die from small-cell lung cancer to give the disease its 6% survival rate, but would you smoke four packs a day with the specific intention of being in that 6%? No, because that's stupid. Well, tenure-track positions in my field have about 150 applicants each. Multiply that 0.6% chance of getting any given job by the 10 or so appropriate positions *in the entire world*, and you have about that same 6% chance of "success." If you wouldn't bet your life on such ludicrous odds, then why would you bet your livelihood?

Don't misunderstand me. There is unquantifiable intellectual reward

2. Thomas H. Benton [William Pannapacker], "Graduate School in the Humanities: Just Don't Go," *Chronicle of Higher Education*, January 30, 2009, https://www.chronicle.com/article/graduate-school-in-the-humanities-just-dont-go/

from the exploration of scholarly problems and the expansion of every discipline — yes, even the literary ones, and even if that means doing bat-shit analysis like using the rule of "false elimination" to determine that Josef K. is simultaneously guilty and not guilty in *The Trial.* But there is one sort of reward you will never get: monetary compensation from a stable, non-penurious position at a decent university.

So you won't get a tenure-track job. Why should that stop you? You can cradle your new knowledge close, and just go do something else. Great — are you ready to withstand the open scorn of everyone you know? During graduate school, you will be broken down and reconfigured in the image of the academy. By the time you finish — if you even do — your academic self will be the culmination of your entire self, and thus you will believe, incomprehensibly, that not having a tenure-track job makes you worthless. You will believe this so strongly that when you do not land a job, it will destroy you, and nobody outside of academia will understand why. (Bright side: You will no longer have any friends outside academia.)

When this happens to you — after you have mailed, at your own expense, the required 60-page dossiers to satellite campuses of Midwestern or Southern universities of which you have never heard; after you endure a deafening silence from most of these institutions but then receive hope in the form of a paltry few conference interviews; after you fork out $1,000 to spend your Christmas amid thousands of your competitors at the Modern Language Association convention; after said convention, where you endure tribunal-style interviews in hotel suites where you are often made to perch in your ill-fitting suit *on the edge of a bed*; after, perhaps, being invited to a callback interview at a remote Midwestern or Southern campus where your entire person will be judged on the basis of two meals and one presentation; after, at the end of all this, they give the job to an inside candidate they were planning to hire all along — when this happens, and it will, it will feel as if the entirety of your human self has been rejected because you are no good at whatever branch of literature-ruining you have chosen.

This is probably not true. On the contrary, you are probably spectacular, due to the manic professionalization of the literary disciplines meant to create PhDs who can compete. Everyone has a book contract, peer-reviewed publications, and stellar teaching evaluations. This was not the case when today's associate professors were hired in the boom of the late 1990s. But don't resent them for insisting that it has "always been hard out there" — just let them buy you lunch. You may also be tempted to resent the generation of full professors teetering ever precariously toward retirement, and thus cleaving ever more resolutely to their positions. Leave them alone — they won't be replaced when they leave anyway; their "tenure lines," as they are called, will die with them.

No, you will not get a job – not because, like Kafka's mouse, you went in the "wrong" direction, but because today's academic job market is a "market" in the sense that one stall selling fiddlehead ferns in the middle of a strip mall is a "farmer's market." In the place of actual jobs are adjunct positions: benefit-free, office-free academic servitude in which you will earn $18,000 a year for the rest of your life.

But how did this happen? Colleges and universities have more students than ever – and charge higher tuition than ever – so whither the humanities professorship amid all the resort-like luxury dormitories and gleaming student centers? Is the humanities professorship extinct because at this very second, thousands of parents of wide-eyed college freshmen are discouraging them from taking literature, philosophy, foreign languages or history (the disciplines that comprised a college education *in its entirety* for thousands of years, but whatever), even though quite unlike humanities PhDs, humanities BA degrees are actually among the most hirable? Or is it, as Rosenbaum and others have suggested, that the overproduction of obtuse torrents of jargon has caused my profession to hasten its own irrelevance?

Who cares? None of this will be sorted out in the five to ten years it takes you to get a PhD. So don't. Sure, you may be drawn to the advanced study of literature like my late grandmother to her three daily packs of Kools – but in the 1950s, smokers didn't know any better. In 2005 when I began my own PhD, I should have known better, but I didn't. Now that you know better, will you listen? Or will you think that somehow you can beat odds that would be ludicrous in any other context?

Look, smarty-pants, let me put this in overcomplicated language you can understand: Ludwig Wittgenstein concluded his *Tractatus Logico-Philosophicus* by proclaiming that anyone who "understood" the work would know to discard everything in it after reading it, to "throw away the ladder" after reaching the top, as it were. But with academia, you don't need to put yourself through five to ten years of the hardest work you will ever do, followed by four years (and counting) of rejection and dejection, simply to conclude that the experience was ill-advised. When it comes to graduate school, you should just chuck the ladder before you try to climb it. You've only got to run the other way.

References

Benton, Thomas H. [William Pannapacker]. "Graduate School in the Humanities: Just Don't Go," *Chronicle of Higher Education*, January 30, 2009. https://www.chronicle.com/article/graduate-school-in-the-humanities-just-dont-go/

Rosenbaum, Ron. "Should You Go To Grad School?" *Slate,* December 27, 2012. https://slate.com/human-interest/2012/12/should-i-go-to-grad-school-ron-rosenbaum-explains.html

Jailbreaking My Academic Career

Jessica Collier

Originally published in *Medium*, April 23, 2013
https://medium.com/altac-chronicles/jailbreaking-my-academic-career-3ec7b0fe1671

I FINISHED MY PhD, in English, in December of 2012. It's been a rough year.

This piece, however, is not of the "just don't go" variety – as in, just don't go to graduate school in the first place, and, if you make it through graduate school, just don't go into academia. This piece is about breaking out once you're in.

While this is not a "just don't go" piece, the "just don't go" conversation is lively and polemical and key to imagining an alternative career path. Most recently, Sarah Kendzior on *Al Jazeera English*, Rebecca Schuman and Katie Roiphe in *Slate*, and Tressie McMillan Cottom on her blog have, respectively, explained the current state of academia for new PhDs; laid bare injured, exiled souls; defended the graduate school experience; and contended that blanket "just don't go" advice ignores racial disparities.[1]

1. Sarah Kendzior, "Academia's Indentured Servants," *Al Jazeera*, April 11, 2013, https://www.aljazeera.com/indepth/opinion/2013/04/20134119156459616.html; Rebecca Schuman, "Thesis Hatement," *Slate*, April 5, 2013, http://www.slate.com/articles/life/culturebox/2013/04/there_are_no_academic_jobs_and_getting_a_ph_d_will_make_you_into_a_horrible.html [pp. 41-45 in the present volume]; Katie Roiphe, "Thesis Defense," *Slate*, April 8, 2013, https://slate.com/human-interest/2013/04/a-literature-ph-d-is-not-a-waste-of-time.html; Tressie McMillan Cottom, "Blanket 'Don't Go To Graduate School!' Advice Ignores Race and Reality?" *Tressie McMillan Cottom* (personal blog), https://tressiemc. com/uncategorized/blanket-dont-go-to-graduate-school-advice-ignores-race-and-reality/

Briefly, the problem behind the conversation is this: In an already volatile higher-ed employment market, the crash of 2008 wiped out 40% of university teaching jobs. Adjunct faculty numbers are at a record high. 76% of university teaching jobs are now adjunct positions, which carry no stability, no benefits, low pay, lower respect, and little chance of mobility. When tenured professors do retire, it is less and less likely that they will be replaced with tenure-track hires. MOOCs and other technology-assisted phenomena, such as software that grades student writing, are radically changing the landscape of higher education.[2] We do not know what college will look like in ten years.

The university is becoming, with a few lucky exceptions, a de facto exploitative labor market. Yet the "total culture" of academia labels those PhDs who choose not to participate as outsiders and failures.[3]

Job market aside, a PhD is a depleting experience. I've written elsewhere about the odd cocktail of exhilaration and exhaustion that attends the process.[4] So, as people like to ask me, what now?

I would not say that I made my decision to "just go" to graduate school under average circumstances. When PhD acceptances and fellowship offers went out, I lay, sweating, in a one-room bungalow in Thailand with a fractured vertebra.

I had taken off for Southeast Asia the previous August, with a teaching job in Malaysia to fund a year of travel. I jumped a Singapore-bound bus one weekend to take the GRE Literature exam. I returned there – Singapore is clean and safe, with minimal distractions and great public transportation – at the end of the semester and holed up in a gaming cave–cum–internet cafe to complete graduate school applications. When the tsunami hit Thailand in December of 2004, I had just traveled north across the Thai border and was relaxing into backpacker mode.

A week or two after the tsunami, I arrived at the Tsunami Volunteer Center (TVC) in Khao Lak, a beach community a few hours from Phuket. I

2. John Markoff, "Essay-Grading Software Offers Professors a Break," *New York Times*, April 4, 2013, https://www.nytimes.com/2013/04/05/science/new-test-for-computers-grading-essays-at-college-level.html

3. Timothy Burke, "Should You Go to Graduate School?" *Easily Distracted* (personal blog), https://blogs.swarthmore.edu/burke/permanent-features-advice-on-academia/features/

4. Jessica Collier, "The Invisible Research," *Medium*, February 1, 2013, https://medium.com/@verbagetruck/the-invisible-research-2936353a78e7

joined a long-term project, rebuilding a nearby village called Tap Tawan, and stayed. In early April, on the morning of the Buddhist 100 days celebration for the dead, the railing of my bungalow's balcony broke, and I fell backwards eight feet down, flat on my back.

I decided this past September, a few months before I was set to file my dissertation, not to go on the academic job market – at least not in the traditional way, which is to apply for every single job in your field and for some jobs that are not in your field, sending messages in bottles from a desolate island of unemployment. I cherry-picked a few from the abysmal job list, less because I wanted those jobs than because I wanted the experience of applying for them.

The job market is a rite of passage for aspiring academics. I needed to obsess over writing samples and statements of teaching philosophy, to groan over the language of the abstract and job letter and other documents that exist only in such a weighty, persnickety way inside academia.

But I couldn't imagine myself in any of the jobs I was supposed to want.

A year or two ago, I realized that I did not self-identify as a teacher. I found teaching fulfilling, and, if student gratitude and evaluations are to be trusted, I was an effective teacher. When I thought about my occupation, however, my mind reverted to "writer." Working with words is intensely difficult – anyone who tells you otherwise is probably not very good at it – and that difficulty for me is analogous to an endorphin rush. All of which is a complicated way of saying that, while teaching is enjoyable, writing makes me happy.

Teaching begets teaching. Most universities do not offer alternative career counseling for graduate students, and PhDs often believe they are not qualified to do anything except teach at the college level, so everyone adjuncts. To afford their lives on adjunct pay, many simultaneously tutor or teach test prep. This work is safe, sanctioned by academic culture as appropriate for young scholars trying to break into a tenure-track job.

I knew the perils of the academic job market. I had friends and colleagues embroiled in it. I also knew that, once finished with the PhD, I was expected to adjunct or take a postdoc and hold on tight through the requisite three or four job market cycles required to get a job or to give up. Each cycle is an academic year.

I knew all of this, and it terrified me. In the final year of my PhD, with a fellowship from a university in London that made it financially feasible not to teach, I began casting around for freelance writing work. I wrote my dissertation in the mornings and afternoons and took on paid work in the evenings. Some of it paid poorly and some, in the end, not at all; initially, billing intimidated me. I made huge mistakes (pro tip: contracts are your best friend) and learned from them. Freelance gigs became longer term consulting gigs. Work follows work.

The world is smarter than academics are trained to believe. In my best moments in private industry so far, the work is stimulating, challenging, intense. It is akin to the best parts of academic life: the moment that you bust through a knotty argument in a chapter or talk, the collegial swelling as strong minds come together at a conference.

There is some tedium everywhere. I don't miss grading papers, scribbling thoughtful end comments and marginal notes on 76 essays, straining to remember that the students who wrote them are individuals and not automated fallacy generators. Similarly, I don't enjoy now the work that involves, say, enumerating directions for the lowest common denominator of user experience.

I do enjoy a sense of possibility and a newfound ownership of my work, unchained from a rigid belief in what makes a career. On that note, in a few days, I leave on a trip to India. Not because, what now? but because the timing is right. Because I can finally kind of afford it. Because a carefully cultivated taste for adventure carried me through the painstaking process of jailbreaking my academic career.

It's been, undoubtedly, a rough year. When it's a choice, rough can be exhilarating: I do not regret how difficult the PhD was in every way. And, while breaking from academia feels like the death of someone close to you, the recompense comes in realizing that not knowing what will happen means anything can happen.

References

Burke, Timothy. "Should You Go to Graduate School?" *Easily Distracted* (personal blog). https://blogs.swarthmore.edu/burke/permanent-features-advice-on-academia/features/

Collier, Jessica. "The Invisible Research." *Medium*, February 1, 2013. https://medium.com/@verbagetruck/the-invisible-research-2936353a78e7

Kendzior, Sarah. "Academia's Indentured Servants," *Al Jazeera*, April 11, 2013. https://www.aljazeera.com/indepth/opinion/2013/04/

20134119156459616.html

Markoff, John. "Essay-Grading Software Offers Professors a Break." *New York Times*, April 4, 2013. https://www.nytimes.com/2013/04/05/science/new-test-for-computers-grading-essays-at-college-level.html

McMillan Cottom, Tressie. "Blanket 'Don't Go to Graduate School!' Advice Ignores Race and Reality?" *Tressie McMillan Cottom* (personal blog). https://tressiemc.com/uncategorized/blanket-dont-go-to-graduate-school-advice-ignores-race-and-reality/

Roiphe, Katie. "Thesis Defense." *Slate*, April 08, 2013. https://slate.com/human-interest/2013/04/a-literature-ph-d-is-not-a-waste-of-time.html

Schuman, Rebecca. "Thesis Hatement." *Slate*, April 5, 2013. http://www.slate.com/articles/life/culturebox/2013/04/there_are_no_academic_jobs_and_getting_a_ph_d_will_make_you_into_a_horrible.html

My Post-Academic Grace Period

Kelly J. Baker

Originally published in *Chronicle Vitae*, November 5, 2013
https://chroniclevitae.com/news/95-my-post-academic-grace-period

IN MAY [2013], I quit my job and moved to Florida. Both decisions might seem big (they were), but they were remarkably easy. My lecturer gig paid little, the teaching load was heavy, and my department was dysfunctional. Leaving behind students, friends, and colleagues was hard. Watching my daughter mourn the loss of her friends was harder.

The move to Florida was unexpected. Out of the blue, my husband was offered a new job with a tech company, which allowed him to telecommute. To my surprise, he took the job, and we decided to move to Florida to be closer to our families. We both walked away from academia, the careers we trained for. That surprised us both. He might go back. I find myself more ambivalent.

Except, I didn't walk away. Not really. Instead, I embraced a safer option, a year hiatus from the academy. Reassess and figure things out, I tell myself, decide whether to stay or not. Delay the inevitable is probably more likely. It is more like a grace period (maybe). Am I going to pay my "debt" to my academic training? Or am I going to do something, anything, else? What I know is that now I have time to breathe, to reflect, to dream, to recreate, and to mourn. I can decide if there is anything that I will miss about academic life. I can decide to take the parts I like (research and writing) and apply them to other careers. I can decide to walk away. The choice, for once, rests on my shoulders.

After six years on the job market, I found myself burned out. I've had conference interviews and campus visits. I've been a second choice for tenure-track jobs multiple times. I applied for jobs while teaching three and four classes a semester. And I finished my first book, wrote articles and book reviews, received a contract for a new book, edited a journal, organized panels, and experimented with an e-book. The harder I worked, I thought naively, the more likely I was to get a job. Optimism is a hard habit to kick.

During this past spring semester, something broke. My tireless drive to research and write dissipated. The latest round of rejections hit harder than previous rounds, and I was tired. Why make myself get up extra early to write if there was no tenure-track job for me? Why spend the time researching when I would rather spend time with my daughter? Why kill myself for a job opportunity that would never materialize? I found that I couldn't do the work I used to love. My motivation stalled. Something broke, and it seemed irreparable.

This was compounded by my increasing frustration with my job as a lecturer. I liked my students, I enjoyed teaching, and I despised the undervaluing of teaching by my department head. I disliked the hierarchy of talents, in which tenure-track and tenured faculty were valued more than those of us who just taught. Being a lecturer meant that my publications could be brushed aside, and that my experience and opinions mattered less. Frustrating doesn't quite cover it.

The desire to throw up my hands and walk away chased me through the day. There must be more to academic life than this. I hoped for something that would make my training and efforts redeemable, and I struggled to find it. Why should I *stay*? That thought is a dangerous one. Once it roots, nothing makes it disappear. It remains and confronts. It pounces on me in Florida now as I try to figure out what I am going to do next.

I mourn what my career could have been, and I struggle to redefine who I am now. Doubt, my old friend, bubbles to the surface as I ponder what I could do alongside what it is possible to do. The grace period is simultaneously too long and too short. Is it a transition? A re-evaluation? A transformation? Is this a shedding of one vision of self to become a better version? Is it a loss of dreams? Is it a moment to dwell in the liminal?

Most days, it is hard to tell. But, I find myself mourning less as days go by. The loss of what could have been is less suffocating and distracting. A transition feels manageable and desirable. The possibilities for what could be are more and more exciting. I might not be an academic after my grace period, and that's okay. I am more than my training. And so are all of you. It is best to never forget that.

My "I Quit" Letter

Melissa Dalgleish

Originally published in *Hook and Eye* (blog), November 7, 2013
https://hookandeye.ca/2013/11/07/my-i-quit-letter/

SARAH KENDZIOR and Rebecca Schuman, two of my favourite pundits on the post-academic problem, have recently agreed that the "I Quit Academia" letter has become an official THING.[1] It's been a thing for a long while – Kenneth Mostern's "What it Means to be Post-Academic" was written in 2001, and I'm sure people penned send-offs long before that – but the genre is proliferating, with Zachary Ernst's "Why I Jumped Off the Ivory Tower," Kendzior's "The Closing of American Academia," Alexandra Lord's "Location, Location, Location" (which I've written about before [in *Hook and Eye*]), Schuman's classic "Thesis Hatement," and Lee Skallerup Bessette's brand-new "Moving Forward."[2]

---

1. Sarah Kendzior (@sarahkendzior), "There needs to be a Norton Anthology of Academics Announcing They Quit," Twitter, October 20, 2013, https://twitter.com/sarahkendzior/status/392095346907557888

2. Kenneth Mostern, "What it Means to be Post-Academic," *Leaving Academia* (blog), March 20, 2001, http://www.leavingacademia.com/blog/career-planning/what-it-means-to-be-post-academic/; [Zachary Ernst's personal blog has since been removed;] Sarah Kendzior, "The Closing of American Academia", *Al Jazeera*, August 20, 2012, https://www.aljazeera.com/indepth/opinion/2012/08/2012820102749246453.html [pp. 133-36 in the present volume]; Alexandra Lord, "Location, Location, Location," *Chronicle of Higher Education*, September 12, 2012, https://www.chronicle.com/article/Location-Location-Location/134264 [pp. 35-40 in the present volume]; Rebecca Schuman, "Thesis Hatement," *Slate*,

For every person who has transitioned into the world of #alt-ac and #post-ac, there's an "I Quit" story to be told. And it seems like more and more people are willing to tell their stories, to throw up their hands and say, openly, that they're through. It's partially a vent, a cry to a world that still believes that professors have it oh-so-easy, that we've all got cushy tenured jobs with summers off and tweed jackets. And it's partially a service: a moment to let others — people like me, people like some of you — see themselves reflected in the words of others, a chance to impart some hard-won wisdom to those who are thinking of academia with stars still in their eyes. Despite being very happily ensconced in a role I would not likely have gotten without having pursued a PhD, I wish someone had told me their story before I started. Like Lee, I'd rather have heard that, and been able to make a clear-eyed choice to still do a PhD, than been given the platitudes and untruths I was.[3]

So then. I quit. And here's my story.

I started my PhD in Canadian literature in 2008. After a year working in publishing after my MA, I started coursework feeling like a bit of a dunce, like I'd forgotten how to speak academese. It took a while to catch up, but I loved it all the same. And then we went on strike. For nearly three months, I did precisely six things. I walked in a circle in the blistering cold, I took the bus, I showered, I ate, I read, I slept. I was exhausted and depressed, and when the strike ended, so did my marriage. I finished coursework, and writing about poetry was my salvation. I started comps, and they were great — because who doesn't love getting paid to hang out with their friends reading and talking about books all day? I mulled over my dissertation proposal for a while, and then wrote it in a weekend. I started working on my dissertation. I published articles and reviews and encyclopedia entries. I gave conference papers. I won grants. I started a peer-reviewed academic journal, helped to run my department's graduate students' association, got great reviews as a teacher. From the outside, I looked like the model of a successful academic-to-be on the rise.

It's hard to tell when exactly it was that the disillusionment crept in. It

April 5, 2013, http://www.slate.com/articles/life/culturebox/2013/04/there_are_no_academic_jobs_and_getting_a_ph_d_will_make_you_into_a_horrible [pp. 41-45 in the present volume]; Lee Skallerup Bassette, "Moving Forward," *Inside Higher Ed*, November 5, 2013, https://www.insidehighered.com/blogs/college-ready-writing/moving-forward

3. Lee Skallerup Bassette, "Journalist or Professor," *Inside Higher Ed*, November 3, 2013, https://www.insidehighered.com/blogs/college-ready-writing/journalist-or-professor

might have been realizing that the adjunct issues we fought so hard for in the strike would soon be, if I kept on this path, my issues. It might have been realizing that in a given year, there were usually about two jobs in my field. It might have been realizing that my partner's mother, despite being a brilliant scholar, struggled to get tenure and then have her excellence recognized by her institution. It might have been recognizing that some of the professors I looked up to most were somewhere between a little and profoundly unhappy on the tenure track. It definitely had something to do with sensing a fundamental disconnect between my desire to exercise control over where I lived and the academy's refusal to admit that as a legitimate desire. It certainly also had something to do with the emotional maelstrom induced by my mother-in-law's death, my partner's grief, a major renovation, and my realization that the project I *really* wanted to do was impossible because of major archival restrictions. Whatever it was, it made me profoundly unhappy. Most of all, I felt very much like every word I wrote of my dissertation was a step closer to the edge of a cliff. Off the end of the cliff was a misty void, a vast nothingness – because if I finished my PhD and didn't become a professor, as I was pretty certain I would not get to become, I would be nothing. My identity was so tied up with being an academic that contemplating not being one was something like contemplating my own death. It was terrifying and paralyzing and profoundly awful. It made me miserable and scared and edgy and sad and eventually, because of all the therapist bills, kinda broke.

That all changed on a sunny afternoon in Winnipeg. I was at the University of Manitoba on an archive trip, and I finished going through all of the boxes I needed a few hours early. One of my earliest #post-ac mentors had recommended that I read *So What Are You Going to Do With That?*,[4] and I decided that I was going to park myself on a bench in the quad in the sunshine and actually take the time to read it. It was, in a word, transformational. Here was a book that was telling me that off the end of the cliff wasn't nothingness. There was a whole world of things that I could do – things that I'd *want* to do, things that I'd *love* to do – that weren't being an academic. They were jobs that would let me have everything I fundamentally wanted – intellectual stimulation, colleagues I liked, financial security, job stability, the ability to have a family on my own timetable, the choice of where I lived – on my own terms. I flew home feeling as though I were the one with wings.

Inevitably, all was not totally peachy thereafter. My desperate desire to stay in academe turned into fury at the system that had taught me that my self-worth lay in conforming to its standards, that those PhDs who didn't

4. Susan Basalla and Maggie Debelius, *So What Are You Going to Do with That? A Guide to Career-Changing for MAs and PhDs* (New York: Farrar, Straus, and Giroux, 2001).

become academics were second-class citizens, lesser, unworthy. Realizing that I was aiming beyond the tenure track certainly removed a lot of the motivation to work on my dissertation, and I spent a lot of time figuring out why I was writing this book, a book that few would read, if not to get a job. Going was very (read painfully) slow until the archival restrictions that had stopped me from pursuing the project closest to my heart were lifted, and I started writing the book I had long wanted to, one that had (and has) intrinsic merit beyond its value on the academic job market.

And then I got lucky. At just the moment when my desire to change what was clearly a broken system was seeking an outlet, an outlet came my way. I got hired as a special research assistant in the faculty of graduate studies, researching and developing policy around graduate student professional and transferable skills development. I got to see how administration worked from the inside, talk to every single program, read the latest research on transferable skills, and find out from students what support they wanted the university to provide for preparing for #alt- and #post-ac careers as well as academic ones. In getting that job, I got luckier than I knew – because I wasn't just researching transferable skills, I was developing them. More accurately, I was recognizing them, recognizing how all of the things that I did as an academic – writing, researching, speaking, analyzing, synthesizing, coordinating, project planning and managing – could be translated into terms that made sense in the working world.

And then I got even luckier – up came a job that required time spent in grad school (but not a PhD), a well-rounded familiarity with my university and its workings, a successful grant-writing record, experience with graduate student professional development, and all of those skills I just listed. I almost missed it. I wasn't even looking for a job. I was planning to spend the year writing, defend, and then look for a job. But this one came up on my Facebook feed, posted by a friend, and – well, you've heard this part of the story. Eh, what the hell, I thought. I scrambled to put together a résumé and a cover letter, sent in my application, and waited. When I got an interview, I went into overdrive and prepared like nobody's business. I met with people who had been in this role, with others at the university with the same job title, with my old boss in the faculty who had worked closely with the person who had just vacated the job. I Googled everyone on the search committee, memorized Vanier guidelines, went shopping for the perfect interview outfit, studied power poses. I agonized over the memories of the interview for my old publishing job, in which my boss basically had to ask me to calm the hell down. But all that prep did just what I wanted it to do. It did calm me the hell down. And without desperate nerves to get in my way, I showed them who I was, and I tried to convince them of two important things: one, that I wasn't biding my time until a tenure-track job came up, and two, that a PhD could be of real value outside of the tenure track.

They bought it, and they gave me the job. And so, I quit. Not as completely as some – I'm still enrolled in the PhD part time, I'm finishing my dissertation because it's a story I'm committed to telling, and I work at the same university as the one I've been doing my doctorate at – but I'll never go on the tenure track. I'll eventually have a PhD, but I'll never be an academic. At one time, if you had told me that, it would have broken my heart. Now, it's just my reality. It took me a long time to believe this, but being an academic is *just a job* – and I have one of those, one that I love. Working in graduate administration has not gotten rid of my resentment for the way academia indoctrinates its graduate students to believe that those who go the #post-ac and #alt-ac route are second-class citizens, or the way it fails to show grad students the ways in which their skills set them apart in the working world, or the way it glosses over the terrible realities of the academic job market in an effort to put on a happy face and keep enrollments up, or the way that it frames precarious labour as a necessary apprenticeship rather than as exploittation. But I'm in a far better position to actually do something about some of that where I am, than I could have where I was headed.

"I quit" isn't the story I thought I'd be telling, back when I started my PhD. But it's one I'm happy to be the main character of all the same.

References

Basalla, Susan, and Maggie Debelius. *So What Are You Going to Do with That? A Guide to Career-Changing for MAs and PhDs.* New York: Farrar, Straus and Giroux, 2001.

Kendzior, Sarah. "The Closing of American Academia." *Al Jazeera*, April 11, 2013. https://www.aljazeera.com/indepth/opinion/2012/08/20128201027492464 53.html

Kendzior, Sarah (@sarahkendzior). "There needs to be a Norton Anthology of Academics Announcing They Quit." Twitter, October 20, 2013. https://twitter.com/sarahkendzior/status/392095346907557888

Lord, Alexandra. "Location, Location, Location." *Chronicle of Higher Education*, September 12, 2012. https://www.chronicle.com/article/Location-Location-Location/134264/

Mostern, Kenneth. "What it Means to be Post-Academic." *Leaving Academia* (blog), March 20, 2001. http://www.leavingacademia.com/blog/career-planning/what-it-means-to-be-post-academic/

Schuman, Rebecca. "Thesis Hatement." *Slate*, April 5, 2013. http://www.slate.com/articles/life/culturebox/2013/04/there_are_no_academic_jobs_and_getting_a_ph_d_will_make_you_into_a_horrible.html

Skallerup Bassette, Lee. "Journalist or Professor." *Inside Higher Ed*, November 3, 2013. https://www.insidehighered.com/blogs/college-ready-writing/ journalist-or-professor

———. "Moving Forward." *Inside Higher Ed*, November 5, 2013. https://www.insidehighered.com/blogs/college-ready-writing/moving-forward

Leaving Academia: "I Can Offer More to the Public Outside University System"

Constantina Katsari

Originally published in *The Guardian*, November 22, 2013
https://www.theguardian.com/higher-education-network/blog/2013/nov/22/leaving-academia-life-beyond-university

FOR THE PAST few years, I have been tormented by inconsistencies in university values and how they put them into practice. Universities in the twenty-first century no longer aspire to become beacons of knowledge, even though they would like to promote themselves as such. Instead, they are trying to turn into large corporations. Their customers are students, their product intellectual property.

In principle, I have no objections to this model of operation. However, it's not why I decided to become an academic in the first place. Almost 20 years ago, graduating in Greece, I was hoping for a life in research. I wanted simply to immerse myself in the study of economic history and fulfil my love of the subject. In order to achieve this, I studied and worked in several European countries, every time leaving behind me loyal friends and a loving family. I was dedicated to my original goal and determined to succeed.

And yet, 20 years later, I found myself caught up in the most absurd situation. On the one hand, I could not conduct any meaningful research as I was working more than 60 hours per week on teaching and administration. On the other, I could not help my students fulfil their dreams; that is, I could not provide them with the right type of education that would allow them to get decent employment in a post-economic crisis. On top of everything else, I felt that I was increasingly removing myself (not just my work) from the real world and the people outside academia who still had an intense interest in my subject area.

The final straw came during a discussion with a Cambridge don. Over dinner he claimed that the last time he had published something he wanted to see published, something he thoroughly enjoyed, was 25 years ago. All of his publications, since then, had been articles commissioned from friends and colleagues, or books that have been negotiated to the last detail with publishers, or pieces of research that complied with the regulations of the few funding bodies. My heart sunk.

The decision to leave my institution – and academia – became the obvious solution, but most of my friends and family were less than supportive. I struggled for almost two years before I took the first step towards freedom. I shared my concerns with a few colleagues who continuously tried to dissuade me from leaving a permanent university post, a job that others "would kill for." Family members reminded me of my newly born twins and their basic needs for sustenance, clothing, housing and ... nappies.

I experienced feelings of guilt and fear that were extremely difficult to overcome. But once I escaped the ivory tower two months ago, encouraged by my husband and brothers, I felt a burden lifting off my shoulders, and a life of possibilities lying in front of me. The plans for my future have already been made. I already knew what I wanted and how to set the process in motion.

I am currently building a business consultancy, helping mostly web-based entrepreneurs in the UK and in Greece. In Leicester, I have entered a partnership with a charitable organisation, Leicester for Business, that teaches startups how to survive and thrive. In Greece, I am collaborating with a local incubator, Colab, to promote the Athens startup scene with courses, pre-accelerator weekends and other exciting ventures.

I have always been an entrepreneur. Ever since I was a kid, I focused on finding business opportunities. I loved the excitement, the ingenuity, the adventure, the unexpected outcomes. I have tried to bring this part of me into university life but it seemed to be incompatible with current processes, practices and expectations. So over my academic career I found myself suppressing a very important part of who I am.

My love of history, of course, remains unabated. I have several pieces of unfinished research that I intend to self-publish over the next few months, as I have a lot more time now than I did in the university. I do not intend to bury my research in inaccessible journals; instead, I will disseminate it digitally. I am also in the process of turning myself into a public historian. I will promote history everywhere and anywhere I go, for as long as I can.

I want to live a meaningful life and feel that I can offer more to the public than I could do under the constraints of a thoroughly bureaucratic and inflexible university system. Wish me luck.

New Game, New Rules

Joe Fruscione

Originally published in *Chronicle Vitae*, February 12, 2014
https://chroniclevitae.com/news/330-new-game-new-rules?cid=vem

MY FIRST DAY of university teaching was August 30, 1999. My last day of university teaching will be April 30, 2014.

A year ago, I was still somewhat optimistic about my chances on the academic job market: *Surely*, I thought, *someone with 14 years of university teaching experience, a book,*[1] *articles and reviews, conference presentations, a Library of Congress lecture, strong connections, and other professional accomplishments (all completed on an adjunct's schedule, no less) can land a tenure-track position, even in this market.*

A year later, the scales have fallen from my eyes. I realize that higher ed is not a meritocracy, and I've been naive. So, instead of drafting academic cover letters and teaching philosophies, I'm writing about why I'm leaving the profession.

The reasons are numerous, and many of them have been discussed on Vitae before.[2] I'm tired of ...

---

1. Joseph Fruscione, *Faulkner and Hemingway: Biography of a Literary Rivalry* (Columbus: Ohio State University Press, 2012).

2. "What We Talk About When We Talk About Quitting," *Chronicle of Higher Education*, December 12, 2013, https://community.chronicle.com/news/215-what-we-talk-about-when-we-talk-about-quitting

- being one of many hundreds of applicants for a single position (for example, I didn't even make the first cut for a job at Marymount University, which drew more than 600 applicants, I was told);
- hearing the words "Just hang in there," or "You're doing such good work; someone is bound to hire you," from those lucky enough to be in stable, tenured positions;
- starting every school year at the same low salary and with the same limited employment and voting rights;
- having no pathway to promotion;
- being asked, "How are you still an adjunct after all you've done?," and knowing I'm qualified and experienced enough to do so much more.

This is not the career I signed up for when I started graduate school in 1998. I've played the game for 16 years and lost: my goal was to land a tenure-track position, and I'm leaving academia without one. If I'm a "failed academic," so be it. I'll be better off as a successful post-academic and future dad.

That doesn't mean I'll be on autopilot for my last semester: There will be no easy A's or needlessly canceled classes or office hours. I'm still engaged in educating my students. I've always been happy balancing my teaching and research interests, and I've dedicated myself equally to both. Lately, though, I've felt wistful about the prospect of leaving the profession I worked so hard – and spent so much money – to enter. I've met some wonderful colleagues who will always be my friends.

Yet I'm also bitter and frustrated about leaving. I've done what I think I'm supposed to do: designed new classes, presented at conferences, published a book, written numerous articles, networked, and generally put my name "out there." I've followed the rules of the game, but the rules keep changing.

I thought I knew what I was getting into when I started graduate school in the humanities (and no, I didn't think I'd have my pick of tenure-track positions). Yet I never imagined that 500 applicants for an Americanist position would become the norm, or that rejection letters would cite "very specific needs" that were never even outlined in the ads.

I also didn't expect to hear stories about search committees *preferring* "fresh" ABD candidates over experienced PhDs. How can more than a decade of teaching and writing experience be so devalued?

So it's time for me to go.

Sydni Dunn said it best in her recent piece on this genre: "Quit Lit isn't about flipping a middle finger to the system. Instead, it's a platform for debunking myths about academics who look beyond the professoriate."[3]

I don't want to burn bridges, fire broadsides at former employers, and shame all tenured or tenure-track faculty for their complicity in a broken, exploitative system – I'm Adjunct Yoda, not Adjunct Hulk, after all.

That said, I've had moments when I've been tempted to scream – like when my former chair emailed me after I left the institution to say the department "never did right by" me. I appreciate the kind words, but I wish s/he'd spoken up when I was there.

And I feel obligated to highlight what's happening in higher ed. As I've told Jennifer Polk of From PhD to Life and the folks at *PBS NewsHour*, it's my sense that universities are deliberately exploiting contingent faculty and citing "budgetary realities" as the excuse.[4] How is it that there are no funds for more tenure-track positions, yet, magically, there's plenty of money for amenities and senior administrative hires who make six-figure salaries?[5]

Which is why the commenters who've sung variations on the "If you don't like it, leave the profession" tune may have a point, vitriol notwithstanding. Perhaps another field or organization will be a better fit for my brain, work ethic, and intellectual integrity.

In the meantime, I've finally accepted that I'll never be admitted to The Club, so I'm taking Rebecca Schuman's sage advice to "never shut up."

Maybe it's time others did, too.

I'm done playing Ivory Tower Calvinball. It's time for a new game and new rules.

References

Dunn, Sydni. "Why So Many Academics Quit and Tell." *Chronicle of Higher Education*. December 12, 2013. https://chroniclevitae.com/news/216-why-so-many-academics-quit-and-tell

3. Sydni Dunn, "Why So Many Academics Quit and Tell," *Chronicle Vitae*, December 12, 2013, https://chroniclevitae.com/news/216-why-so-many-academics-quit-and-tell [pp. 141-47 in the present volume].

4. Jennifer Polk, "Transition Q&A: Joseph Fruscione," *University Affairs*, December 2, 2013, https://www.universityaffairs.ca/career-advice/from-phd-to-life/transition-q-a-joseph-fruscione/; "Why Adjunct Professors are Struggling to Make Ends Meet," *PBS News Hour*, February 6, 2014, https://www.pbs.org/video/why-adjunct-professors-are-struggling-to-make-ends-meet-1398981858

5. "Rocking the Economic Boats of Higher Education," *The Unarmed Education Mercenary* (blog), January 30, 2015, https://theunarmededucationmercenary.blospot.com/2014/02/rocking-economic-boats-of-higher.html

Fruscione, Joseph. *Faulkner and Hemingway: Biography of a Literary Rivalry*. Columbus: Ohio State University Press, 2012.

Polk, Jennifer. "Transition Q&A: Joseph Fruscione." *University Affairs*, December 2, 2013. https://www.universityaffairs.ca/career-advice/from-phd-to-life/transition-q-a-joseph-fruscione/

"Rocking the Economic Boats of Higher Education." *The Unarmed Education Mercenary* (blog). January 30, 2015. https://theunarmededucationmercenary.blogspot.com/2014/02/rocking-economic-boats-of-higher.html

"What We Talk About When We Talk About Quitting." *Chronicle of Higher Education*. December 12, 2013. https://community.chronicle.com/news/215-what-we-talk-about-when-we-talk-about-quitting

"Why Adjunct Professors are Struggling to Make Ends Meet." *PBS NewsHour*. February 6, 2014. https://www.pbs.org/video/why-adjunct-professors-are-struggling-to-make-ends-meet-1398981858

Goodbye to All That: Why I Left the Academic Life

Josh Marshall

Originally published in *Talking Points Memo*, February 24, 2014
https://talkingpointsmemo.com/edblog/goodbye-to-all-that-2

THERE'S BEEN A rollicking debate in the generally non-rollicking and pretty small world of academics, political types and journalists about why academics are so obscure and boring and why they won't get in the game and start contributing and carrying their weight in our country's public debates. That was the framing at least of the [*New York*] *Times* piece by Nick Kristof which (though iffy in itself) kicked the conversation off.[1] One response, for instance, [came] from Daniel Drezner,[2] a very publicly outspoken academic, who was in the curious position of having the publisher of his main outlet, *Foreign Policy*, not only agree with Kristof's thesis but further crap on academics who try to write for a popular audience as "opaque, abstract, incremental, [and] dull," and goes on to say he's going to stop publishing them anymore.[3]

1. Nicholas Kristof, "Professors, We Need You!" *New York Times*, February 15, 2014, https://www.nytimes.com/2014/02/16/opinion/sunday/kristof-professors-we-need-you.html

2. Daniel W. Drezner, "What Nick Kristof Doesn't Get About the Ivory Tower," *Politico*, February 21, 2014, https://www.politico.com/magazine/story/2014/02/nick-kristof-academics-rebuttal-103786

3. David Rothkopf (@djrothkopf), "Kristof gets why we at FP are dialing back academic contributions – too many are opaque, abstract, incremental, dull," Twitter, February 16, 2014, https://twitter.com/djrothkopf/status/435028506984980480

As a general matter, I think Drezner and a bunch of other generally youngish academics are right in their pushback when they say that contrary to Kristof's claims, academics are actually a lot more involved in public debates today than they have been in a while. And a lot of that is because of the Internet and the paths to contact with the larger public has made possible. Think about Juan Cole. A vast contribution to the public conversation about the Middle East, entirely because of the Internet. There's really little precedent in recent decades for anything like him in his area of study. And there are many other academics who have made public names for themselves via online writing, though in many cases writing themselves out of the academy in the process of doing so. If they manage both, it's most likely they have tenure, which likely puts them well into their thirties or beyond.

As I thought about this though, I couldn't help but see it through the particular prism of the decisions I made in my own life, which cut pretty hard to the core of this discussion.

I was supposed to be a history professor. And a good bit of my decision to leave grew out of my growing sense of the deeply conventional, channeled nature of the profession, one in which I found paradoxically little outlet for creativity or novelty.

This wasn't an idea I just came to when I was thinking about what to do after college.

Sometime in high school I zeroed in on history and, because the college I went to allowed you to, I actually declared to have my application evaluated as a potential history major. Through college, with some very momentary exceptions, I never seriously considered doing anything else but getting a doctorate in history and making a career as a professional historian. And after one year out of college — a course chosen entirely because I knew I needed my better, late college grades on my transcript to be able to get into a good program — I enrolled in the history program at Brown University.

Brown wasn't the very best program in the country. There were three or four other programs that had a claim on that title. But it was one of the very best. And I had the additional advantage that I was there to study with a man who was and is unquestionably and rightly one of the most renowned academic historians of his generation, Gordon S. Wood.

Before going any further, I should state explicitly that my situation was significantly different from that of most of the people who are having this debate. If you study the Middle East or macroeconomics or international relations or public policy, your input should be pretty germane to many public questions. If you specialize in English settlers in New England in the mid-17th century, your knowledge is distinctly less relevant.

Still, things got off to a very good start. In fact, going into my preliminary exams toward the end of my second year in the program, I was doing quite well. Already I had a journal article scheduled for publication in a respected peer-reviewed journal, coming out of my first year in the program. I made the cut on year one and then passed my exams at the end of the year. Then I hit something like a brick wall. It was like an anti-epiphany and, though I'm not certain, I think it hit me the night I was out celebrating having passed my prelims. Like a shock, I just thought to myself: "This isn't enough."

It's difficult for me to convey the degree of personal crisis this triggered about my future, since I had been planning on this path for going on a decade. I simply hadn't considered anything else. The trigger, I think, was paradoxically that I was doing quite well. As long as you're trying to climb some new rung or fighting to prove yourself, it's pretty easy not to step back and question the whole premise of what you're doing. Of course, I'd only survived my first year or two of grad school and had the lucky break to get an article published. But I felt like I was doing about as well as I could at that point, enough to let me think about how what I was doing would unfold into the future. And when I looked, I just felt, as I said, "this isn't enough."

The key for me was that I realized that I wanted to do something like what I'm doing today. Obviously, I couldn't imagine quite how things turned out. (It was only around that time that I saw the first primitive web browser, Mosaic – coded, as it happens, by a guy who many years later would become a very minor – in terms of percentage stake – but greatly appreciated investor in [Talking Points Memo], Marc Andreessen.) But I wanted to write about the great issues of the day, about politics and the culture at large. I was pretty sure I had something to say and I wanted to be part of that world.

The only problem was I had no idea how to do it. And I also wasn't sure I had the courage to cut my ties to my plan for my own life. I toyed and more than toyed with the idea of going to law school for the not very good reason that I knew that Mike Kinsley and a number of other writer and pundit types had taken that path into the profession. I did the whole test prep thing; took the LSAT; filled out the applications and at the very last moment decided not to apply to any of them because I realized that I was already half way to one degree that had no clear relation to what I now realized I actually wanted to do. So why was I going to start another?

But even though I was realizing I'd probably just chosen the wrong career, it is important to understand that every incentive in academic life is geared against engagement with the world outside of academics. There's no other way to put it. This has perhaps changed slightly in the intervening 15 or 20 years – with the Internet being a major part of that. But I suspect that's more people acting in spite of these incentives and reacting to the increasingly straitened job opportunities in the profession.

So I settled back down to the business of teaching my classes and finding a dissertation topic with the vague idea that I'd be something like what Kristof has in mind: a professor who also writes for a public audience about the big issues of the day.

But with all of this upheaval in my own plans for my life I started seeing what was now my nominal, chosen profession in a new light. It just seemed too confining than anything I could ever manage. One of the things Kristof misses but Joshua Rothman gets in [a] piece in *The New Yorker* are all the professional pressures that militate against what Kristof seems to imagine is simply a matter of a better attitude or more effort.[4] The paradoxical incentives for conformity, hyper-specialization, ever-narrowing job prospects, the sheer smallness – judged in terms of numbers of people – of the whole enterprise. These are each related and mutually reinforcing.

Once when I was trying to figure out what I was doing I headed up to Wood's office to discuss it with him. Wood was generous and kind and always encouraging to me but rather distant as an advisor. At one point in our conversation, he laid it on the line. "You need to decide whether you'll be satisfied with writing for an audience of two or maybe three hundred people."

Clearly, the correct answer to this was "yes." And as Wood said it, then and now I have the sense he thought posing it in this way would get me back on track with a focus on the scholarly community we were a part of. But hearing it so starkly, in my mind my response was something more like, "Holy Crap, no way! That's definitely nowhere near enough people. And worse yet, I *know* some of those people. And I *definitely* don't want to write for them."

More and more graduate school – both my program and the folks from other schools who I'd meet at conferences – struck me as a sort of institutionalized depression. Much has changed and stayed the same since the mid-90s. But consider the sociology of graduate education in the humanities. To get into a strong PhD program you need to be fairly bright and, even more important, you need strong academic credentials. At least then, those attributes gave you a pretty good shot at a life of at least some and maybe a lot of financial comfort and stability. Law school, medical school, consulting, business or other opportunities.

In this case, you're spending at least 5 or 6 years in school with the distinct possibility you'll never get a full-time tenure-track position. Think about it, the better part of your twenties for the *chance* to get a job. If you do

4. Joshua Rothman, "Why Is Academic Writing So Academic?" *New Yorker*, February 20, 2014, https://www.newyorker.com/books/page-turner/why-is-academic-writing-so-academic

get a job it will likely be somewhere you've never lived or wanted to live and your main goal will be working like crazy to build up enough publishing capital to move on to some other more desirable position. Many end up piecing together various contract gigs with little prospect of finding a permanent job with a future, benefits or anything. Needless to say, this can be a bit depressing. And all the while folks are seeing their college peers getting their first adult incomes in various professions or business or whatever else.

Perhaps unsurprisingly this can generate some pretty toxic intra-group dynamics. And the negativity this involves, I think, pervades a lot of academic life.

Clearly, if it's absolutely what you want to do, you do it. But if there's any doubt, why put yourself through that? As it happens my two best friends from graduate school both ended up with great and very prestigious positions. Mostly that was because they are both extremely bright, dedicated historians. But they also had good timing – graduating during the minor hiring renaissance of the late 90s.

For my part, for a while I figured I'd be one of those professors who professors and also writes magazine articles and columns. But eventually I realized that would mean I would end up mediocre at both. So I scrapped that idea and committed myself to making a career as a writer. After various false starts I was blessed, through a totally fortuitous set of circumstances, to be taken under the wing of the novelist and journalist James Carroll who among other things helped me land my first job in journalism. That was in 1998. The volume of work forced me to set the dissertation aside but I kept myself enrolled for the next four years before finally carving out time in 2002 and 2003 to finish it and get the degree.

I was about to turn 34 and I could feel like the logic and probabilities of the situation were about to turn definitively against me. It barely made sense that going on five years into another profession I'd really shift the car into neutral and start back to work on something so unrelated to the life I was living. If I didn't do it then I never would. And I could not leave it unfinished.

I should say here if it's not already obvious that this is at least as much about me as the academic profession. At the end of the day it just wasn't for me. If we're lucky we know ourselves better as we get older. In retrospect, the idea that I would ever operate well in that sort of confining institutional setting simply made no sense.

For myself I wouldn't change a thing. I learned a huge amount in graduate school about how to think and also how to write. I feel like I use what I learned every day in doing what I do today. Journalism provides very few incentives for going really deep into a topic or, more importantly, a discipline of thinking to think critically about what you know and don't. In some ways, I've barely changed. I rarely read anything but history and almost never about anything that happened in the last century or two.

Because I've achieved some prominence in life, I'm sometimes contacted by academic professional organizations to find out more about what I do as an example that there are other things graduating PhDs can do beside jump and dance for an assistant professorship. For me, as I said, it's all perfect. But really, why would you spend that kind of time getting a degree if in any real sense you weren't going to use it? It would be hard for me to justify that to someone else unless they simply really wanted to spend 5 or 6 years studying history (or whatever else). For my part, I *did* enjoy it. But I realized I'd enjoy being a professor much, much less.

All the incentives of academic life drive against having the time, the need and in many cases the ability to communicate with a larger public. In some cases, that's as it should be. In others, it's about the straitened nature of academic life, specialization driven by bad job prospects, an over-abundance of PhDs, and a deep, *deep* conventionality driven by risk aversion rooted in all of the above.

References

Drezner, Daniel W. "What Nick Kristof Doesn't Get About the Ivory Tower." *Politico*, February 21, 2014, https://www.politico.com/magazine/story/2014/02/nick-kristof-academics-rebuttal-103786

Kristof, Nicholas. "Professor, We Need You!" *New York Times*, February 15, 2014. https://www.nytimes.com/2014/02/16/opinion/sunday/kristof-professors-we-need-you.html

Rothkopf, David (@djrothkopf). "Kristof get why we at FP are dialing back academic contributions – too many are opaque, abstract, incremental, dull." Twitter, February 16, 2014. https://twitter.com/djrothkopf/status/435028506984980480

Rothman, Joshua, "Why Is Academic Writing So Academic?" *New Yorker*, February 20, 2014. https://www.newyorker.com/books/page-turner/why-is-academic-writing-so-academic

Why I'm Leaving Academia

Anonymous

Originally published in *The Guardian* blog, "Academics Anonymous," May 1, 2014.
https://www.theguardian.com/higher-education-network/blog/2014/may/01/academic-anonymous-leaving-academia

IN A FEW WEEKS, I will be leaving my career in academic research. The pleasure of contributing to scientific knowledge has disappeared and I am overworked and undercompensated with no semblance of a work-life balance. The cons of academia now far outweigh the pros, so I am walking away.

I am currently working as a postdoc, which is the purgatory between finishing a PhD and obtaining a long-term fellowship or permanent position. According to the 2013 Careers in Research Online Survey (CROS), 77% of research staff are on temporary, fixed-term contracts, and 87% of these are for less than three years.[1]

The expectation is that you move institutions after one or two contracts. I am currently working as a part of a large physics collaboration and am one-and-a-half years into my first postdoc. I will be told to leave and find another one in two years.

Prospects Are Poor

We put up with this in the hope that we will be rewarded with a permanent

1. Careers Research and Advisory Centre [CRAC], *Careers in Research Online Survey (CROS), 2013 UK Aggregate Results* (Cambridge, UK: Vitae, 2013), 8, fig. 1. https://www.vitae.ac.uk/vitae-publications/reports/cros-report-vitae-2013.pdf/view

position at a university in a town or city we would actually like to live in. Unfortunately, as reported in CROS:

> it seems likely that the expectations of many respondents seeking a long-term career in higher education will not be fulfilled. It is unrealistic to expect that two thirds of current research staff, or even half of those in the early stage of their career, will be able to secure a long-term career in higher education, particularly in the UK.[2]

Postdocs have unrealistic, 24/7 demands placed on us. Because competition for permanent positions is so fierce, the expectation is that we will do anything and everything to boost our career. Physics collaborations are becoming larger and more international, and this means a constant demand for activity throughout the day. Calls are arranged around working hours for the US and western Europe, but unless it is in the middle of the night, there is an expectation of attendance.

There is a non-stop barrage of emails throughout the night and weekend asking for work. For example, I will receive an email at 7 PM asking for it to be taken care of by the end of the day. With the advent of email on mobiles, this expectation has only increased.

Holidays Are Frowned Upon

It used to be that the perks of an academic career included flexitime and more holiday time than industry. These days more and more companies understand the benefits of allowing their employees flexitime, so it is becoming standard in industry.

While we might try to take holiday time as postdocs, it is frowned upon, as you are taking away from time that could be spent publishing papers. If you do go on holiday, there is an expectation that you are checking your emails and keeping in touch, because we are all competing for those holy permanent positions.

I have sat with a colleague on the verge of tears because they had to cancel a weekend away under pressure from their supervisor, who had expressed a desire that an experiment get checked over the weekend.

I never dreamed of becoming a professor; I simply love doing research and I always thought (naively) that after my PhD – during which I worked long hours, slept little and operated under unhealthy stress levels – I would be able to have a hobby again. I signed up for workshops and programmes to develop new, non-research passions and loved every minute.

2. CRAC, *CROS 2013*, 12.

However, it quickly became apparent that this was unfeasible and I was putting my career and reputation at risk by not being able to meet, work or respond to emails during the courses I attended twice a week between 7 PM and 9 PM. I had to give them up after six months and it was extremely difficult, as they were something I truly enjoyed and looked forward to.

Goodbye to a Permanent Job

I have had to force myself to not look at emails throughout the night, mostly because it put great strain on my relationship to have to drop everything late at night to take care of an issue. If I was not able to take care of it, I would obsess over how I would deal with the fallout the next day.

Unfortunately, my decision to switch off was met with this exact statement: "Well, of course you are free to turn off your emails in the evening, but you can say goodbye to any permanent job if you choose to do so for the long term."

I am not oblivious to the fact that many jobs demand extensive travel, long hours, constant email and communication. However, are the low pay (relative to peers in industry), the short, fixed-term contracts, the expectation that you constantly move universities and countries with no guarantee of a permanent position, worth it? Not for me.

This experience (and failed first attempt at a career) has taught me that I personally have to love what I do, and only then will I be happy to work hard and place high demands on myself.

Next month my partner and I will move somewhere we want to live, with the aim of living there for more than two-to-four years, and I will take my resumé to pubs and coffee shops. I just want to find a job now that will give me time to relax, focus on my hobbies and find what I want to do with the rest of my life, and I am actually looking forward to it.

References

Careers Research and Advisory Centre [CRAC]. *Careers in Research Online Survey (CROS), 2013 UK Aggregate Results.* Cambridge, UK: Vitae, 2013. https://www.vitae.ac.uk/vitae-publications/reports/cros-report-vitae-2013.pdf/view

I Have One of the Best Jobs in Academia. Here's Why I'm Walking Away.

Oliver Lee Bateman

Originally published (under the name Oliver Lee) in *Vox*, September 8, 2015

https://www.vox.com/2015/9/8/9261531/professor-quitting-job

MY GRANDMOTHER worked in a school cafeteria. My mother taught second grade. Nearly two decades ago, I resolved to enter public education, too, but with plans to rise even higher. I would become a college professor, advancing the scholarship of my discipline, free from the petty bureaucratic concerns that hamstrung my mother's career.

From 1998 until 2012, I pursued that objective with extraordinary focus. I graduated from college at 19. I went to law school and passed the bar exam. At 24, I was admitted to the history PhD program at the University of Pittsburgh. There, I made connections with brilliant academics, won prestigeious fellowships and grants, and, at the age of 29, just five years after starting graduate school, I landed a tenure-track job.

I can't understate how rare this opportunity is: Tenure-track jobs at large state universities are few and far between.[1] Landing one without serving a postdoctoral appointment or working as a visiting assistant professor is about as likely as landing a spot on an NBA team with a walk-on tryout – minus the seven-figure salary, naturally.

1. See Rebecca Schuman, "Why Your Cousin With a Ph.D. Is a Basket Case," *Slate*, September 23, 2014, http://www.slate.com/articles/life/education/2014/09/how_do_professors_get_hired_the_academic_job_search_explained.html

I had read all of the doom-and-gloom think pieces about the status of the American university system,[2] of course, but it felt like none of that applied to me. I had a full-time position, secured early in my career — the possibilities were endless. Although a legal historian by training, I viewed myself as beyond such simple labels: I was a *cultural* historian, in command of critical theory and immersed in the latest and best work on gender and sexuality. Activism informed my teaching; I exhorted my students to transcend and transform the status quo. I coached my university's legal debate team to a national championship bid and served on nearly a dozen PhD and EdD dissertation committees. I launched several digital humanities initiatives and curated a museum exhibit about professional wrestling, attracting main-stream attention in the process.

I had not just survived the academic *Hunger Games* — I had emerged triumphant.

Then it all began to fall apart.

First there was sniping, from peers and administrators. Critiques of my teaching and debate team coaching, often made through backchannels and delivered to me secondhand or not at all, centered on my easygoing personal style (He doesn't use the title "doctor!" He teaches in T-shirts!), my effusive student evaluations (If he's pleasing them, he must be doing something wrong!), and my relatively calm demeanor (If a young academic doesn't seem stressed beyond capacity, he's not working hard enough!).

Then there was official pushback and politics. A proposal to create interactive teaching materials from archival materials was derided as bewildering and gimmicky. I learned that the public outreach in which I engaged — that is, publishing in popular magazines — had ruffled certain feathers. I watched administrators and donors who had championed my career be shown the door, or at least swept under the rug, by an incoming presidential administration — proving that the autonomy I had imagined upon entering academia really was an illusion.

Finally, I realized not even students were too invested. When my best friend visited my campus to give a talk, he observed one of my lectures. I've got many shortcomings as an academic, but lecturing isn't one of them. I've been on TV, radio, podcasts — you name it.[3] By professor standards, which admittedly aren't that high, I could rock the mic. But while my friend sat there, semi-engrossed in the lecture, he found himself increasingly distracted

2. E.g., Rebecca Schuman, "Thesis Hatement," *Slate*, April 5, 2013, http://www.slate.com/articles/life/culturebox/2013/04/there_are_no_academic_jobs_and_getting_a_ph_d_will_make_you_into_a_horrible.html [pp. 41-45 in the present volume].

3. Oliver Lee Bateman, personal blog, http://www.oliverbateman.com/in-the-media/

by the student in front of him. That student, who like all in-state students was paying $50 per lecture to hear me talk, was watching season one of *Breaking Bad.* In a class with no attendance grade, where the lectures were at least halfway decent, he was watching *Breaking Bad.*

Later during that same visit, my friend asked me, in total sincerity, "Why aren't you doing something meaningful with your life?"

"This *is* important," I insisted. But there was no passion behind my words. I was a priest who had lost his faith, performing the sacraments without any sense of their importance.

Op-eds about the failings of higher education are like certain unmentionable body parts: Everybody's got one. Professors are or aren't afraid of their liberal students, adjuncts are underpaid and exploited, grade inflation is rampant, college graduates can't find jobs, student loan debt will doom us all.[4]

But these are just parts of a larger and even more troubling story. After spending four years working in higher education, trying to effect piecemeal improvements, I'm convinced that the picture is more dire than most people realize: There's no one single problem to fix or villain to defeat, no buzzword-y panacea that will get things back to normal.

And so now, after devoting nearly 20 years to this life, I've decided to walk away. I'm quitting my tenure-track position; by May of [2016], I'll be out of this side of academia forever.

Here are some departing thoughts.

1) Too Many People Go to College

As recently as a year ago, I remained willing to work inside that fractured system of pay-to-play higher education. If students wanted to take out federal loans to buy degrees, who was I to stop them? Let the chips fall where they may; graduate them all and let the invisible hand sort them out.[5]

But that system is unsustainable. Liberal arts programs, and the humanities in particular, have become a place to warehouse students seeking

4. Edward Schlosser, "I'm a Liberal Professor, and My Liberal Students Terrify Me," *Vox*, June 3, 2015, http://www.vox.com/2015/6/3/8706323/college-professor-afraid; Rachel Riederer, "The Teaching Class," *Guernica*, June 16, 2014, https://www.guernicamag.com/features/the-teaching-class/; Oliver Lee Bateman, "Confessions of a Grade-Inflating Professor," *The Atlantic*, June 27, 2014, http://www.theatlantic.com/education/archive/2014/06/the-case-for-grade-inflation/373251/; Leah McGrath Goodman, "Millennial College Graduates: Young, Educated, Jobless," *Newsweek*, May 27, 2015, http://www.newsweek.com/2015/06/05/millennial-college-graduates-young-educated-jobless-335821.html

5. Lee Bateman, "Confessions of a Grade-Inflating Professor."

generic bachelor's degrees not out of any particular interest in the field, but in order to receive raises at work or improve their position in a crowded job market.

Once upon a time, in a postwar America starved for middle managers who could file TPS reports, relying on the BA as an assurance of quality, proof of the ability to follow orders and complete tasks, made perfect sense. But in today's world of service workers and coders and freelancers struggling to brand themselves, wasting four years sitting in classes like mine makes no economic sense for the country or for the students – particularly when they're borrowing money to do so.

Every so often, we're treated to an essay about how liberal arts majors can prepare students to make creative contributions to an employer's bottom line.[6] Do you know how else you can prepare to make these vague creative contributions, much more cheaply and efficiently? By sitting around in your parents' basement and reading great works of literature. Yes, lectures and classroom discussions might help open your mind to new possibilities, but so will skillfully produced videos that are freely available on YouTube.[7] Expert oversight is valuable – but how valuable is it really? I imagine most people wouldn't fork over $50 an hour for the privilege, regardless of their respect for the stellar minds whose contributions to society can rather easily be accessed and understood for free.

2) Online Education Isn't the Solution

Despite my department boasting more than 20 full-time faculty with solid research and teaching credentials, a majority of history students don't come anywhere near their classrooms. Instead, they're remote students, enrolled in an online education.

For some, online degree programs are a solution to the cost and time problem. If there's mass demand for BAs, but the time and expense of real college doesn't make sense for most people, why not provide a similar service digitally? Online classes could unite knowledge seekers from around the world, advocates say, allowing them to get a version of the university experience more compatible with the demands of the modern world.

But in practice, online education isn't a solution – it's a Band-Aid on an infected wound.

6. Jessica Kleiman, "Why Getting A Liberal Arts College Education Is Not A Mistake," *Forbes*, April 28, 2014, http://www.forbes.com/sites/work-in-progress/2014/04/28/why-getting-a-liberal-arts-college-education-is-not-a-mistake/

7. See, e.g., the Khan Academy channel, https://www.youtube.com/user/khanacademy.

In place of thought-provoking video chats and genuinely creative software applications the theory promises, most online students get Blackboard – a cumbersome and inefficient program that only a bureaucracy could love. The "lectures" amount to little more than uploaded PowerPoints that may or may not be accompanied by instructor narration. Usually a single module serves as the university-wide template for an entire mandatory subject, such as US history to the Civil War, allowing professors to be replaced by "graders" capable of administering these courses for even less than the pittance paid to adjuncts. At my university, for example, a grader for one of our online courses supervises approximately 30 to 50 students for an entire course. The grader typically makes $700.

Meanwhile, online classes are – in defiance of all reason – generally longer and more involved than in-person classes. To make up for the lack of in-person instruction, they gorge on assignments, sometimes featuring as many as 60 quizzes in a term. The consequence is cheating as often as education; if you've got a willing partner or three, you could theoretically divide up the coursework and hope the underpaid grader doesn't notice.

Completion rates for online courses are dismal as well, especially at places such as the University of Phoenix Online, which has invested heavily in front-end services like financial aid advising but far less in teachers and student support.[8]

All of this makes perfect sense from an economic standpoint: University administrators are rational actors, and what they're incentivized to maximize are paid student enrollments. There's still no real penalty for failing to graduate students, so why not chase that easy federal money and focus all the effort on upfront enrollment? But what's clear is that this system does not offer a viable, sensible alternative for students; it just allows administrations to exploit the crisis in education to make even more money with even less effort or investment.

3) Tenured Professors Pity Adjuncts. But We Can't Help Them.

We all went into this business with the best of intentions. Those of us who sought PhDs in overpopulated and declining fields knew that the market was not only rough but absolutely brutal; dark humor about the impossible odds facing PhD seekers is part and parcel of the whole grad student experience.[9]

Among the handful of academics who do land tenure-track jobs, one

8. Christopher Beha, "Leveling the Field," *Harper's*, October 2011, http://harpers.org/archive/2011/10/leveling-the-field/

9. See, e.g., Jorge Cham's *PhD Comics*, http://www.phdcomics.com/.

finds little sympathy for the less fortunate. Lip service, to be sure, but academia is a bloodless, endless game of *Survivor* in which every winner is saying to himself or herself, "There but for the grace of God go I" — or, more likely, "Sucks for them, but what can you do?"

As someone who has sat in department meetings, served on hiring committees, and powwowed with other "real" academics at conferences, I can offer the following statement with confidence: No matter how bad things are for the adjuncts, they're effectively non-people to their ostensible colleagues. We won't save you. It's not that we full-timers don't care; it's that we can't. The rules of the game for tenure are simple and terrible — "do twice as much as you think you need to do" — and there's no time to worry about the fallen when your own pay lags well behind the national average.

Life for the liberal arts adjuncts, who surely deserve better, is only getting worse as enrollments climb. University administrators maximize the bottom line, and the bottom line at most non-elite schools is tuition-paying customers. If you can pay someone to teach five history classes for $15,000 or pay someone else $60,000 to teach those same five classes, why bother with the latter? People complain, but there's no real evidence showing that loss of business from students turned off by less-qualified instructors is even close to competing with the savings.

The incentives are especially destructive in the humanities. When administrators do decide to invest in faculty, they tend to favor STEM professors. Those guys rake in the valuable grant money, and thanks to the miracle of co-authored papers, they produce far longer CVs with far better citation counts, a valuable asset when chasing a higher school ranking and the cash that comes with it.

The situation has become dire enough that I often think the only feasible solution would be to eliminate tenure altogether. Morally, such a plan would be repugnant: Academics deserve the freedom to work at their pace and without the fear of too much administrative interference. But economically, it might be the only thing that allows for real labor market flexibility, forcing out elderly and ineffective professors and driving a rise in the standard of living for those many talented adjuncts who are unable to find work under prevailing conditions.

4) "Alt-academia" Isn't a Solution — It's Surrender

So if not to the wretched life of an adjunct, whither our underpaid, over-educated PhDs? The notion of "alternative academic" careers has become a rallying cry for many, particularly those whose alternative academic position involves finding alt-ac jobs for other PhDs.[10]

Briefly put, "alternative academia" is a catchall term for the process wherein individuals, unsuccessful in their quest to become university professors or disillusioned with that sort of work, seek alternative employment at places like libraries, nonprofits, university presses, and private sector think tanks.

These positions are typically filled by people with master's degrees or other terminal credentials; those with doctorates, goes the reasoning, would be able to use their critical thinking skills to excel in such fields, which lack many of the pressures associated with the tenure track but still offer opportunities to undertake meaningful, exciting work.

The concept is good enough in theory, but in practice it's just another way of phrasing the problem: There's not enough room in academia. Go find a job in a different field.

Some blame scholars themselves for the problem — claiming that today's PhD holders aren't as capable or as qualified as generations past. But after sitting on hiring committees and reading hundreds of CVs and writing samples, I refuse to blame the earnest applicants whose sole crime was being told scholarship was a worthwhile pursuit and believing it. If anything, market pressures have resulted in the production of some of the finest scholarship in generations, with even many adjuncts having a handful of great publications under their belts.[11] The problem is that the system is more than happy to take their money and use their services from undergrad all the way to their doctoral graduation, but when it comes time to pay it off with a real job? Sorry — best look somewhere "alternative."

Recently, an article circulated that urged PhD seekers to view their degrees as a six-year, time-limited job, after which they should expect to move on to something else.[12] That's all well and good, but like my $50-a-pop lectures, is that something you'd want to invest in? When presented with such stark questions, I'd imagine most people would say no. Forcing people to master multiple languages, paleography, archival research, coding, yet all

10. Ashley Sanders, "Going Alt-Ac: How to Begin," *Inside Higher Ed*, January 26, 2014, https://www.insidehighered.com/blogs/gradhacker/going-alt-ac-how-begin

11. David Wescott, "Survival of the Fittest in the English Department," *Chronicle of Higher Education*, May 1, 2015, https://www.chronicle.com/article/survival-of-the-fittest-in-the-english-department/

12. Chris Humphrey, "A PhD is a Fixed-Term Job, Not a Passport to a Professorship," *Jobs on Toast* (blog), July 20, 2015, http://jobsontoast.com/phd-fixed-term-job-not-passport-to-professorship/

the while reminding them they need to be ready to retool as academic advisers or advertising executives, isn't a solution to the academic crisis – it's outright surrender to it.

5) The Students and Professors Aren't the Problem; the University System Is

All of these issues lead to one, difficult-to-escape conclusion. Despite all the finger-pointing directed at students ("They're lazy! They're oversensitive! They're entitled!"), and the blame heaped on professors ("Out of touch and irrelevant to a man"), the real culprit is systemic. Our federally backed approach to subsidizing higher education through low-interest loans has created perverse incentives with disastrous consequences. This system must be reformed.

When I started out, I believed that government regulation could solve every problem with relatively simple intervention. But after four years of wading though this morass, I'm convinced these solutions should be re-evaluated constantly. If they're not achieving their objectives, or if they're producing too much waste in the process, they ought to be scrapped. We can start with federal funding for higher education.

The quickest and most painful solution to the crisis would involve greatly reducing the amount of money that students can borrow to attend college. Such reductions could be phased in over a span of years to alleviate their harshness, but the goal would remain the same: to force underperforming private and public universities out of business. For-profit universities – notorious for their lack of anything resembling good academic intention – should be barred altogether from accessing these programs; let them charge only what consumers in a genuinely free market can afford to pay for their questionable services.[13]

Without the carrot of easy access to student loans, enrollments would shrink. Universities would be forced to compete on a cost-per-student basis, and those students still paying to attend college would likely focus their studies on subjects with an immediate return on investment. Lower tuition costs, perhaps dramatically lower at some institutions, would still enable impoverished students eligible for Pell Grant assistance to attend college. Vocational education programs, which would likely expand in the wake of such a massive adjustment, would offer inexpensive skills training for

13. Aaron Glantz, "'Degree Mills' Are Exploiting Veterans and Making Millions Off the GI Bill," *The Daily Beast*, June 28, 2014, http://www.thedailybeast.com/articles/2014/06/28/degree-mills-are-exploiting-veterans-and-making-millions-off-the-gi-bill.html

others.[14] The liberal arts wouldn't necessarily die out – they'd remain on the Ivy League prix-fixe menu, to be sure, and curious minds of all sorts would continue to seek them out – but they'd no longer serve as a final destination for unenthusiastic credential seekers.[15]

In the time that's allotted to us to in life, we have to make many choices. Opting to pursue an unmarketable career solely because one loves it is an available option. But that decision has consequences. In a university system like ours, where supply and demand are distorted, many promising young people make rash decisions with an inadequate understanding of their long-term implications. Even for people like me, who succeed despite the odds, it's possible to look back and realize we've worked toward a disappointment, ending up as "winners" of a mess that damages its participants more every day.

Had I known sooner, I would've given up on this shrinking side of academia many years ago, saving myself plenty of grief while conserving the most valuable quantity of all: time. No one should have to wait so long or sacrifice so much of it for a system like this. Time is money, and we must spend it wisely. Until something is done – something that isn't just a quick fix, something that looks long and hard at the structure of the present university system and tears it up from the foundation, if that's what it takes – the academy is no longer an investment of time worth making.

References

Beha, Christopher. "Leveling the Field." *Harper's*, October 2011. http://harpers.org/archive/2011/10/leveling-the-field/

Deresiewicz, William. "The Neoliberal Arts." *Harper's*, September 2015. http://harpers.org/archive/2015/09/the-neoliberal-arts/

Glantz, Aaron. "Degree Mills' Are Exploiting Veterans and Making Millions Off the GI Bill." *The Daily Beast*, June 28, 2014; http://www.thedailybeast.com/articles/2014/06/28/degree-mills-are-exploiting-veterans-and-making-millions-off-the-gi-bill.html

Humphrey, Chris. "A PhD is a Fixed-Term Job, Not a Passport to a Professorship." *Jobs on Toast* (blog), July 20, 2015. http://jobsontoast.com/

14. Harold L. Sirkin, "What Germany Can Teach the U.S. About Vocational Education," *Bloomberg*, April 29, 2013, http://www.bloomberg.com/bw/articles/2013-04-29/what-germany-can-teach-the-u-dot-s-dot-about-vocational-education

15. William Deresiewicz, "The Neoliberal Arts," *Harper's*, September 2015, http://harpers.org/archive/2015/09/the-neoliberal-arts/

phd-fixed-term-job-not-passport-to-professorship/

Kleiman, Jessica. "Why Getting A Liberal Arts College Education Is Not A Mistake." *Forbes*, Apr 28, 2014. http://www.forbes.com/sites/work-in-progress/2014/04/28/why-getting-a-liberal-arts-college-education-is-not-a-mistake/

Lee Bateman, Oliver. "Confessions of a Grade-Inflating Professor." *The Atlantic*, June 27, 2014. http://www.theatlantic.com/education/archive/2014/06/the-case-for-grade-inflation/373251/

McGrath Goodman, Leah. "Millennial College Graduates: Young, Educated, Jobless." *Newsweek*, May 27, 2015. http://www.newsweek.com/2015/06/05/millennial-college-graduates-young-educated-jobless-335821.html

Riederer, Rachel. "The Teaching Class." *Guernica*, June 16, 2014. https://www.guernicamag.com/features/the-teaching-class/

Sanders, Ashley. "Going Alt-Ac: How to Begin." *Inside Higher Ed*, January 26, 2014. https://www.insidehighered.com/blogs/gradhacker/going-alt-ac-how-begin

Schlosser, Edward. "I'm a Liberal Professor, and My Liberal Students Terrify Me." *Vox*, Jun 3, 2015. http://www.vox.com/2015/6/3/8706323/college-professor-afraid

Schuman, Rebecca. "Thesis Hatement." *Slate*, April 5, 2013. http://www.slate.com/articles/life/culturebox/2013/04/there_are_no_academic_jobs_and_getting_a_ph_d_will_make_you_into_a_horrible.html

———. "Why Your Cousin With a Ph.D. Is a Basket Case." *Slate*, September 23, 2014. http://www.slate.com/articles/life/education/2014/09/how_do_professors_get_hired_the_academic_job_search_explained.html

Sirkin, Harold L. "What Germany Can Teach the U.S. About Vocational Education." *Bloomberg*, April 29, 2013. http://www.bloomberg.com/bw/articles/2013-04-29/what-germany-can-teach-the-u-dot-s-dot-about-vocational-education

Westcott, David. "Survival of the Fittest in the English Department." *Chronicle of Higher Education*, May 1, 2015. https://www.chronicle.com/article/survival-of-the-fittest-in-the-english-department/

Why the Audit Culture Made Me Quit

Liz Morrish

Originally published in *Times Higher Education*, March 2, 2017.
https://www.timeshighereducation.com/features/why-audit-culture-made-me-quit

When, in 2015, I started my blog critically analysing marketisation, consumerism and audit culture in universities, I was aware that a large number of academic staff in anglophone universities seemed to be leaving the profession. I didn't expect to be joining them quite this soon.

Late last summer, for instance, Sara Ahmed very publicly resigned as director of the Centre for Feminist Research at Goldsmiths, University of London, over the alleged sexual harassment of students by staff.[1] At about the same time, I too found myself at a point of feminist snap — the moment at which your faith in academia finally yields to terminal antipathy — albeit for different reasons.

It all happened quite quickly. Last year saw the intensification of outcomes-based performance management in many universities, and I chronicled this on my blog, *Academic Irregularities: Critical University Studies*. This led to invitations to speak at several universities.

In the UK, much of the rush to management by metrics is in response to shifting government incentives and policy changes, which, fed through the mechanism of the research excellence framework, affect institutional prior-

1. Sara Ahmed, "Resignation Is a Feminist Issue," *Feministkilljoys* (personal blog), August 27, 2016, https://feministkilljoys.com/2016/08/27/resignation-is-a-feminist-issue/

ities, reputations and funding levels. Many of these metrics are quite outside the control of academics. Nevertheless, they have been weaponised as tools of performance management, and the very nature of the scrutiny creates a hostile environment for academic freedom.

The most objectionable expectation is that of research grant "capture." According to a 2015 investigation in *Times Higher Education*, one in six UK universities had some form of financialised targets for at least some of its academics, and the trend seems to be continuing even though grant success rates are as low as 12% in one UK research council.[2] I have found it profoundly disturbing to bear witness to an unforgiving climate that seems to privilege economic values to the complete neglect of academic values – or even academic value to a discipline. It is akin to judging athletes on their commercial endorsements rather than on how many gold medals they win.

Other institutions have imposed more granular surveillance under the guise of new "robust" policies of performance management that construct academics as liabilities, not as creative institutional assets. So, for example, at a number of UK research-intensive universities, professors are required to defray their own salaries with grant income, and this "key performance indicator" eclipses any contribution to teaching, scholarship or academic mentoring. At best, this myopic view of performance restricts how that "human resource" may operate, from shifting conceptions of what constitutes research, or work at all, to the narrowing of institutional definitions of "competence" to exclude non-compliant personality types. In more encouraging news, however, management at Newcastle University conceded last summer that it was time to abandon coercive metrics and adopt a consultative and collegial approach to improving research.[3]

Another pernicious development has been the spread of anticipatory performance management, including the requirement to declare intent to publish in designated high-impact-factor journals and in preferred research areas. Even when those "outputs" are peer reviewed and published, they may often be subject to internal reviews, whereby close colleagues are obliged to deliver graded verdicts on them. It is hard to think of a more effective way to pollute collegial relationships and increase personal stress, as well as constrain academic freedom. These career-defining judgements are often

2. "Grant Income Targets Set at One in Six Universities, *THE* Poll Suggests," *Times Higher Education*, June 11, 2015, https://www.timeshighereducation.com/news/grant-income-targets-set-one-six-universities-poll-suggests; "UK Grant Success Rates Prompt Worldwide Comparisons," *Times Higher Education*, October 6, 2016, https://www.timeshighereducation.com/news/uk-grant-success-rates-prompt-worldwide-comparisons

3. Jack Grove, "Newcastle University 'to Drop Draconian Research Targets'," *Times Higher Education*, June 8, 2016, https://www.timeshighereducation.com/news/newcastle-university-to-drop-draconian-research-targets

repurposed as a tool of academic fracking – separating out researchers from teachers. Having been fortunate enough to have a career of more than 30 years in academia, I know that these two endeavours are inseparable.

Sara Ahmed and I are by no means the only feminist academics over the past couple of years to have resigned, after decades of claiming space for collaborative, interdisciplinary and slow scholarship, as well as personal development transformation and reflexive practice.[4] These notions recognise the value of research in contributing to a conversation about power and privilege. And they highlight the fact that apparently objective research may nevertheless reflect the social location of the researcher. Feminists have brought to the academy the theoretical and practical tools to ensure that the impact of different experiences of race, class and gender on academic labour are understood. Feminist scholarship has advanced the argument that there should be no one-size-fits-all performance expectations in the academy.

But although universities may have policies on diversity and inclusion, these principles have evidently been poorly internalised because we now see an embrace of processes guaranteed to amplify structures of inequality. All researchers are now measured against the most exceptional, often unencumbered, scholars, regardless of individual location or ambition. Academics are required to be productive within the tightly delimited notions invoked by management, and to be visibly competitive while never being quite sure what the competition involves.

I have found this to be utterly alienating. Universities in the UK, the US, Australia and many other systems that have adopted a neoliberal model have been turned into what Richard Hall, professor of education and technology at De Montfort University, calls "anxiety machines."[5] In a 2016 paper, "Re-engineering Higher Education: The Subsumption of Academic Labour and the Exploitation of Anxiety," he and Kate Bowles, senior lecturer in communication and media studies at the University of Wollongong in Australia, argue that this anxiety is intentional and inherent in a system driven by improving performance.[6]

There are also emerging threats to academic freedom in the form of

4. Alison Mountz, et al., "For Slow Scholarship: A Feminist Politics of Resistance through Collective Action in the Neoliberal University," *ACME* 14.4 (2015), https://www.academia.edu/12192676/For_Slow_Scholarship_A_Feminist_Politics_of_Resistance_through_Collective_Action_in_the_Neoliberal_University

5. Richard Hall, "On the University as Anxiety Machine," *Richard Hall's Space* (personal blog), March 19, 2014, http://www.richard-hall.org/2014/03/19/on-the-university-as-anxiety-machine/

6. Richard Hall and Kate Bowles, "Re-engineering Higher Education: The Subsumption of Academic Labour and the Exploitation of Anxiety," *Workplace* 28 (2016), https://ices.library.ubc.ca/index.php/workplace/article/view/186211

slippage between the audit and disciplinary functions of performance management. Until recently, I had spent my entire career without having encountered a single colleague undergoing disciplinary action or performance improvement monitoring. Now, recourse to these procedures has become almost commonplace in some universities. It is not clear what results managers expect to emerge from a system that torments staff with unattainable targets, constant surveillance, constant audit and the knowledge that any dip in "performance" may result in their contracts being terminated. But the suicide of Imperial College London professor Stefan Grimm in 2014 after he was told that he was "struggling to fulfil the metrics of a professorial post" should have brought this kind of punitive regime to a swift halt in any ethical institution.[7] Instead, in some universities, the system of "incentives" would be instantly recognised by the subjects of Stanley Milgram's infamous psychology experiments, which tested the willingness of individuals to obey authority even to the point of causing severe pain and distress to others.

My recent work has been situated in the expanding field of critical university studies. This is an approach that invites scholars to be critical of the structures, assumptions and power relations that govern the academy. After all, in the UK at least, academic freedom is enshrined in law, and most university statutes and articles of government reflect this. Yet it is clear that, in practice, universities have rather different thresholds of tolerance for critics of higher education practice. At one extreme is the controversial suspension of Thomas Docherty, professor of English and comparative literature at the University of Warwick, for insubordination after he allegedly made ironic comments and used negative body language towards his head of department. At the other is the defence by the vice-chancellor of the University of Sheffield, Sir Keith Burnett, of the right of one of his academics, Craig Brandist, to write an article likening UK higher education policy to that of Stalin's Soviet Union, after the professor of cultural theory and intellectual history was chastised for doing so by Sheffield's HR department.

This capriciousness of managerial commitment to academic freedom means that to be a critical scholar is to live with uncertainty. Far from being reassured by the published statutes, those of us who blog and tweet must adopt a strategy of academic defensive driving, hoping to avoid what Bowles calls an episode of social media "gotcha" by university management.[8] And if

7. Chris Parr, "Imperial College Professor Stefan Grimm 'Was Given Grant Income Target'," *Times Higher Education*, December 3, 2014, https://www.timeshighereducation.com/news/imperial-college-professor-stefan-grimm-was-given-grant-income-target/2017369.article

8. Kate Bowles, "Networked Professionals," *Music for Deckchairs* (personal blog), June 6, 2016, http://musicfordeckchairs.com/blog/2016/06/06/networked-professionals/

established academics feel threatened, imagine the vulnerability of a young scholar who is called to this kind of work.

In March last year, *Times Higher Education* republished a blog piece that I wrote on the causes of stress and threats to mental health in academic life. The piece recounted how, on University Mental Health Day, I opened up to students about some of the pressures their lecturers were under. Many readers were kind enough to retweet the link, respond under the line or email me personally to let me know that my article resonated for colleagues around the world. But after it had received 10,000 hits on my own blog and spent four days trending on *THE*'s website, my previous employer objected to it and I was obliged to ask for it to be taken down. This inaugurated a disciplinary process that I felt curbed my ability to write further on the topic, or to have a frank dialogue with students on mental health in universities. So I decided to reclaim my academic freedom – outside the academy.

Research in critical university studies inevitably involves being critical of our local working practices and conditions, inasmuch as these have their origin in institutional as well as governmental policy. We must be free to document those experiences and make them available for analysis in terms of power and privilege. Indeed, I regard this as an obligation, and I am sustained in this belief by the generous and encouraging responses posted on my blog.

As I was beginning to write this article [in autumn 2016], I saw a draft of the Copenhagen Declaration cross my Twitter timeline. It offers some principles for ensuring university autonomy, academic freedom and a humane workplace: "These include the right to intellectual and professional self-determination within the context of the organisation's welfare, the right not to be fired at will, the right to a workplace that does not tolerate bullying and other abuses of authority, the right to criticise the institution in public, and the right to reject inappropriate forms of assessment."

I had thought that I and others in the UK already had those rights, but what I see in universities is a repeated failure to align actions with stated principles. There is a widespread perception that when management revokes established rights, this has the effect of eroding academics' trust in the system, and it has certainly contributed to my own disenchantment. Academia badly needs a manifesto for academic citizenship to counteract the project of managerial colonisation. It is obvious that there can be no self-determination or academic freedom within a working environment that is censorious and authoritarian, regardless of how many times "empowerment" features in the strategic plan.

In his seminal 1950 article, "The Idea of a University," the political scientist Michael Oakeshott assumed that "intellectual hooligans" were safely beyond the walls of academia, but now we encounter members of this constituency installed in its plushest offices. At this point, what I value more than anything is the opportunity for activism to reclaim the academy from them, and to write according to my conscience. Unfortunately, this kind of rearguard action can only properly be fought from the outside. And so I have resigned.

References

Ahmed, Sara. "Resignation Is a Feminist Issue." *Feministkilljoys* (personal blog), August 27, 2016. https://feministkilljoys.com/2016/08/27/resignation-is-a-feminist-issue/

Bowles, Kate. "Networked Professionals." *Music for Deckchairs* (personal blog), June 6, 2016. http://musicfordeckchairs.com/blog/2016/06/06/networked-professionals/

"Grant Income Targets Set at One in Six Universities, *THE* Poll Suggests." *Times Higher Education*, June 11, 2015. https://www.timeshighereducation.com/news/grant-income-targets-set-one-six-universities-poll-suggests

Grove, Jack. "Newcastle University 'to Drop Draconian Research Targets'." *Times Higher Education*, June 8, 2016. https://www.timeshighereducation.com/news/newcastle-university-to-drop-draconian-research-targets

Hall, Richard. "On the University as Anxiety Machine," *Richard Hall's Space* (personal blog), March 19, 2014. http://www.richard-hall.org/2014/03/19/on-the-university-as-anxiety-machine/

Hall, Richard, and Kate Bowles. "Re-engineering Higher Education: The Subsumption of Academic Labour and the Exploitation of Anxiety," *Workplace* 28 (2016). https://ices.library.ubc.ca/index.php/workplace/article/view/186211

Mountz, Alison, et al. "For Slow Scholarship: A Feminist Politics of Resistance through Collective Action in the Neoliberal University." *ACME* 14.4 (2015). https://www.academia.edu/12192676/For_Slow_Scholarship_A_Feminist_Politics_of_Resistance_through_Collective_Action_in_the_Neoliberal_University

Parr, Chris. "Imperial College Professor Stefan Grimm 'Was Given Grant Income Target'." *Times Higher Education*, December 3, 2014. https://www.timeshighereducation.com/news/imperial-college-professor-stefan-grimm-was-given-grant-income-target/2017369.article

"UK Grant Success Rates Prompt Worldwide Comparisons." *Times Higher Education*, October 6, 2016. https://www.timeshighereducation.com/news/uk-grant-success-rates-prompt-worldwide-comparisons

Postscript
September 28, 2020

It is now four years since I left my post at a UK university. It was an unplanned departure, but I found myself unexpectedly ready to make the move. The fact is, I was suffering from severe burnout which had endured for several years and which lasted two and a half months past my leaving. Nevertheless, my commitment to my colleagues and to the future of critical university studies was not subdued by the malaise I felt. I retained the hope that I would continue to make a contribution.

By September 2016, I had been writing a blog, *Academic Irregularities*, for about a year. It had been designed to accompany a book project of the same name, co-authored with Professor Helen Sauntson.[1] It was this blog that had got me into what the recently deceased US congressman, John Lewis, called "good trouble." It had also built me an audience of readers who offered many kind affirmations that my words made a difference to their understanding of the academy and conditions of labour there.

My original piece was published in the *Times Higher Education* in early 2017. I wanted to comment on the pernicious environment of management by metrics that had caused so many of my colleagues at multiple institutions to become ill through anxiety and overwork. They had become subject to a ruthless form of performance management which held them to continually increasing standards of "performance," although much actual work was obscured by new, tightly delimited academic workload models. Even some of their research was rendered inadmissible; we have seen the status of the single-authored monograph fall from humanities gold standard to being considered an output of lesser significance because metrics such as impact factor of the publisher and citations cannot be easily tracked.

I simply became exhausted and despondent at the thought of facing years of such treatment and the knowledge that any perceived deficit might result in further punitive measures as policies designed to support academics were repurposed as instruments of coercion and discipline. There was an increased invocation of measures such as "improving performance," "capacity procedures," and a new and unforgiving regime of staff appraisal.

1. Liz Morrish and Helen Sauntson, *Academic Irregularities: Language and Neoliberalism in Higher Education* (London: Routledge, 2020).

Termination of employment was understood to be a very realistic prospect by many who were told their careers were at risk. My point in the original blog piece in 2016 was to argue that if professors had been made to join the precariat, then all academics were vulnerable to insecure employment. The targets were shifting all the time; not just the level of achievement, but also the choice of particular metrics was as uncertain as capricious.

Since leaving the academy, I have not been short of projects that have kept me busy and, importantly, connected to other academics. Twitter has been particularly important in this regard. I have published many more blog posts and journal articles, and have managed to finish the book. I was also commissioned to write pieces for some higher education policy platforms. Along the way I have been invited to give talks to research and trade union groups at universities including Vigo (Spain), Birmingham, Nottingham, Exeter, Cardiff, and Oxford. A series of strikes were called by the University and College Union in 2018 over threats to the Universities Superannuation Scheme amid allegations of a flawed evaluation of the scheme's financial viability. I spoke at several strike rallies. These were all significant events, rewarding to be part of, and important for maintaining a sense of community.

But the big project was a 2019 report on the state of staff mental health commissioned by the Higher Education Policy Institute (HEPI). Drawing on universities' own figures (accessed by freedom of information requests) on increases in referrals to occupational health and counselling by university staff, I was able to substantiate with evidence the argument that the mental health of university staff was declining. The increases were staggering, in some cases between 300% and 400% since 2012. The report attributes the deterioration to factors such as excessive workloads, insecure employment, and punitive metrics-driven performance management policies.[2]

A follow-up publication in 2020 confirmed a further rise in referrals to mental health services. These pieces received extensive press attention, and because of the credibility of HEPI as a higher education think tank, they have been widely quoted.

Many of the forums I have written for are funded by subscription from universities and other stakeholders in higher education. It has amused me to think that the very university which went to such lengths to silence me, now has to pay to read my opinions.

This year, I was finally able to write about the circumstances of my leaving academia in a piece published in March 2020, entitled "Don't Frighten

2. Liz Morrish, "Pressure Vessels: The Epidemic of Poor Mental Health among Higher Education Staff," Higher Education Policy Institute, Occasional Paper 20, May 23, 2019, https://www.hepi.ac.uk/wp-content/uploads/2019/05/HEPI-Pressure-Vessels-Occasional-Paper-20.pdf

the Students: The Crisis of Academic Freedom in the Managed University."[3] This narrated the sequence of events that led to the disciplinary process that culminated in a finding of two charges of gross misconduct: one for "frightening" the students, another for writing a piece which had the potential (unrealised) for bringing the university into disrepute. I had done neither, of course, but that wasn't the objective of the process.

At this point these events are well back in the rear-view mirror, but I still think they are worth sharing and discussing. I understand the reaction of some academics who find the emergence of quit lit objectionable. Why should they read the embittered reflections of those whose privilege has enabled them to leave their posts? However, I think if they read a little further, they would find that very few of these contributions take that stance. What is interesting is why this genre exists in academia and in so few other areas. The fact that academics are by nature critical and reflective should be celebrated, not suppressed.

Nevertheless, it is important to recognise the dimensions of privilege — social, cultural and financial — that allow the genre to emerge. I was able to leave, and sacrifice a salary, because I had the financial capacity to do so. There is a paradox of privilege that attends quit lit, which is that at least I have had something to quit from. Indeed, in writing that, I have defined quit lit as the provenance of the formerly secure. But it is important to recognise, especially for the emphasis of this volume, that as Dave Webster and Niki Rivers point out, most academics who leave the profession are invisible and uncounted when they leave temporary and precarious posts.[4] And I continue to be privileged in that, although the last few years of my career were arduous and frustrating, that adversity allowed me to develop the critique that sustains my work presently. Critical university studies is a field that benefits from the perspective of an insider on the outside.

To be redeemed and justifiable, quit lit should point the academy toward a more ethical and humane future. It should not appear triumphant or condescending to those who remain. I hope it contributes to a conversation about what can be improved for successive generations, including sustainable careers, realistic workloads, and kind, humane and democratic institu-

---

3. Liz Morrish, "'Don't Frighten the Students': The Crisis of Academic Freedom in the Managed University," Council for the Defence of British Universities, April 20, 2020, http://cdbu.org.uk/dont-frighten-the-students-the-crisis-of-academic-freedom-in-the-managed-university/

4. Nicola Rivers and Dave Webster, "Why It's Always Personal ... Rejection, Failure, and the University as a Bad Boyfriend," *Fruits of the Pedagogic Life* (personal blog), April 18, 2018, https://davewebster.org/2018/04/18/why-its-always-personal-rejection-failure-and-the-university-as-a-bad-boyfriend/

tions that see a value in their workers that exceeds a reliance on spurious "metrics."

References

Morrish, Liz. "'Don't Frighten the Students': The Crisis of Academic Freedom in the Managed University." Council for the Defence of British Universities, April 20, 2020. http://cdbu.org.uk/dont-frighten-the-students-the-crisis-of-academic-freedom-in-the-managed-university/

———. "Pressure Vessels: The Epidemic of Poor Mental Health among Higher Education Staff." Higher Education Policy Institute, Occasional Paper 20, May 23, 2019, https://www.hepi.ac.uk/wp-content/uploads/2019/05/HEPI-Pressure-Vessels-Occasional-Paper-20.pdf

Morrish, Liz, and Helen Sauntson. *Academic Irregularities: Language and Neoliberalism in Higher Education*. London: Routledge, 2020.

Nicola Rivers and Dave Webster. "Why It's Always Personal ... Rejection, Failure, and the University as a Bad Boyfriend." *Fruits of the Pedagogic Life* (personal blog), April 18, 2018. https://davewebster.org/2018/04/18/why-its-always-personal-rejection-failure-and-the-university-as-a-bad-boyfriend/

The Sublimated Grief of the Left Behind

Erin Bartram

Originally published in *Erin Bartram*, personal blog, February 11, 2018.

http://erinbartram.com/uncategorized/the-sublimated-grief-of-the-left-behind/

IT HAPPENED during AHA.

I was sitting at home, revising my manuscript introduction and feeling jealous of all of my historian friends at the conference, when I got an email telling me my last (and best) hope for a tenure-track job this year had evaporated.

I'd promised myself that this would be my last year on the market. Now, I'd promised myself that *last* year, and I'd decided to try again, but this time, I knew it was over.

I closed my laptop and walked out of my office. In that moment, I couldn't bear to be surrounded by the trappings of a life that had just crumbled around me. The perfect reading lamp, the drawer of fountain pen ink, the dozens of pieces of scratch paper taped to the walls, full of ideas to pursue. The hundreds of books surrounding me, collected over nearly a dozen years, seemed like nothing more than kindling in that moment.

I cried, but pretty quickly I picked myself up and started thinking about the future. The circumstances of the job I didn't get were particularly distressing, so I discussed it with non-academic friends, explaining over and over again that yes, this is the way my field works, and no, it wasn't surprising or shocking to me, and no, I won't be able to "come back" later, at least in the way that I'd want to, and yes, this was probably what was always going to happen. And then I started looking forward.

Only now do I realize how messed up my initial reaction was.

I was sad and upset, but I didn't even start to grieve for several weeks, not because I hadn't processed it, but because *I didn't feel I had the right to grieve.* After all, I knew the odds of getting a tenure-track job were low, and I knew that they were lower still because I didn't go to an elite program. And after all, wasn't this ultimately my failure? If I'd been smarter, or published more, or worked harder, or had a better elevator pitch – if my brain had just been better, maybe this wouldn't have happened. But it had happened, and if I were ultimately to blame for it, what right did I have to grieve?

Despite the abundance of quit lit out there, we're still not, as a community of scholars, doing a great job dealing with this thing that happens to us all the time. The genre is almost universally written by those leaving, not those left behind, a reflection of the way we insulate ourselves from grappling with what it means for dozens, hundreds, thousands of our colleagues to leave the field.

Quit lit exists to soothe the person leaving, or provide them with an outlet for their sorrow or rage, or to allow them to make an argument about what needs to change. Those left behind, or, as we usually think of them, those who "succeeded," don't often write about what it means to lose friends and colleagues. To do so would be to acknowledge not only the magnitude of the loss but also that it was a loss at all. If we don't see the loss of all of these scholars as an actual loss to the field, let alone as the loss of so many years of people's lives, is it any wonder I felt I had no right to grieve? Why should I be sad about what has happened when the field itself won't be?

Even in our supportive responses to those leaving, we don't want to face what's being lost, so we try to find ways to tell people it hasn't all been in vain. One response is to tell the person that this doesn't mean they're not a historian, that they can still publish, and that they *should.* "You can still be part of the conversation!" Some of you may be thinking that right now.

To that I say: "Why should I?"

Being a scholar isn't my vocation, nor am I curing cancer with my research on nineteenth-century Catholic women. But more importantly, no one is owed my work. People say, "But you should still write your book – you just *have* to." I know they mean well, but actually, no, I don't. I don't owe anyone this book, or any other books, or anything else that's in my head.

"But your work is so valuable," people say. "It would be a shame not to find a way to publish it."

Valuable to whom? To whom would the value of my labor accrue? And not to be too petty, but if it were so valuable, then why wouldn't anyone pay me a stable living wage to do it?

I don't say this to knock any of my many colleagues who write and publish off the tenure track in a variety of ways that they find fulfilling. I just want us to be honest with ourselves about who exactly we're trying to comfort when we offer people this advice and what we're actually asking of those people when we offer it.

We don't want these people to go and we don't want to lose all the ideas floating around in their heads, so we say, "Please give us those ideas, at least. Please stay with us just a little bit." But we're also asking people to stay tethered to a community of scholars that has, in many ways, rejected them, and furthermore, asking them to continue contributing the fruits of their labor which we will only consider rigorous enough to cite if they're published in the most inaccessible and least financially rewarding ways.

We also try to avoid grappling with the loss of so many colleagues by doing just what we do with our students: reminding the departing scholar about all the amazing *skills* they have!

I'm not saying I don't have skills, or that my professional training hasn't refined them. But when we talk to our students about the thinking skills they learn as history majors, we're talking about how they can use those skills to be things *other than historians*. You can use those skills in finance! Insurance! Non-profits! All sorts of regular jobs that your concerned parents will recognize!

Here's the thing, though. I got a PhD in history because I wanted to be a historian. That's what I am trained to be. I didn't write a dissertation on nineteenth-century Catholic women to learn the critical thinking skills of history and then go work in insurance. I didn't spend my twenties earning so little *I ended up helping unionize my coworkers* because I wanted to be in non-profit work.

Obviously, when we're confronted with a colleague in the situation I'm in – someone who didn't want to leave and who doesn't know how she's going to pay the rent after May – we emphasize those skills because we want to reassure this person (and ourselves) that they can find gainful employment, if not necessarily fulfilling work.

But we also emphasize it, I think, for the same reasons we encourage the departing colleague to keep publishing. We don't want to face how much knowledge that colleague has in their head that's just going to be *lost* to those who remain, and even worse, we don't want to face how much knowledge that colleague has in their head that's going to be utterly *useless* in the rest of their lives.

I teach my undergrads skills through content, and I keep the amount of content low, but as both a teacher and a scholar, I personally know *so much stuff*. I have forgotten more about Martin Van Buren than most people around me will ever know. I might find a job that uses that content, but in all likelihood, I won't. I knew what job would pay me to know a lot about stuff that happened in the past. I just couldn't get that job, and now I have to do something else.

Now, there are people who get PhDs and don't want to be professors, and that's great for them and I'm glad they find the PhD a useful part of their personal and professional lives. But let's be honest: most graduate programs in history are preparing students to be history professors. We can talk all we want about alt-ac careers, but when it comes down to it, few of them actually require a PhD, and almost none of them need you to have learned as much as I've learned about the day-to-day operations of rural nineteenth-century parishes. I learned all that because I wanted to be a history professor, and because that's what my program trained me to be. I certainly didn't learn all that because I wanted to find a new career at 35.

I started as a VAP where I currently teach in the fall of 2015 and defended my dissertation that December. I remember feeling really sad at the end of that first month, coming out of the first A&S faculty meeting. I wasn't sad because I didn't think I could do the job, I was sad because I realized that I could do it *really well*. Of course I could do it really well! This was what I had been trained to do. This was what I wanted to do. I was sad because I knew that I might already be on borrowed time – that I probably wouldn't get to do it for my whole life.

And now I know that I won't get to do it for my whole life. I probably won't publish my book, at least not in its current iteration. I won't teach anymore. I won't sit on all those committees that I actually wanted to sit on. If that article that's been under review *for seven months* ever comes back, I probably won't do the work to publish it in a prestigious, paywalled journal. After about half a dozen tries, I finally got accepted to SHEAR, but couldn't even be happy about it. All the stuff in my head – Emerson's ideas of vocation, how to interpret what a dean actually means, the collections at MHS I still need to go through, the entire life story of a woman I've spent the last eight years researching and writing about – doesn't matter in the way that I hoped it would matter: as part of a life spent researching, writing, thinking, and teaching as a member of an institution of higher ed and a broader scholarly community.

I've been writing this in my head for over a month, and after siphoning off about five other significant arguments that will appear later in this [blog] space, I'm finally making myself put it out there. It's become too painful to keep up the facade in public (let's be honest, on Twitter), and I also need to put it out there so I can extinguish the last ember of hope that somehow this has all been a big mistake and I'm actually the recipient of a newly created named chair in Nineeenth-Century American Lady Studies at Literally Any

University-Anywhere.

I don't know what I'm going to do. I don't know what I'm good for. I don't know how to come to terms with the fact that I have so much in my head, and so much in my Google Drive, that is basically useless right now. I don't know how to come to terms with the fact that the life I imagined is not going to happen. I've already stopped doing my scholarship, other than editorial work for forthcoming pieces. In a few months, I'll be done teaching. I don't know how to come to terms with never doing those things again.

Most of all, though, I don't know how to come to terms with the fact that I'll probably never see most of my colleagues again. I won't get to work with so many of you that I'd hoped to work with. I won't even ever get to *meet* some of you. My friends.

I've lost a huge part of my identity, and all of my book learning on identity construction can't help me now. What hurts the most, in a way, is that my loss has been replicated a thousand times over, and will be replicated a thousand times more, barring some mass rejection of capitalism, and rather than face what that means, we have, as a profession and as people, found ways of dealing with it that largely erase the people we lose, erase their pain and grief, and erase our own.

I'm not asking you to feel sorry for me. I'm not sure what I'm asking you to do. All I know is that it was easier for those few weeks when I didn't grieve, but it wasn't honest and it wasn't ever going to get me to a better place emotionally. I suppose I just wonder what would happen if we, as a community, stopped saying, "he's gone to a better place," bringing a casserole, and moving on. What would happen if we acknowledged the losses our discipline suffers every year? What would happen if we actually grieved for those losses?

A few final points:

- No, I don't want to teach high school, either private or public.
- No, I don't want to adjunct or VAP anymore.
- Yeah, this is a highly emotional piece of writing and paints with a broad brush and you might disagree with a lot of the ways I've characterized academia.
- No, I don't care that you disagree. My feelings, thank heavens, are not subject to peer review.
- And finally, the part of this post that makes me most uncomfortable. If this or anything else I've ever written or tweeted has been interesting or helpful to you, you can buy me a cup of tea: https://ko-fi.com/erinbartram.

Just Another Piece of Quit Lit

Joseph Conley

Originally published in *The Chronicle of Higher Education*, March 8, 2018
https://www.chronicle.com/article/Just-Another-Piece-of-Quit-Lit/242756

A FEW YEARS AGO I quit my PhD program. It was the second-best decision I've ever made. They don't write novels or make movies about us quitters. That honor is reserved for people who never gave up, believed in themselves, didn't listen to all the naysayers, and persevered. However, with graduate-school attrition rates at around 50 percent,[1] half of us never reach the PhD promised land. I'm a quitter. And, honestly, I think some of you should be, too.

It is hard to tell people that you've quit something. I remember feeling a powerful terror, expecting people I told to cut ties with me. I know that sounds terribly hyperbolic, but since my parents had said they were proud of me for pursuing a doctorate, I assumed they would be ashamed of me for quitting. Over the years, my friends had overshot me in life markers, but that was easy to justify based on my "higher pursuits." With that ego-crutch removed, I was forced to face what I hadn't accomplished.

As it turned out, (almost) no one abandoned me because of my loss of faith in graduate study. Instead, my relational terror was replaced by an existential terror as I realized that all of those specialized topics we study so

1. Leonard Cassuto, "PhD Attrition: How Much Is Too Much?" *Chronicle of Higher Education*, July 1, 2013, https://www.chronicle.com/article/PhD-Attrition-How-Much-Is/140045

deeply for so long in graduate school are – for the most part – of zero interest to anyone else.

I wish I could tell you that, at least professionally, it was easy to make the transition into the "real" world. But that would be a lie. I spent my first post-academic summer and fall working at a marina in Maine. I had, in my heart, given up on academe but had not yet done so on paper. The marina was a romantic, clichéd, self-imposed exile, and if I hadn't been so depressed I would have been happy.

From there, I got work as a hospital security guard. I was punched, kicked, bit, scratched, and hit with every substance the human body can produce. I liked it more than my doctoral program, and so I officially severed ties.

Remember when I said that most people have no interest in our research? They also don't see it as viable work experience. And as much as I tried to tout my soft skills, application after application went unanswered – or so it seemed in those early months. The whole process sucked. But it (and therapy) gave me plenty of opportunity to reflect on graduate school and why I left.

Most "quit lit" articles I've read focus on the dismal tenure-track job market, the particulars of the student-adviser relationship, and the support that a doctoral program can (but often doesn't) provide. To be sure, all of those were factors in my decision to leave graduate school. But at the end of the day, and after much soul searching, I've concluded that I never should have been there in the first place.

I entered college bright-eyed and bushy-tailed but directionless. I had a vague idea that maybe I would become a lawyer but no real commitment to it. What I did have a commitment to was pleasing the adults around me. And that meant mirroring their career choices. It just so happened I was surrounded by professors.

All of my training up to that point had made me exceptionally proficient at being a student, so jumping through the hoops required to get into a PhD program was right in my wheelhouse. I had heard the warning: "Only pursue a PhD if there is literally nothing else you can imagine yourself doing." Every time I heard it, I nodded in agreement, confident that that was me.

But I knew nothing. I had assumed that the entire business world consisted of salespeople and paper pushers. I could either: (a) be a professor or (b) endure the soul-crushing monotony of corporate life. I didn't choose the professoriate so much as I thought it was the only appealing choice.

And it was great – for a while. I loved my master's program and looked up to the doctoral students, eager to join their ranks. It wasn't until I started the PhD program that a cynicism began to creep in.

The work I was doing became increasingly less inspiring. Time in the library, once an adventure, became a chore. Conference presentations seemed like nothing more than an attempt to get an additional line on my CV, with no one on the panels particularly interested in what anyone else had to say. Some presenters showed up on stage with nothing more than a few hastily scribbled notes, indicating that even *they* didn't care what they had to say. I got an article in a peer-reviewed journal; only the reviewers ever read it.

As the voices of existential dread grew louder in my head, I did more to drown them out. I started drinking more. Soon I forgot what it was like to wake up without a headache. Lacking funds, I survived on coffee and cheap whiskey – and not always in the expected order. I even started smoking.

My one real complaint against academe is that it doesn't problematize that sort of behavior. In fact, it romanticizes alcoholism, isolation, and poor health choices, as graduate students convince themselves that loneliness and excessive drinking somehow make them an intellectual.

But there is nothing heroic about that lifestyle, and if life choices are driving you to self-destructive behavior, it is time for new life choices. It is time to quit. Unfortunately, I didn't figure that out right away. So instead, I became a cynical, misanthropic drunk who terrified my parents and torpedoed a relationship with a great girl who deserved better. Don't do that. Don't be that person. You, and the people in your life, deserve better.

So I quit. And ... life is pretty great now. As I've noted, it took some time to reach this point. It also took some crappy jobs and some therapy. But life on the other side is so much better. My job (they actually pay me to do this) is to teach technical and fund-raising skills to nonprofit professionals. Most months I'll train about 200 people, all of whom will immediately use the skills they've learned to make the world a better place. How cool is that?

I earn enough to pay my bills (including student loans), put money away in savings, and still have some left over to go out to dinner with my wife on date night.

To be honest, I've found the for-profit world to be far more supportive of me as a person than academe ever was. Rather than being soul-crushing, working for "the man" has been liberating and allowed me to be who I want to be in the world. Plus, my parents aren't terrified anymore, which is a nice perk.

Maybe none of what I've said resonates with you. Maybe for you, graduate school has been wonderful and supportive, and achieves all the ideals that it promised. Maybe you are thrilled to be a doctoral student. Maybe you are even angry that I would threaten your beloved institution. Well, this article isn't for you, and, anyway, shouldn't you be writing?

Perhaps you completed your PhD, and are languishing in adjunct purgatory. Does what I've said apply to you? I don't know. I didn't make it far enough to earn the right to answer that question.

This essay is for people who, reading along, thought, "Yeah, that sounds like me." You don't have to finish your PhD. Even if you did, you don't have to stay in academe. You aren't stuck. You aren't trapped. This isn't your only option. If working on your PhD and pursuing a faculty career are making you someone you don't like, then stop being that person. I promise, no one cares about your research topic anyway, and people will still be your friend.

There are amazing, fulfilling, supportive, and meaningful jobs outside of higher education. So just quit. Or, rather, realize that deciding you are stuck doing something that is destroying you because of a decision you made when you were 21 is the real quitting.

References

Cassuto, Leonard. "PhD Attrition: How Much Is Too Much?" *Chronicle of Higher Education*, July 1, 2013. https://www.chronicle.com/article/PhD-Attrition-How-Much-Is/140045

On Quitting Academia

Malcolm Gaskill

Originally published in the *London Review of Books*, vol. 42, no. 18, September 24, 2020

https://www.lrb.co.uk/the-paper/v42/n18/malcolm-gaskill/diary

IN MAY, I gave up my academic career after 27 years. A voluntary severance scheme had been announced in December, and I dithered about it until the pandemic enforced focus on a fuzzy dilemma. Already far from the sunlit uplands, universities would now, it seemed, descend into a dark tunnel. I swallowed hard, expressed an interest, hesitated, and then declared my intention to leave. A settlement agreement was drafted, and I instructed a solicitor. Hesitating again, I made a few calls, stared out of the window, then signed.

My anxiety about academia dates back to my first job, a temporary lectureship in history at Keele University. I had drifted into doctoral research with a 2.1 from Cambridge and an unclassifed O-Level in self-confidence. My friends from university, many headed for work in London, had initially been sceptical. One of them, later the deputy prime minister, worried that academic pay was crap and I'd have to read everything. Besides, decent posts were scarce. But I liked my subject, was taken on by a charismatic professor, scraped a grant, and switched Cambridge colleges as a gesture towards a fresh start. Reality had been evaded. To an extent unthinkable today, arts postgrads were left alone to read. At lamplit tutorials and seminars, held in book-lined rooms in dark courtyards, it was hard not to feel like an impostor, though, looking back, I now realise that others were also straining to suspend disbelief in themselves. Then, suddenly, I was out of time and needed a job. It was the end of what feels now like one long autumn of snug teas and cycling through mists.

The day I arrived in Keele, it was raining. I'd split up with my girlfriend and had arranged to share a house with a colleague I'd never met; my office was still in the process of being built. Ahead lay the prospect of cobbling together dozens of lectures while at the same time somehow writing up my PhD. I was gloomy and apprehensive, but things fell into place. My housemate hadn't finished his thesis either: we laboured through early mornings and evenings, eventually submitting on the same day. The teaching was exciting and rewarding. There were a lot of mature students, some of them displaced by the closure of the Staffordshire collieries, all eager to learn. My impostor syndrome went into remission. I had articles accepted by peer-reviewed journals, passed my PhD viva, and ascended through a series of jobs. In 2007 I joined the University of East Anglia and four years later was made a professor. I published books, essays and reviews, received grants and fellowships, spoke at seminars and conferences, assessed manuscripts, supervised postgraduates, served as an external examiner and sat on committees. I had become the person I once impersonated. There were still Billy Liar moments: doodling in meetings, dreaming up titles for novels, imagining the present as prelude. But the masquerade was over. What I did was who I was.

Then, two years ago, things took a turn. A viable application for a big research grant fell at the first hurdle. Two articles I'd spent months on were rejected, one quite quickly, the other after a long ordeal of consideration and resubmission. Some of the assessors, cloaked in anonymity, seemed affronted by what I was trying to say. It was crushing, but also an awakening. They had pecked so viciously because I was an injured hen in the brood. They sensed disingenuousness, ebbing engagement, slippage from relevance, and, behind it all, a loss of faith. When I felt I'd been faking it I was the genuine article; now I was established I'd become an interloper. I realised I'd said all I had to say. So when my wife accepted a job in Dublin and I took a career break to look after our children, settling into non-academic life was easy. I didn't miss it, any of it.

It used to be more interesting. In 1993, Keele still bore a resemblance to the world Malcolm Bradbury captured in *The History Man* (1975): lecturers taught whatever enthused them – one medievalist offered a course on the Holocaust – and the cooler professors held parties to which students were invited. There were eccentrics straight out of Waugh's *Decline and Fall:* loveable cranks who had written one or zero books, drank at lunchtime and liked a flutter. They smoked in their offices and let ferrety dogs roam the corridors. They were amused by the arrival of career-minded scholars, and panicked when the Higher Education Funding Council for England (HEFCE) demanded to know how taxpayers' money was being spent. The Research Assessment Exercise found them wanting in research, and a dawning age of inspection exposed worryingly heterodox teaching methods.

Immediately before a HEFCE visit, a dusty sculpture was rinsed under the tap to make a good impression, as if the inspectors were a bevy of exacting aunts rather than fellow academics pressed into public service. In my next job, a wall of photocopied 'evidence' was adduced in the department's cause, and a crate of booze was bought, in contravention of HEFCE rules, to relax the inspectors. Alas, it was stolen by some students.

These were in many respects the bad old days, unworthy of anyone's nostalgia. There was too little transparency, permitting countless small abuses. There was favouritism and prejudice; a policy of laissez-faire concealed unequal workloads and, in some cases, sheer indolence. The tightening of central controls in the 1990s introduced accountability to the system, and the expansion of the higher education sector generally, which happened around the same time, did good by allowing more young people from working-class backgrounds to earn a degree, something that, to their parents as to mine, had previously represented a social distinction as remotely glittering as a knighthood. When I began my PhD, there were fewer than fifty universities in the UK, awarding around 80,000 first degrees annually; twenty years later the number of HE institutions had nearly trebled, and the number of degrees had increased by a factor of five. In 1999 Tony Blair vowed that the 33% of school-leavers then in higher education would rise to 50% in the next century, a goal that was reached in 2018.

Widening opportunity in education is the noblest of social and political projects. But the cost is now clear. In the 'bad old days' students were, as they are today, taught with commitment and passion, but sometimes eccentricity added a spark. Provided he — and it was usually a he — turned up fully dressed and sober and didn't lay hands on anyone, the crazy lecturer could be an inspiration. Expectations were less explicit, the rhetoric and metrics of achievement were absent, which made everyone feel freer. Even applying to a university seemed less pressured, because it was so unclear what it would be like when you got there. You absorbed teachers' anecdotal experiences and sent off for prospectuses, including the student-produced 'alternative' versions mentioning safe sex and cheap beer. Even after matriculation I had only a vague sense of the structure of my course. The lecture list was to be found in an austere periodical of record available in newsagents. Mysteries that today would be cleared up with two clicks on a smartphone had to be resolved by listening to rumours. This news blackout has been replaced by abundant online information, the publication of lucid curricular pathways, the friendly outreach of student services and the micromanagement of an undergraduate's development. Leaps of progress all, if it weren't for the suspicion that students might develop better if they had to find out more things for themselves. We learned to be self-reliant and so were better prepared for an indifferent world; we didn't for a moment see the university as acting in loco parentis. Excessive care for students is as reassuring as a comfort blanket and can be just as infantilising.

Academics lament the local autonomy that has now been arrogated to the centre, where faculty executive committees and senior management teams call the shots. Lecturers no longer exercise the discretion that once supported students' pastoral welfare, and are instead trained to spot mental health problems and to advise students to consult GPs and book university counselling sessions (waiting lists tend to be long: anxiety is the new normal, sometimes reported as dispassionately as one might do a cold). Instances where essay extensions have been granted only on submission of proof of bereavement are not unheard of: procrustean bureaucracy in the name of consistency. Team-teaching is preferred to the one-lecturer show because university managers have an aversion to cancelling an advertised module should the lecturer take research or parental leave, move to another university, or run off screaming into the night. This was once an acceptable risk; now it threatens to infringe students' consumer rights. Overseeing such concerns are marketing departments of burgeoning complexity and swagger, which manage public relations and promote the brand. National rankings based on several 'key performance indicators' – research, teaching, student satisfaction (a revered metric deriving from an online survey) – are parsed and massaged by these departments into their most appealing iterations, in the hope of pushing their institution as close as possible to pole position in an intensely competitive race. The Russell Group, a self-selecting club of 24 elite UK universities, content to be thought of as 'the British Ivy League', admits some new members and excludes others. Those refused entry make ingenious claims to be as good as those inside the charmed circle. But it's a struggle. The Russell Group's members attract three-quarters of all research income, which matters not least because world-class research-led teaching is a strong selling point for recruiting undergraduates.

The key factor is tuition fees – currently £9250 per annum for full-time study – which in 2012 replaced most direct funding of universities. Today half of UK universities' £40 billion annual income comes from fees. Universities are businesses forced to think commercially, regardless of any humane virtues traditionally associated with academic life. Academic heads of department – otherwise known as 'line managers', some of whom control their own budgets – are set aspirational admissions targets which often prove unachievable due to the vicissitudes of an unstable market. The usual outcome, in Micawberish terms, is misery over happiness. Academics, already demoralised by declining real wages, shrinking pensions and the demands of the Research Excellence Framework – not least the demand to demonstrate the public 'impact' of their research – report feeling not just overburdened by marketisation, but victimised. Some administrators, especially those without teaching duties, can make 'underperforming' academic staff feel like spanners in the works, rather than labourers who own the means of production and create the very thing marketing departments have to sell.

University mottos, with all their classical hauteur, have been displaced by vapid slogans about discovering yourself and belonging to the future. Universities are centres of excellence, hubs of innovation, zones of enterprise. The gushing copy has limited relevance on the shop floor. Lecturers deserve more respect than is found in Dalek-like emails demanding 100% compliance with this or that directive. An infinitely expanding bureaucratic universe displays authoritarian indifference to variety and nuance in the very work exalted in their promotional material. Vice-chancellors and deans always remember to give thanks and praise at graduation ceremonies and other festal moments; but what lecturers want is understanding, not least about the manifold claims on their time.

So how has all this affected 'the student experience'? Undergraduates today can't know how it felt to belong to a state-funded institution whose low-pressure otherworldliness allowed for imagination and experimentation, diversity and discovery. The student experience didn't need defining because it wasn't for sale: it magically happened within a loosely idealistic, libertarian countercultural framework. The last thing anyone at a university wanted to wear was a suit: now you can't move for them. Today's watchwords are value and satisfaction. Even if it's a good thing for fee-paying students to have a say in what their money buys, a transactional mentality has led to paradoxical demands for more contact hours and the right not to use them. Whereas lectures have long been optional, seminars and tutorials have remained compulsory. This is now under threat, along with the basic principle that attendees at a lecture are passive consumers and seminar participants are active producers. These days the customer is usually right and the lecturer more like a generic service provider. Supporting observations include students' failure to learn their tutor's name after 12 weeks, a tendency to refer to 'teachers' and 'lessons', dependence on prepackaged fillets of text – whatever happened to 'reading round the subject'? – and unabashed admissions that set work has not been done. Why pretend the dog ate your homework when you own the homework?

Students miss out if they duck challenges they imagine to be beyond their capabilities. Punching above your weight can be stressful and tiring, but without doing a bit of it students ironically fail to develop the independent learning skills and confident self-expression that employers value (here I'm talking mainly about the arts and humanities). Unlike other commodities and services, where typically the customer wants no involvement in the manufacture or delivery of their purchases, students get out of a degree what they put in. One of the worst outcomes would be if they unwittingly believed that fees entitled them to a good degree, and when awarded a 2.2 (or that endangered species, a third) reflexively blamed anything and anyone other than themselves. As bad would be a reluctance to award degrees below a 2.1 for fear of complaint, even legal action.

Universities obsessed with student satisfaction are finding it harder to navigate their obligations. It doesn't help that students have been hit by waves of strikes, followed by the further disruption caused by Covid-19. As for academic staff, feelings of discontent, disenfranchisement, disillusionment and disorientation are increasing, as academic careers become less and less appealing. The financial impact of the pandemic on universities has been catastrophic, with individual losses over the next financial year predicted to be in the tens of millions. In July, the Institute for Fiscal Studies estimated a combined long-term deficit of £11 billion. Deprived of fees from foreign students (especially for postgraduate courses), revenue from rental accommodation, income from the conference trade and returns from other investments, universities are facing Herculean challenges – hence redundancies both voluntary and, in due course, compulsory. The IFS predicts that, without cutting workforces, universities will save only £600 million. I jumped while there was still a lifeboat in the water. UEA has a broad regional base, and will survive with some belt-tightening and structural changes. According to some reports, however, 13 institutions will go bust without government bailouts, which no doubt they will receive in exchange for pruning courses devoid of obvious vocational benefit.

What will the student experience be now? A new order of one-way corridors, social distancing, teaching bubbles, screened and sanitised everything, and 'dual-delivery synchronous and asynchronous learning activities': a minimal amount of face-to-face teaching combined with online lectures, prerecorded so that lecture theatres can be freed up for use as spacious seminar rooms. Lecturers have been racing to refine lockdown protocols into coherent products, now widely advertised as 'blended learning'. Many have spent their summers taking training modules in 'generic breadth and depth e-learning provision', the warp and weft of embedded skills that look neat on a 'weave diagram' but are harder to apply in real life. To keep class discussion buoyant, lecturers are told to 'encourage students to practise the verbalisation aspect of knowledge'. Multiple 'learning outcomes', sacred buzzwords before the pandemic, have been supplemented with 'learner journeys', promising against the odds a positive experience as well as a realistic hope of achieving something. But mostly lecturers have been tasked with filming multiple bite-size video 'segments' suited to modern attention spans (complete with subtitles and credited imagery), setting 'interactive tasks' and building bespoke websites for their modules.

Who knows how long this set-up will last. Currently we can only applaud the pragmatism and stamina of lecturers, beg the forbearance of students, and wish them well. But if the R-number creeps up, or if there are more strikes (a prospect made likely by redundancies), even the contingency plan will stall and dissatisfaction will soar. School-leavers may question the wisdom of paying so much for so little. As it is, calls for universities to refund fees and rent have fallen on deaf ears. The student experience has already been compromised and the brand damaged. The path to recovery is pegged out with proposals for retrenchment, mostly effected by shedding staff. I had dreaded telling colleagues in my field that I was quitting, imagining incredulity and a hushed inference that I was terminally ill or at least having a breakdown. Academia is vocational: people don't usually pack it in or switch careers – although that may become more common. When I finally broke the news, most of the people I told said they would retire early if they could afford it – a few had made calculations about payouts and pensions and most had at least contemplated it in glummer moments. It's just no fun any more, they said. One or two admitted that their self-identity was so bound up with academic life they could never give it up, but even this wasn't a judgment on my decision: they were entirely sympathetic and acknowledged that a wonderful career had lost a lot of its glamour.

Of course, none of us is lost in space, rounding the lip of a black hole. Higher education will always be worthwhile, if only because for students it provides three unique years removed from family, school and a career. In spite of uncertainty and austerity, versatile and resourceful young people will create their own networks and forums conducive to study and sociability. Academics will carry on doing research that informs their teaching. Learning for its own sake may suffer as courses are honed to a fine utilitarian edge and students evolve into accomplished grade accountants, expert in the work required for a 2.1 – playing the system they themselves finance. But degrees will retain value, and, for those who find graduate entry-level jobs, they will remain value for money. Above all, even allowing for a likely contraction of the HE sector, our universities will still promote social mobility, having already transformed the profile of the typical student, in terms of gender as well as class. There will be no return to sixty years ago when only 4% of 18-year-olds went on to higher education, most of them men. The change is permanent. I'm glad to have played my part in this revolution.

Perhaps this is why I feel uneasy, and why my future feels more suspenseful than exciting. I've had dreams in which I've strolled across a platonically perfect ivy-clad campus, been enthralled by a perfect seminar, and had engaging discussions with old colleagues, including my Cambridge supervisor and the people I knew when I was doing my PhD, back in the halcyon days when everything had a point and a purpose. There's guilt there: a sense of loss, of potential squandered and maybe even betrayed. UEA has made me an emeritus professor, which is an honourable discharge and something to cling to, and my wife insists we can live on her salary. But I still can't decide whether I've retired or just resigned, or am in fact redundant and unemployed. I'm undeniably jobless at 53, able-bodied (I hesitate to say 'fit'), with a full head of hair and most of my teeth, and haunted by St Teresa of Avila's dictum that more tears are shed over answered prayers than unanswered ones.

I keep thinking about a short story we read at school, Somerset Maugham's 'The Lotus Eater'. It is the cautionary tale of a bank manager who drives off the toads of work, gives up his comfy pension and goes to live like a peasant on a paradisal Mediterranean island. Needless to say it doesn't end well: his annuity expires, his mind atrophies, he botches suicide. He sees out his days in a state of bestial wretchedness, demoted in the great chain of being as a punishment for rebelling against nature. I don't see the story as a prediction, and would always choose industry over idleness, but Maugham's contempt for someone who dodges life's challenges – the story satirised an effete acquaintance from Heidelberg – resonates. Still, I couldn't go back. Goodbye to all that.

Graduate School Is a Foreign Country

Susan Ferber

PERHAPS IT should have occurred to me that I was more suited for publishing (where I have now made a happy professional home for almost a quarter-century) than for academia when my favorite activity in history graduate seminars was preparing to give presentations on other people's books. I loved digging into all the published reviews and getting a sense of the different perspectives on the scholarship and contextualizing the books within that scholarly literature. Finding archival documents thrilled me, but the rest of what being an academic would entail — chiefly lecturing — had already proved terrifying. Spending hours in the library going through print journals and microfilm (there were no digital, searchable databases then!) to find reviews of books — that was the kind of investigation I craved. I remember so vividly reading the many reviews of Ramón Gutiérrez's *When Jesus Came, the Corn Mothers Went Away*, then trying to synthesize all the different opinions on that work, then trying to explain the new horizons its approaches opened up.

While there were a few memorable exceptions, too often the actual seminars fell flat for me. It wasn't the fault of my cohort; they were and are bright and fascinating (and today a few of them are even my authors). But like all new graduate students, they were eager to make their mark, and I still shake my head thinking about a few filibusterers who dominated conversation every week. Surely, we all wanted to know what the scholars and our professor, the seminar leader, had to say about the works, didn't we? We had years of learning ahead of us, but the greenest among us attacked the books on our syllabus as if they themselves knew firsthand how easy it was to write a book and get it published. There was a lot of posturing and trying on of academic jargon to convey ideas in a way that we thought would impress the authors of those books and our professors. By the end of each seminar, it almost always felt as though there was no value in those books, that the authors had structured them badly, that their research questions were inadequate, that their archival source base was too thin, that the analysis had failed to take into account all the strands it should, that they were bad reads. There must have been a reason that these books had made it onto our syllabus, if not as models for our own work then as examples of important scholarship. Yet, that wasn't how it felt after the books had been torn to shreds.

At the same time, we were being heavily encouraged to write first- or second-year seminar papers as the drafts of publishable articles. In retrospect, I appreciate the professionalization that this encouraged, but at the time I thought that it was much too soon for most of us to have anything original to say. I continue to think that we should have been more humbled as apprentices and not been encouraged to believe that anything we said or wrote was ready for peer review. It didn't seem as if any of us thought about how we would feel were our articles read by a vicious group of first-year graduate students.

For as long as I could remember, I had loved books – loved digging into their prose, thinking about the worlds created in them. Like so many other high achievers, I had had my nose in a book since I could first read by myself at around age four. And I thought, perhaps mistakenly, that graduate school would allow me to keep my nose there professionally. Never in my undergraduate seminars or tutorials or sections where we discussed and debated books had I come away feeling like books had no value or joy. However, in graduate school, all those years of research and writing seemed just to lead to works that could be demolished in two-hour seminars.

Increasingly unhappy, I was thinking about what kind of life might further the activities that fascinated me. A few years earlier, a career counselor had suggested I try publishing for a little while before going to graduate school, as if it were a preparatory job for academia. I found myself daydreaming about what kind of life would help authors improve their books *before* they got published. What if, instead of deconstructing books between hard covers in graduate seminars, I could somehow work with authors to construct them *before* they were read?

Such were my inchoate and uninformed takes on what the publishing industry was all about. Until I met with publishing professionals, I hadn't thought a great deal about market research, about financial modeling, about how bricks and mortar and online sales outlets drove the industry, or even about competitive acquisition and the roles agents play in a segment of the industry. To me, it was about the craft of working on texts with authors, the kind of one-on-one work that I somehow imagined dominated editors' days.

In many ways, it wasn't graduate school that had best prepared me for what I thought was that kind of editorial work. When I was an undergraduate, there was a Writing Fellows Program that I had benefited from, first as a student, then as a writing fellow myself. Trained students worked with other students on developing the ideas for their essays before they were submitted for class. And from the other side, I had learned about how to give feedback to my peers to improve their written work. Even before that program, others in my dorm had brought their unfinished papers to me to ask if I could read the drafts and edit them, so I knew that I could do this. I had found it deeply satisfying to be able to help someone else do something better. One day seeing my name on the cover of a book felt less important than doing this kind of collaborative work.

Collaboration – that didn't seem to be a skill much prized in grad school. I'm sure this was partially because of the discipline, which was and is not one that prioritizes group projects, lab work, joint writing projects, or co-teaching. Despite some friendships I made and still maintain, it felt like an intensely lonely period. I missed the feeling that had been so present in my undergraduate seminars: all of us being involved in a collaborative enterprise of learning. Instead, graduate school felt like a competition, which no doubt better prepared those who succeeded to compete for scarce resources, like teaching assistantships, fellowships, eventually academic positions, and the rest of the world of academia ahead. But it left me feeling cold and increasingly depressed, especially when the crisp fall days turned to gloomy, damp winter ones and the sun set even before afternoon seminars ended.

When I finally decided to leave, I thought getting a job in publishing would satisfy elements of my intellectual and personal life that had been feeling squashed. Perhaps I didn't give graduate school enough of a chance at either institution I attended; I might have grown and changed more to adapt to it; I might have developed sharper elbows, a more outspoken persona, and thicker skin. Thinking back, I was young and I could have grown more *with* graduate school, rather than seeing myself as increasingly alienated from it. But that has come with hindsight. At the time, I desperately wanted to feel happy in the activities that filled my days and nights. I didn't want to come to hate school, which I had loved for decades. It wasn't the fault of the institution; it was my inability to make myself into the model of a graduate student.

Meanwhile, on the publishing job market, my time in graduate school made me *less* appealing in the eyes of human resources departments. I'm sure the assumption was that I would be entitled and think myself above the nitty-gritty administrative work that dominates the lives of entry-level employees in the book trade, despite my having previously held administrative jobs. HR interviewer after HR interviewer looked over my résumé, seeing numerous elite universities, and asked: why was I not teaching? In fact, teaching – standing up in front of a lecture hall or even a small classroom and commanding the room for an hour – was the activity most unsuited to my personality.

At first, I aimed to get far away from the kinds of books I had read in grad school. I needed a fresh start, perhaps literary fiction, where I could apprentice myself to an editor and learn a new skill set and hear different voices, not those of professional historians. As I did informational interviews and applied for virtually every entry-level editorial job advertised (in pre-Internet HR site days, they were listed in the Sunday classified section) around the cities of New York and Boston, I talked with people who did self-help, romance, reprints, cookbooks, textbooks, novels, commercial nonfiction. As part of an interview, I had to write a reader's report for a book proposal on the emotional education of boys. In my report, I declared the project too derivative of scholarship and too much a rip-off of a parallel book on girls; it went on to become a national bestseller. Clearly, I did not fully understand trade publishing or the tastes of the mass market. Perhaps I would have come to better appreciate them had I been hired. So it seemed I probably would be a better fit for a university or academic press. Yet at those presses too, I wasn't getting beyond the interview stage to a job offer. Having studied both fiction and Latin for years, I thought I was perfectly suited for an opening for an assistant to a literature and classics editor, yet I failed to get anything beyond a return postcard acknowledging receipt of my application from an HR department.

Then, suddenly, a stroke of luck: someone in that HR department gave my résumé to a different hiring editor a few months later, someone who himself had been a history graduate student and left to get into publishing. Perhaps he saw something of his own path in my résumé. When he hired me, he said he knew I was the one because I was so hungry to learn.

I was and remain utterly grateful for that chance, especially after 11 months of a frustrating job search for an entry-level job. When I got the offer, I reasoned that, since I had held office jobs before and done many hours of archival and curatorial work of a highly detailed nature, my graduate training should somewhat increase my starting salary. After all, I was going to be an assistant working in the same discipline in which I had trained. What about all the literature reviews I had done? What about my knowledge of the key players in the field and the universities where I would be looking for reviewers and, if I was lucky, authors? In the end, $500 above the starting salary of $20,000 was what that was worth — and I was advised not to push my luck.

Nonetheless, I derived more than $500 from the mostly unhappy years of graduate school that went before. They had taught me that it would be okay to leave a path, one I had chosen and worked so hard to follow. They had taught me that highly ranked programs at strong universities could look right on paper but in practice feel wrong for me. And they had taught me that I had to find a way to be happy in my daily life and to feel that the career path I was on would be more satisfying than the present. Walking away — not even taking a leave of absence, as I was advised to do — could provide a fresh start. In the end, doing that was the smartest decision I made about grad school. It would have been unfair for an institution to fully train someone, to use its scarce financial resources on her, to shape an academic for the market and then for her not to want what she had been given — at least this was what I convinced myself. Better to relinquish the fellowship and allow someone else to have that opportunity, someone who would be a better fit.

On a daily basis now, I use those skills of researching reviews, thinking through critiques, positioning a new work in a body of literature, and deciding whether the voice of the author speaks to me. There are projects I have signed hubristically, thinking I could, behind the scenes, improve the work to the point where a grad seminar would read the finished book and see all of its glowing qualities and perhaps allow the seminar to constitute a fan club and end early that day. That, of course, will never happen. It is the nature of grad students to critique and to think that they themselves could do better. Some of the most acclaimed and prizewinning books I have edited get dissected in seminars just the way books in my day did. But I know about the quiet work, done with pencil on paper, behind the scenes, one-on-one with the author, that went into making the final text, as well as the shortcomings and often overwriting that were in early drafts. That's between an author and an editor.

Occasionally I am invited to graduate seminars now by author friends when I am on campus. Sometimes this has even coincided with a discussion of a book I have edited. It's a very different experience coming in as an observer, no longer feeling I have to prove myself and falling short. In some of them, the professors say that the first part of seminar has to be devoted to positive feedback about the book, something I wish had been true in my classrooms. Last fall I spontaneously attended a seminar that had turned into a discussion about creative non-fiction techniques and different forms that authors have chosen for writing history, sometimes inside and sometimes outside the academy. It was one of the most exciting and engaging days I'd had in a long time. The students wanted to hear what I had to say. I was able to hear their reactions to various techniques and what they thought about their reading that week, Sarah Bakewell's *At the Existential Café*. Since I had only just been invited that morning, I hadn't read the whole book in advance, but I didn't break out in a cold sweat about not finishing the reading, the way I used to in grad school. Instead, I could just appreciate the discussion.

The past, it has been said, is a foreign country. I love visiting so many of those countries through my manuscripts and books, seeing them through the eyes of my authors as well as those who write for other publishing houses. But my own graduate school past isn't one I feel the need to reinhabit, even as intensely gratifying as it is to visit occasionally.

The Afternoon I Decided to Quit Academia

L. Maren Wood

Solicited for this volume and published in slightly different form at Beyond the Professoriate, June 2021
https://beyondprof.com/the-afternoon-i-decide-to-leave-academia

I REMEMBER THE day I decided to leave academia with crystal clarity.

It was the end of my third year on the academic job market. I had spent the fall and winter teaching as an adjunct, paying my way to conferences, applying and interviewing for academic jobs, and losing sleep over what might happen if I didn't land a more secure position.

It was June. I had lined up a few adjunct classes for the Fall, but was hoping to land something more permanent.

That day, I learned that I had come in second for a visiting assistant professorship. It was four courses per semester and it paid $38,000. Not enough, I was told, to really live in the town where the university was located.

If I had landed the job, it would have meant living across the continent from my partner. He had accepted a dream consulting job in Washington, DC.

And I had come in second.

I walked down the road a few blocks to where one of my faculty mentors lived. I told her my disappointing news. With encouragement, she said, "but you were so close!"

But close to what?

That afternoon, this dream job I had been pursuing for my entire adult life suddenly looked more like a disappointing nightmare. Rather than providing me with secure pay, meaningful work, and the life of the mind, academia had delivered underemployment, stress, depression, and anxiety.

I returned home and called my best friend, Harry.

"I'm done. I can't do this anymore." I told him. I felt emotionally depleted, but also liberated by the decision. I had no idea what else I was going to do; I just knew I couldn't go on being this depressed, feeling hopeless about my future.

Harry understood. He was finishing his PhD in English literature and had struck out on the job market. Although he'd won a university prize for the best dissertation and had secured a book deal, he couldn't even land an interview.

The academic job market had collapsed in 2008, had upended all of our planning, and ended our dreams.

I had wanted to be a professor from my sophomore year of university. I wanted the life of the mind, to teach and study history, and to be surrounded with people who were creative, innovative, and passionate about their work. It seemed like a charmed life.

When the job market collapsed, it felt like a bait-and-switch. We had been admitted into our PhD programs because we were promising scholars. Then the jobs disappeared and we were left to figure out what on earth we were going to do with our humanities PhDs.

That Fall, I poured my heart into my teaching, knowing it would probably be my last time in a university classroom teaching history. At the end of my last class, my last semester, I took photos of the empty classroom, cried, and closed the door.

Despite the sadness of letting go of my dream job, I knew I was making the right decision.[1]

The problem was, I had no idea what else I could do, how to begin exploring career options, or applying for non-academic jobs.

In January, I moved to DC to join my partner. I was totally lost, lonely, and depressed.

I started my job search asking the question most PhDs ask: what can I do with my degree *in this very specific discipline.* It turns out, that's the wrong question to ask. Focusing on subject matter expertise instead of skills traps you into narrow career opportunities.

In DC, I did informational interviews with people who worked at the

1. See L. Maren Wood, "Walking Away From Academia When It Was Your Dream Job," Beyond the Professoriate, n.d., https://beyondprof.com/walking-away-from-academia-when-it-was-your-dream-job/

archives, but that didn't align with my interests, and I would probably have needed to earn a library science degree. I already had student loan debt, so taking on more loans for yet another degree seemed like a bad idea.

I started volunteering at an historic house and did an internship at an historical preservation society, hoping to break into historical preservation or public history. But I quickly realized that those organizations seldom hired historians; they wanted project and program managers, fundraisers, volunteer coordinators, and event planners.

I read job ads, but nothing seemed like an obvious fit.

This all left me even more demoralized and depressed.

After a few months in DC, *I felt like I wasn't qualified for any job.*

If that's how you feel, I empathize completely.

One day, my partner came home to find me in frustrated tears about my lack of progress on landing a new career.

"I don't know what I want to do with my life!" I exclaimed.

His advice: "Maren, nobody does. We just say yes to opportunities, and then a new one comes along, and you evaluate it and decide if you'll take that or stick with what you're already doing."

That was such a *revelation.* I had been thinking of "careers" in an outdated sense: the thing that I was going to do for the rest of my life.

That's easy to do when you leave academia. You are used to thinking of your career trajectory as graduate student > postdoc > assistant professor > associate professor > full professor > professor emeritus > death.

But that's not how careers work for most professionals in today's economy. People apply their education, skills, interests, and talents in a variety of different roles across a wide range of organizations. In fact, most people change jobs every three to five years, especially at the beginning of their careers.[2]

A professional career is not one thing. It's the sum of all the opportunities we say yes to.

That has been very true for me.

Becoming an entrepreneur and launching a small startup was not the end result of years of planning. It was the product of a series of events, or opportunities. It also reflects my own interests, values, and skills.

Being the founder of a startup is not a job for an historian. But it's a job this historian decided to try.

When I was struggling so much in DC to figure out what I wanted to do,

---

2. Alison Doyle, "How Often Do People Change Jobs During a Lifetime?" The Balance Careers, updated June 15, 2020, https://www.thebalancecareers.com/how-often-do-people-change-jobs-2060467

I started to conduct research about the career paths of history PhDs. That resulted in a publication in *The Chronicle of Higher Education*. The editor, Denise, took a chance on an unknown junior scholar who had dug up some interesting research.

From there, the chair of the UNC-Chapel Hill history department (my alma mater) hired me to conduct a study of alumni career pathways for our department. And he paid me. He was so impressed by my research that he recommended me to the director of the American Historical Association. I worked on a series of research projects for the AHA. That in turn led to work as a researcher for *The Chronicle of Higher Ed.*

As I built up my expertise through freelance and part-time work, I was able to generate more and more opportunities for myself. It wasn't a career in and off itself, but it was work experience, and it allowed me to become a thought-leader in the field of careers and professional development for PhDs.

This research also helped me realize that my personal struggle to transition from academia into a meaningful full career was not unique. Everyone struggled.

Leaving academia is really, really difficult. The PhDs I work with through Beyond the Professoriate are making similar mistakes to the ones I made. When I interview PhDs who now have successful careers, they also highlight how difficult it was to transition, until they learned the formula of a successful job search.

It's hard, and we need help.

This is what led me to start Beyond the Professoriate. I wanted to teach graduate students and PhDs how to launch successful non-academic job searches because *we have so much to offer.*

Beyond Prof's research shows that there are so many ways that PhDs can leverage their education.

Looking back, here's what I wish someone would have told me about leaving academia.

You are not your degree.

This is the biggest mistake PhDs make.

In academia, we are conditioned to think of ourselves by our subject matter expertise. The entire institution is structured around departments where everyone teaches and studies a specific discipline.

Asking "what can I do with my degree in this very specific field" is the wrong question because it traps us into a narrow list of career opportunities.

And, your subject matter expertise might not even be the thing you're most passionate about.

Instead ask yourself "why did I earn this degree in the first place". If you say, it's because I love history, or Shakespeare, dig deeper. Why? What is it about this very niche thing that is satisfying to you?

The truth is, you're pursuing this discipline not because it is the definition of your interests, but because it allows you to express and explore things that you find intellectually interesting.

Then, ask yourself: what is it that I love about my work? If you say teaching, dig deeper. What is it about your teaching that you love? Is it the opportunity to talk about your subject matter expertise? That's not teaching, that's knowledge transfer. Or perhaps you love talking about ideas or facilitating conversations. Maybe you really love curriculum design and development.

My point is, you are not defined by your degree, and what you do next is not limited to your subject matter expertise.

For me, I was interested in history because I'm interested in the power of stories, and the way we use stories to make sense out of our reality. It's why I studied narratives of sexual danger in the eighteenth century.

It's also why I love helping PhDs define and articulate their career stories during their job search.

It's also why marketing is my favorite part of running a business.

I would never have thought that marketing would be a subject I would find as fascinating as history.

And guess what? If I'm looking for career opportunities for communicators, storytellers, and marketers, there are *numerous* opportunities and career pathways. That's very different than public history, museums, and historic houses.

It's your skills that open doors.

Leaving academia requires us to have a different relationship to our degrees. Rather than seeing the degree as an integral part of our identity, we need to see it as something we accomplished through the application of our skills.

Your expertise and all the things you did while earning your PhD – your course papers, dissertation, publications, courses you designed and taught – those are examples of how you applied your skills, with success, to execute projects.

In your next career, you'll apply those same skills to conduct new research and deliver new projects.

You are not an historian, or anthropologist, or ecologist. You're a highly educated professional with a rich set of skills that you've applied, with success, for the past number of years.

Now, you will take your education and these skills that you've developed and apply them to solve new problems, and overcome new challenges, in a different setting.

You're taking your PhD with you – but it will be the skills, not the subject matter expertise – that will be of most value to employers.

You don't have to know what you want to do for the rest of your life, just what you'd like to try next.

Just get started!

The hardest job to land will be your first job out of academia. Why? Because you'll lack a lot of the linear work experience employers value in job candidates.

This means you may need to do contract work, part-time, freelance, or entry level positions in order to get your foot in the door.

That's OK.

Hiring managers operate on the idea that past behavior is the best prediction of future behavior. If you've been successful in a similar role in a different organization, that increases your chances of being hired.

Once you have evidence to show hiring managers, you'll have greater opportunity to advance in your career.

So, get started. Say yes to interesting opportunities and see where they take you.

Remember, people change jobs every three to five years, so if you don't like your first non-academic job, that's OK. You can pivot.

But the next time you move, you'll have work experience in the professional workspace, and it will be easier for you to find new opportunities.

Finally, experiential learning is critical in deciding what jobs, roles, and responsibilities you will find most valuable. You simply can't know that you'll love or hate marketing or project management until you've given it a shot.

Through non-academic work experience, you'll learn more about yourself, professional workspaces, the kind of managers you work best with, and the kind of organizations where you'll thrive.

You can't do this alone.

There are so many reasons why networking is critical to career success but you have to build a community of people who can help you.

You'll have so many questions about your career transition – what entry-level positions should you aim for, what do hiring managers value in candidates, what does pay and compensation look like in this field – and so many more.

The best people to answer those questions will be professionals who work in that space. They are your subject matter experts who can give you advice.

Plus, did you know that 80% of jobs are filled through networking, and an estimated 70% of jobs are never posted?

You need a community of professionals who can help you by telling you when jobs come up in their organizations.[3]

It's not uncommon to leave academia and need to build a new professional network from scratch. But we've interviewed hundreds of PhDs at Beyond the Professoriate and they were able to build new networks.

Get active on LinkedIn and start connecting with alumni. Join the Beyond the Professoriate LinkedIn group. Reach out to people who work at employers of interest.

Finally, you are employable.

Just remember, there are so many ways for smart, creative people to build meaningful careers. The skills you've developed while earning your PhD are in demand.

The biggest challenge will be to provide those concrete examples of work experience that hiring managers are looking for.

If you're still in graduate school, or if you have a few months before your current academic contract runs out, get started building those skills.

Take online courses, or freelance, or volunteer. Get creative!

Lots of PhDs leave academia every year and successfully make the transition. There is nothing special about them.

What they do is leverage their skills, cast a wide net for new opportunities, and build a community of professionals who can help them.

You can make it happen for you, too.

References

Doyle, Alison. "How Often Do People Change Jobs During a Lifetime?" The Balance Careers. Updated June 15, 2020. https://www.thebalancecareers.com/how-often-do-people-change-jobs-2060467

Freeland Fisher, Julia. "How to Get a Job Often Comes Down to One Elite

3. See Julia Freeland Fisher, "How to Get a Job Often Comes Down to One Elite Personal Asset, and Many People Still Don't Realize It," CNBC @Work, updated February 14, 2020, https://www.cnbc.com/2019/12/27/how-to-get-a-job-often-comes-down-to-one-elite-personal-asset.html

Personal Asset, and Many People Still Don't Realize It." CNBC @Work. Updated February 14, 2020. https://www.cnbc.com/2019/12/27/how-to-get-a-job-often-comes-down-to-one-elite-personal-asset.html

Wood, L. Maren. "Walking Away From Academia When It Was Your Dream Job." Beyond the Professoriate, n.d. https://beyondprof.com/walking-away-from-academia-when-it-was-your-dream-job/

PART TWO

REFLECTIONS ON THE GENRE

The Closing of American Academia

Sarah Kendzior

Originally published in *Al Jazeera*, August 20, 2012
https://www.aljazeera.com/indepth/opinion/2012/08/
201282010274924 6453.html

It is 2011 and I'm sitting in the Palais des Congres in Montreal, watching anthropologists talk about structural inequality.

The American Anthropological Association meeting is held annually to showcase research from around the world, and like thousands of other anthropologists, I am paying to play: $650 for airfare, $400 for three nights in a "student" hotel, $70 for membership, and $94 for admission. The latter two fees are student rates. If I were an unemployed or underemployed scholar, the rates would double.

The theme of this year's meeting is "Traces, Tidemarks and Legacies." According to the explanation on the American Anthropological Association website, we live in a time when "the meaning and location of differences, both intellectually and morally, have been rearranged." As the conference progresses, I begin to see what they mean. I am listening to the speaker bemoan the exploitative practices of the neoliberal model when a friend of mine taps me on the shoulder.

"I spent almost my entire salary to be here," she says.

My friend is an adjunct. She has a PhD in anthropology and teaches at a university, where she is paid $2,100 per course. While she is a professor, she is not a Professor. She is, like 67% of American university faculty, a part-time employee on a contract that may or may not be renewed each semester. She receives no benefits or health care.

According to the Adjunct Project, a crowdsourced website revealing adjunct wages – data which universities have long kept under wraps – her salary is about average. If she taught five classes a year, a typical full-time faculty course load, she would make $10,500, well below the poverty line. Some adjuncts make more. I have one friend who was offered $5,000 per course, but he turned it down and requested less so that his children would still qualify for food stamps.

Why is my friend, a smart woman with no money, spending nearly $2,000 to attend a conference she cannot afford? She is looking for a way out. In America, academic hiring is rigid and seasonal. Each discipline has a conference, usually held in the fall, where interviews take place. These interviews can be announced days or even hours in advance, so most people book beforehand, often to receive no interviews at all.

The American Anthropological Association tends to hold its meetings in America's most expensive cities, although they do have one stipulation: "AAA staff responsible for negotiating and administering annual meeting contracts shall show preference to locales with living wage ordinances." This rule does not apply, unfortunately, to those in attendance.

Below Poverty Line

In most professions, salaries below the poverty line would be cause for alarm. In academia, they are treated as a source of gratitude. Volunteerism is par for the course – literally. Teaching is touted as a "calling," with compensation an afterthought. One American research university offers its PhD students a salary of $1,000 per semester for the "opportunity" to design and teach a course for undergraduates, who are each paying about $50,000 in tuition. The university calls this position "Senior Teaching Assistant" because paying an instructor so far below minimum wage is probably illegal.

In addition to teaching, academics conduct research and publish, but they are not paid for this work either. Instead, all proceeds go to for-profit academic publishers, who block academic articles from the public through exorbitant download and subscription fees, making millions for themselves in the process. If authors want to make their research public, they have to pay the publisher an average of $3,000 per article. Without an institutional affiliation, an academic cannot access scholarly research without paying, even for articles written by the scholar itself.

It may be hard to summon sympathy for people who walk willingly into such working conditions. "Bart, don't make fun of grad students," Marge told her son on an oft-quoted episode of *The Simpsons*. "They just made a terrible life choice."

But all Americans should be concerned about adjuncts, and not only because adjuncts are the ones teaching our youth. The adjunct problem is emblematic of broader trends in American employment: the end of higher education as a means to prosperity, and the severing of opportunity to all but the most privileged.

In a searing commentary, political analyst Joshua Foust notes that the unpaid internships that were once limited to show business have now spread to nearly every industry. "It's almost impossible to get a job working on policy in this town without an unpaid internship," he writes from Washington, DC, one of the most expensive cities in the country.[1] Even law, once a safety net for American strivers, is now a profession where jobs pay as little as $10,000 a year – unfeasible for all but the wealthy, and devastating for those who have invested more than $100,000 into their degrees. One after another, the occupations that shape American society are becoming impossible for all but the most elite to enter.

The Value of a Degree

Academia is vaunted for being a meritocracy. Publications are judged on blind review, and good graduate programs offer free tuition and a decent stipend. But its reliance on adjuncts makes it no different than professions that cater to the elite through unpaid internships.

Anthropologists are known for their attentiveness to social inequality, but few have acknowledged the plight of their peers. When I expressed doubt about the job market to one colleague, she advised me, with total seriousness, to "re-evaluate what work means" and to consider "post-work imaginaries." A popular video on post-graduate employment cuts to the chase: "Why don't you tap into your trust fund?"

In May 2012, I received my PhD, but I still do not know what to do with it. I struggle with the closed-off nature of academic work, which I think should be accessible to everyone, but most of all I struggle with the limited opportunities in academia for Americans like me, people for whom education was once a path out of poverty, and not a way into it.

My father, the first person in his family to go to college, tries to tell me my degree has value. "Our family came here with nothing," he says of my great-grandparents, who fled Poland a century ago. "Do you know how incredible it is that you did this, how proud they would be?"

And my heart broke a little when he said that, because his illusion is so

1. Joshua Foust, "The Uneven Playing Field of Unpaid Internships," *Need to Know*, PBS, May 9, 2012, https://www.pbs.org/wnet/need-to-know/opinion/the-uneven-playing-field-of-unpaid-internships/13785

touching – so revealing of the values of his generation, and so alien to the experience of mine.

References

Foust, Joshua. "The Uneven Playing Field of Unpaid Internships." *Need to Know*. PBS. May 9, 2012. https://www.pbs.org/wnet/need-to-know/opinion/the-uneven-playing-field-of-unpaid-internships/13785

"I Quit Academia," An Important, Growing Subgenre of American Essays

Rebecca Schuman

Originally published in *Slate*, October 24, 2013
https://slate.com/culture/2013/10/quitting-academic-jobs-professor-zachary-ernst-and-other-leaving-tenure-and-tenure-track-jobs-why.html

SARAH KENDZIOR, *Al Jazeera English*'s firebrand of social and economic justice, suggested this week that there should be a *Norton Anthology of Academics Declaring They Quit*, among whose august contributions she would place Zachary Ernst's "Why I Jumped Off the Ivory Tower."[1] Ernst's Oct[ober 20, 2013] essay is a deeply honest account of his acrimonious departure from what many would consider a dream job: a tenured position as a philosophy professor at the University of Missouri.

Ernst's contribution is indeed part of a raucous subgenre of "I Quit Lit" in (or rather, out of) academe, which includes Kendzior's own acidic "The Closing of American Academia," Alexandra Lord's surprisingly controversial "Location, Location, Location," and my own satirical public breakdown.[2] All

1. Sarah Kendzior (@sarahkendzior), "There needs to be a Norton Anthology of Academics Announcing They Quit," Twitter, October 20, 2013, https://twitter.com/sarahkendzior/status/392095346907557888

2. Sarah Kendzior "The Closing of American Academia," *Al Jazeera*, August 20, 2012, https://www.aljazeera.com/indepth/opinion/2012/08/2012820102749246453.html [pp. 133-136 in the present volume]; Alexandra Lord, "Location, Location, Location," *Chronicle of Higher Education*, September 12, 2012, https://www.chronicle.com/article/Location-Location-Location/134264/ [pp. 35-40 in the present volume]; Rebecca Schuman, "Thesis Hatement," *Slate*, April 5, 2013, http://www.slate.com/articles/life/culturebox/2013/04/

of us faced, and continue to face, the impressively verbose wrath of a discipline scorned, which itself is the completing gesture of initiation into the I Quit Oeuvre.

Ernst's "Why I Jumped" is thus not unusual in and of itself: Academe is a profession full of erudite free-thinkers who feel disillusioned by a toxic labor system in which criticism is not tolerated – so those who leave often relish the newfound ability to say anything they want (talking about "a friend" here).[3] In its insularity and single-mindedness, academe is also very similar to a fundamentalist religion (or, dare I say, cult),[4] and thus those who abdicate often feel compelled to confess.

But there's an important way that Ernst's essay distinguishes itself: Most I Quitters are like me, which is to say failed academics, or like Lord, whose disillusion hit her midway down the tenure track. Ernst is part of the *sub*-subgenre of quitters who did the unthinkable, giving up tenure. He joins, for example, scientist Terran Lane, who left the University of New Mexico for Google, and writer Anne Trubek, who ditched idyllic Oberlin when freelance writing was able to pay her bills.[5]

It is still exceptionally rare for a tenured academic to publicly and voluntarily *leave the field*. (To understand the way the concept is viewed by academics, please say that phrase aloud the way you'd say "contract syphilis.") Despite their widespread and documented unhappiness, most associate professors (the rank one achieves upon being granted tenure) stick it out until the end, for numerous reasons. First, while tenure does not actually mean "a job for life *no matter what*," it does offer a level of security absent from other professions. Moreover, by the time a professor makes tenure, she has usually been so heavily socialized by the "Total Institution" of the Academy that to leave it would be almost akin to death.[6]

---

there_are_no_academic_jobs_and_getting_a_ph_d_will_make_you_into_a_horrible.html [pp. 41-45 in the present volume]. On the reaction to Lord's piece, see Karen Kelsky, "Location, Location ... What?" The Professor Is In, September 14, 2012, http://theprofessorisin.com/2012/09/14/location-location-what/.

3. See Rebecca Schuman, "Take Your 'Love It' and Shove It," *Pan Kisses Kafka* (blog), April 26, 2013, https://pankisseskafka.com/2013/04/26/take-your-love-and-shove-it/

4. See Sarah Kendzior, "Academia's Indentured Servants," *Al Jazeera*, April 11, 2013, https://www.aljazeera.com/indepth/opinion/2013/04/20134119156459616.html

5. Terran Lane, "On Leaving Academe," *Chronicle of Higher Education*, August 19, 2012, https://www.chronicle.com/article/on-Leaving-Academe/133717 [pp. 29-34 in the present volume]; Anne Trubeck, "Giving Up Tenure? Who Does That?" *Chronicle of Higher Education*, April 8, 2013, https://www.chronicle.com/article/giving-up-tenure-who-does-that/

6. Wikipedia, s.v. "total institution," last modified April 26, 2021, https://en.wikipedia.org/wiki/Total_institution

What further distinguishes Ernst's giant middle finger to the profession, Mizzou, and the chair of his department (what approximates in academe for a direct "boss"), is that he does not succumb to either of these trappings. He is cynical about the "academic freedom" of the tenured, whom he believes have been hand-selected for mediocrity and obsequiousness (and since he is among their ranks, one wonders if he begrudgingly includes himself in this indictment). He also has no delusions about the relative importance of hyper-specialized research, and has sought to publish innovative multi-disciplinary articles that involve the scientific disciplines — for which he has then been heavily penalized. And finally, in a rare coup for humanists, Ernst is departing for a lucrative job in the private sector.

His essay has ignited academic Facebook, and may be pilloried by those who find his departing huff to be immature, ungrateful or unprofessional. But even to his detractors, his climactic critique of the "corporatization" of the American university should be unassailable (at least until the end). As has become common in higher education, the University of Missouri system now hires former multinational CEO's as presidents, on the basis of what Ernst criticizes as nebulous and irrelevant "business experience" — but not because Ernst is himself "anti-business." Rather, he explains, a multinational CEO focuses on "marketing, cutting costs, and improving outcomes that are based on short-term economic measures. This means serving more customers with a smaller number of employees while cutting costs." This actually makes no *business* sense in the university world.

Indeed, a conservative approach may have worked (or not!) at Sprint, where former University of Missouri System President Gary Forsee spent a universally maligned tenure, but even the staunchest professor-hater can see why this is not a good model for education. The goal of a multinational corporation is to make its shareholders and highest executives rich. This is — I hope we can all agree — not the goal of the American research university, nor should it ever be. If anything, Ernst argues, the university's affinity to business should share the ethos of the plucky startup, as fledgling ventures are status-quo-rejecting "intruders" that "succeed only if they cause some kind of disruptive change that gives them the advantage over their vastly more well-established competitors."

Ernst's solution — that the corporatized university emulate Instagram rather than Microsoft — is, to be sure, a supremely provocative idea sure to incur academic scorn. But whether you agree — or, as I do, you object to the corporate model wholesale and reserve a special loathing for startup culture — Ernst's farewell should offer those outside the university a powerful glimpse into why a successful academic would want to add another entry to the I Quit Canon.

References

Kelsky, Karen. "Location, Location ... What?" The Professor Is In, September 14, 2012. http://theprofessorisin.com/2012/09/14/location-location-what/

Kendzior, Sarah. "Academia's Indentured Servants." *Al Jazeera*, April 11, 2013. https://www.aljazeera.com/indepth/opinion/2013/04/20134119156459616.html

———. "The Closing of American Academia." *Al Jazeera*, August 20, 2012. https://www.aljazeera.com/indepth/opinion/2012/08/2012820102749246453.html

Kendzior, Sarah (@sarahkendzior). "There needs to be a Norton Anthology of Academics Announcing They Quit." Twitter, October 20, 2013. https://twitter.com/sarahkendzior/status/392095346907557888

Lane, Terran. "On Leaving Academe." *Chronicle of Higher Education*, August 19, 2012. https://www.chronicle.com/article/on-Leaving-Academe/133717

Lord, Alexandra. "Location, Location, Location." *Chronicle of Higher Education*, September 12, 2012. https://www.chronicle.com/article/Location-Location-Location/134264/

Schuman, Rebecca. "Take Your 'Love It' and Shove It." *Pan Kisses Kafka* (blog), April 26, 2013. https://pankisseskafka.com/2013/04/26/take-your-love-and-shove-it/

———. "Thesis Hatement." *Slate*, April 5, 2013. http://www.slate.com/articles/life/culturebox/2013/04/there_are_no_academic_jobs_and_getting_a_ph_d_will_make_you_into_a_horrible.html

Trubeck, Anne. "Giving Up Tenure? Who Does That?" *Chronicle of Higher Education*, April 8, 2013. https://www.chronicle.com/article/giving-up-tenure-who-does-that/

Wikipedia, s.v. "total institution." Last modified April 26, 2021. https://en.wikipedia.org/wiki/Total_institution

Why So Many Academics Quit and Tell

Sydni Dunn

Originally published in *Chronicle Vitae*, December 12, 2013
https://chroniclevitae.com/news/216-why-so-many-academics-quit-and-tell

STRAIGHT OUT OF graduate school, Matt Welsh landed a pretty choice gig. As an assistant computer science professor at Harvard University, he had a home in a highly respected department; he had his own office, with polished furniture and stocked bookshelves; and best of all, he had a pathway to tenure.

"The best, the top, the most high-caliber graduate students went on to be professors," Welsh said. "Anything else would have been a tremendous failure. A few years down that path, my whole life was focused on getting tenure. So much of my self-worth was centered on reaching that bar."

Which makes it all the more surprising that shortly after attaining his goal – becoming a full professor at Harvard – he quit. And then, on his personal website, he explained why.[1]

"I joined Harvard because it offered the opportunity to make a big impact on a great department at an important school, and I have no regrets," he wrote. "But my own priorities in life have changed, and I feel that it's time to move on."

When Welsh took to the Web to make his announcement, he was ahead

1. Matt Welsh, "Why I'm Leaving Harvard," *Matt Welsh* (personal blog), November 15, 2010, http://matt-welsh.blogspot.com/2010/11/why-im-leaving-harvard.html [pp. 19-22 in the present volume].

of the curve. But he's now in good company: Recently, there's been a surge of cathartic columns in which scholars – with tenure and without – explain why they're leaving academia. (We [at *Chronicle Vitae* have] listed the essays we've read in a Google Doc; take a look and add pieces we've missed.)[2]

There's nothing new, of course, about academics leaving the ivory tower. But the exploding genre of "Quit Lit" demonstrates that saying goodbye is becoming an increasingly public act.

We've been collecting these pieces for a while, in part because we wanted to get a sense of what was driving the writers to move on.

But then we came to an even more basic question: Why are so many ex-scholars motivated to write? So I asked a bunch of the stars of Quit Lit for their thoughts.

The Explainers

Welsh's reason to blog about his big decision was simple: It's not typical for a tenured professor to jump ship.

"Any time anyone decides to leave, rumors fly and people jump to conclusions," he said. "Maybe I didn't get tenure, maybe I had a problem with my institution, maybe there was a falling out. None of those things were the case. I felt I had to be very open about why the change was happening."

It wasn't just a matter of heading off the rumor mill, he added: "Some of me put it out there to solicit feedback and check my own reasons, to put my thoughts out there and try to justify it."

Because even if you're confident in your decision to leave, it's a scary process, said Peter Larson, a biology professor of 10 years who left to become a full-time running blogger, coach and exercise physiologist. After you've invested so many years into a single career, he said, the idea of giving it up is "very final."

"I got to the point where I was at a crossroad," Larson said. "I wasn't unhappy doing what I was doing, but I knew I would be happier doing other things. I realized I'd never forgive myself if I never took the chance."

Starting last school year, Larson told his department that his resignation was a possibility. He was granted a one-year leave of absence to explore the idea. "By the spring, I realized the leave of absence was delaying the inevitable," he said.

Larson sent his resignation letter to the dean April 15, [2013,] and he published "Leaving Academia: One Chapter Ends, Another Begins" one

2. "Quit Lit: The Vitae List" is no longer available online.

week later.[3]

"There were a lot of factors that went into making the final call," he wrote. Chief among them: "I've come to realize that though I love teaching, I'm not in love with academia."

After Larson sent his resignation letter, he said, he felt instant relief. He wanted others to understand what happened and realize a professor could make it in the outside world.

"It was a story worth telling," he said.

The same is true for young academics who got out before they spent much time seeking tenure-track jobs, said Blithe Rocher, a physical chemist who took a job as a web developer after a two-year research fellowship.[4] She, too, felt like she had to back up her choice.

"The main purpose was to say, 'Here's something I've worked my whole life for, and I'm pretty much stopping my path'," Rocher said. "I wanted to explain to people why – and maybe it wasn't even for others, maybe just for myself – this was the right decision."

The Statement-Makers

For some writers, the decision to publish their reasoning was the equivalent of yelling "take this job and shove it" to their home institutions, and to a higher-education system that they feel is heading in the wrong direction.

Zachary Ernst, a former associate professor of philosophy who now works as a software engineer, was among the most prominent writers to take this approach. His account, "Why I Jumped Off the Ivory Tower," went viral in October [2013].[5]

"My decision to leave isn't really about my department or university in particular, but about a perverse incentive structure that maintains the status quo, rewards mediocrity, and discourages potentially high-impact, interdisciplinary work," wrote Ernst, who declined a request for an interview. "My complaints are really about the structural features of the university, and not about the behavior of particular people. Although I believe that my university is unusually bad in these respects, I think these structural features are quite common."

3. Peter Larson, "Leaving Academia: One Chapter Ends, Another Begins," *Runblogger* (blog), April 22, 2013, https://runblogger.com/2013/04/leaving-academia-one-chapter-ends.html

4. Blithe Rocher, "From Scientist to Developer: Why I Restarted My Career as a Big Nerd Intern," Big Nerd Ranch, July 22, 2013, https://bignerdranch.com/blog/from-scientist-to-developer-why-i-restarted-my-career-as-a-big-nerd-ranch-intern

5. Zachary Ernst's personal blog has since been removed.

And then he unleashes.

Alessandra Lopez y Royo, a former reader of visual culture in the United Kingdom who took early retirement in August, was another who didn't shy away from highlighting the shortcomings of higher ed. In a column for *Times Higher Education,* she equated universities to money-hungry machines and criticized new research expectations.[6] (Several Quit Lit authors expressed concern about the corporatization of academia.)

"I feel I can no longer sacrifice my dignity and integrity within a university," she wrote. "I feel part of an oppressive and hierarchical structure that demands the compromise of individuality and creativity in order to fit the mould."

Some readers thought her piece was a "case of sour grapes," taking issue with her decision to name her university and department. But she said she felt like she needed to voice her opinion.

"This is what happens," she said. "There's nothing wrong with telling people what things are like."

The Destigmatizers

For others, Quit Lit isn't about flipping a middle finger to the system. Instead, it's a platform for debunking myths about academics who look beyond the professoriate.

One of those beliefs is that PhD's who don't land tenure-track jobs aren't trying hard enough, said L. Maren Wood, a former adjunct who now runs an education consulting and research group. She said she has learned firsthand that this isn't true, and that higher ed just isn't for everyone.

"Some people who have written these pieces had an inkling it wasn't for them in graduate school," Wood said. "That had never been the case for me. Ever since I was little, I wanted to be a teacher."

But when she entered her third year on the academic job market with no security in sight, she said, she hit a brick wall. She phoned a friend and told him she planned to quit. His response: "I don't blame you."

"I cried at the end of the phone call and cried a lot more in the following months," Wood wrote in *The Chronicle of Higher Education.*[7] "I was angry — at myself, at the system, at the administrators who were cutting

---

6. Alessandra Lopez y Royo, "Why I'm Quitting the Academy," *Times Higher Education,* August 22, 2013, https://www.timeshighereducation.com/comment/opinion/why-im-quitting-the-academy/2006622.article

7. L. Maren Wood, "'The Afternoon I Decided to Leave Academe' — and What Happened Next," *Chronicle of Higher Education,* August 8, 2013, https://www.chronicle.com/blogs/phd/2013/08/08/the-afternoon-i-decided-to-leave-academe-and-what-happened-next

tenure-track jobs, at those who'd caused the 2008 economic crash. I kept looking at job boards, trying to find a reason my decision to leave was wrong."

When she finally felt confident in her decision to leave, she shared her experience with others.

"I wanted to write it for people who assume we didn't want it bad enough, who say perseverance is all you need," she said. "That's not true. You can work as hard as you want and have an amazing CV, but – in a saturated job market – not get an opportunity."

There's another myth worth debunking, said Melissa Dalgleish, a PhD candidate who decided early on to take an alt-ac job as a university research officer: the notion that academics have failed if they deviate from the classroom. Leaving traditional academia carries a stigma, she said, but it shouldn't; it's not shameful to pursue an alternate career.

Dalgleish, who wrote about her choice to accept an alt-ac job for *Hook and Eye*, said her motivation to write was to help normalize the act of leaving and to help students recognize that there's life outside academia.[8]

"I was attempting to get close to a world in which people won't have to go through the stressful experience of renegotiating their entire identity when they decide not to remain in academia," she said. "If we, the people writing, can counteract the stigma, the sense of alienation for people going through the same thing, then our purpose is fulfilled."

"It Definitely Struck a Chord"

There's a long way to go before people stop questioning those who flee, Dalgleish said, but openly discussing the act is a start. Quit Lit has worked as a catalyst for that conversation, she said.

For one thing, this stuff definitely draws eyeballs. "It was our most-read post this year," says Dalgleish of the *Hook and Eye* essay, "and one of all time. It definitely struck a chord in some way."

Other authors agree: They've seen spikes in their reader traffic when they discuss breaking out of higher ed, and they've received a range of feedback from commenters and colleagues alike.

"People within academia understand the want to get out," Rocher said, noting that the response to her piece was mostly positive and supportive. "But some of the younger academics, those who are still in grad school, were disillusioned. 'Oh, no. Why is Blithe leaving?'"

In more extreme cases, Quit Lit has inspired others to take action.

---

8. Melissa Dalgleish, "My 'I Quit' Letter," *Hook and Eye* (blog), November 7, 2013, https://hookandeye.ca/2013/11/07/my-i-quit-letter/ [pp. 55-60 in the present volume].

Mark Smithers, who left academia more than a decade ago, happened upon Rebecca Schuman's "I Quit Academia: An Important, Growing Subgenre of American Essays," published by *Slate* in October [2013]. It was only then that he decided to write about his own departure.[9]

Schuman's column "got me thinking about my own reasons for leaving the academy in 1999 and also my gradually decaying anger with higher education before and since leaving," Smithers wrote, before detailing his own track record.

After years searching for a full-time gig, he left the classroom to do higher education consulting work. But the new job didn't dissolve his frustration with what went wrong in his own academic career. "My anger seems to have a half-life of about seven years," he joked.

When all of his pent-up emotions resurfaced, he said, he turned to writing as a "cathartic exercise." "I decided I needed to get it all out of my system," he said. "I wrote things I've been thinking about over a long time. I let it splurge."

And through his prose, he found assurance: "Rebecca Schuman's piece talks about those that quit as 'failed academics.' I think she's right. I am a 'failed academic.' A proud one."

Welsh agreed, saying he knows he made the right decision when he left Harvard to be a software engineer at Google — even if he did lose the fancy office and title.

"I basically sit at a desk with no walls," he joked. "But it suits me. I'm very happy in my role. In some sense, the reason I became a computer scientist was to write software. I'm returning to my roots."

References

Dalgleish, Melissa. "My 'I Quit' Letter." *Hook and Eye* (blog), November 7, 2013. https://hookandeye.ca/2013/11/07/my-i-quit-letter/

Larson, Peter. "Leaving Academia: One Chapter Ends, Another Begins." *Runblogger* (blog), April 22, 2013. https://runblogger.com/2013/ 04/ leaving-academia-one-chapter-ends.html

Lopez y Royo, Alessandra. "Why I'm Quitting the Academy." *Times Higher Education*, August 22, 2013. https://www.timeshighereducation.com/ comment/opinion/why-im-quitting-the-academy/2006622.article

---

9. Rebecca Schuman, "'I Quit Academia,' An Important, Growing Subgenre of American Essays," *Slate*, October 24, 2013, https://slate.com/culture/2013/10/quitting-academic-jobs-professor-zachary-ernst-and-other-leaving-tenure-and-tenure-track-jobs-why.html [pp. 137-40 in the present volume]. Mark Smithers' post has since been removed.

Rocher, Blithe. "From Scientist to Developer: Why I Restarted My Career as a Big Nerd Intern." Big Nerd Ranch, July 22, 2013. https://bignerdranch.com/blog/from-scientist-to-developer-why-i-restarted-my-career-as-a-big-nerd-ranch-intern

Schuman, Rebecca. "'I Quit Academia,' An Important, Growing Subgenre of American Essays," *Slate*, October 24, 2013. https://slate.com/culture/2013/10/quitting-academic-jobs-professor-zachary-ernst-and-other-leaving-tenure-and-tenure-track-jobs-why.html

Welsh, Matt. "Why I'm Leaving Harvard." *Matt Welsh* (personal blog), November 15, 2010. http://matt-welsh.blogspot.com/2010/11/why-im-leaving-harvard.html

Wood, L. Maren. "'The Afternoon I Decided to Leave Academe' – and What Happened Next." *Chronicle of Higher Education*, August 8, 2013. https://www.chronicle.com/blogs/phd/2013/08/08/the-afternoon-i-decided-to-leave-academe-and-what-happened-next

The Grief of the Ex-Academic

Leonard Cassuto

Originally published in *The Chronicle of Higher Education*, February 25, 2018

https://www.chronicle.com/article/The-Grief-of-the-Ex-Academic/242612

ERIN BARTRAM IS a visiting assistant professor of history who has been looking for a tenure-track position since she earned her PhD in 2015. A few weeks ago, she decided to stop trying. She made her decision public in an essay – "The Sublimated Grief of the Left Behind" – that she posted on her blog and republished in *The Chronicle*.[1]

"I got a PhD in history because I wanted to be a historian," Bartram wrote. "Now I have to do something else." At first, she said, she suppressed the sadness she felt – "I didn't feel I had the right to grieve" – and then she released it.

Bartram's essay has generated a vesuvian outpouring of responses from all over the virtual academic quad.[2] There are scores of comments on her blog post. Her essay has been retweeted more 2,000 times on Twitter, and repeatedly reblogged.

1. Erin Bartram, "The Sublimated Grief of the Left Behind," *Erin Bartram* (personal blog), February 11, 2018 http://erinbartram.com/uncategorized/the sublimated grief of the left-behind/ [pp. 97-101 in the present volume); Bartram, "Why Everybody Loses When Someone Leaves Academe," *Chronicle of Higher Education*, February 15, 2018, https://www.chronicle.com/article/why-everybody-loses-when-someone-leaves-academe/

2. Sarah Brown, "She Wrote a Farewell Letter to Colleagues. Then 80,000 People Read It," *Chronicle of Higher Education*, February 15, 2018, https://www.chronicle.com/article/she-wrote-a-farewell-letter-to-colleagues-then-80-000-people-read-it/

What does all of this attention mean? To answer that, we must first understand that this sort of essay isn't new.[3] Contemporary academe supports a genre that has been dubbed "quit lit."[4] The storyline – "I am leaving academe because ..." – has proved catnip to academic readers. Some read quit lit out of curiosity, because they can't comprehend how anyone could just walk away from our profession. Others clearly sympathize with a fellow traveler walking a hard road.

Bartram's essay has quickly gained a prominent place in a quit-lit subfield that might be called "pushed-out lit." Up to now, the best-known work in that category is probably Rebecca Schuman's anguished "Thesis Hatement," which was published [in 2013].[5]

A scholar of German literature, Schuman checked all the right professional boxes and still didn't get a tenure-track job. Like Bartram, she treaded water for a few years in the contingent labor market, and then decided that she had had enough. Her account of her departure from academe blazes with anger.

Like Bartram, Schuman made a loud noise when she slammed the door shut on the academic job market. Her essay attracted thousands of comments, and eventually got her a job as a higher-education columnist for *Slate*. Today she writes about a variety of topics. As a successful freelance writer, she still criticizes the doings at colleges and universities, but her tone isn't quite so angry. Now she sometimes defends professors, and this year she even went back on the academic job market, although her bid ended without a job offer.[6]

Bartram is obviously angry too, but grief animates her above all. Her grief leads her to question the value of her scholarly work ("Valuable to whom?"), her learning ("utterly useless"), and how the time she spent in academe "doesn't matter in the way that I hoped it would."

We need to respect Bartram's feelings – and from where I sit, that starts with trying to understand them. We also need to look at the meaning of those feelings to Bartram's thousands of readers. The academic job market has

3. Alexandra Lord, "Every PhD Needs a Plan B," *Chronicle of Higher Education*, March 16, 2009, https://www.chronicle.com/article/every-ph-d-needs-a-plan-b/

4. Sydni Dunn, "Why So Many Academics Quit and Tell" Chronicle Community, December 12, 2013, https://community.chronicle.com/news/216-why-so-many-academics-quit-and-tell [pp. 141-47 in the present volume].

5. Rebecca Schuman, "Thesis Hatement," *Slate*, April 5, 2013, http://www.slate.com/articles/life/culturebox/2013/04/there_are_no_academic_jobs_and_getting_a_ph_d_will_make_you_into_a_horrible.html [pp. 41-45 in the present volume].

6. Rebecca Schuman, "A Fine Rejection Season," *Chronicle of Higher Education*, February 7, 2018, https://www.chronicle.com/article/a-fine-rejection-season/

fallen to historic lows since the 2008 recession but it also has been true for years — generations, it must be said — that plenty of PhDs don't get tenure-track jobs. Why has Bartram's story of not getting one gone viral?

"I sent Bartram's blogpost to a number of different types of friends and colleagues," wrote Nathan Ballantyne, an associate professor of philosophy and a colleague of mine at Fordham University, in an email, "and the reactions I got are radically different. Nobody is reading this powerful piece in the same way." Some of his respondents focused on Bartram, others on the scene of her sadness: the academic workplace. Some felt for her, but others questioned her decision to leave the discipline along with the profession. For Ballantyne, the varied responses reflect how the issues Bartram raises "are connected to our identities as scholars and students, gatekeepers and outsiders."

So we might say that her story is a Rorschach blot that shows each of us who we are as academics.

As for Bartram, she sees herself as a failed academic. Now that she's ending her academic career, she says, "I don't know what I'm going to do. I don't know what I'm good for."

Maybe it's just my Rorschach moment, but that's the comment that jumps out of the essay for me. When someone with a PhD doesn't know what she could be good for, it surely says something about how she's feeling, but it also says something about graduate training and academic culture.

When we say that graduate school teaches a lot of valuable skills, that's not just puffery. Doctoral students learn to work with information in sophisticated ways, and to communicate to different kinds of audiences.

Yet graduate school also teaches students that only a professorship truly justifies the long chase for the PhD. The message that a tenure track job is the only honorable career goal can be implicit, and not always intentional. But the fact is: The doctoral curriculum is modeled on the work of a professor at a research university. It emphasizes research skills over pedagogical and collaborative ones, and we who dispense that curriculum too easily allow our students to default into the singular pursuit of a professorship and the foreclosure of all other alternatives.

For me, Erin Bartram's grief raises an instrumental question: How can we change graduate education so that it doesn't set people up to feel like failures in the face of a likely outcome? We might start by honoring the range of career possibilities that students face. The wider world needs more PhDs — but (and here's the rub) only if they're happy to be in the wider world. When we treat diverse careers with scorn, we invite graduates like Erin Bartram to mourn as they contemplate those non-academic paths.

Bartram may stand out for her beautiful rendering of her sadness, but there's nothing unusual about her story. Most PhD's don't become professors, but that's only a problem if we teach them to feel like failures when that happens. Bartram herself knows that; she says her sad employment outcome is "probably what was always going to happen."

Susan Basalla and Maggie Debelius know it, too. They've been writing about it for more than 15 years, in multiple editions of *So What Are You Going to Do With That? Finding Careers Outside Academia*, first published in 2001. When they write, "We understand that being forced to leave a career you love because of a weak job market is heartbreaking," they might have been speaking directly to Bartram.[7]

Their book is also talking to people like Bartram when they warn that "if you think that you can't possibly be happy outside academia, you probably won't be." Despair can be its own self-fulfilling prophecy.

One of my own doctoral students recently described the academic job market as "a desert." (She now works in the corporate world.) We should teach and prepare our students with that reality in mind. Above all, we have to respect the diversity of career options they will have to choose from, not just the one we occupy.

That doesn't mean encouraging graduate students to abandon scholarly pursuits, but it does mean integrating other skills they will need outside of the university as well as within it. For example, students pursuing PhDs in the humanities and social sciences need to learn how to work collaboratively. Not only do employers value such experience, but it would also help with scholarship. When we teach with our students' career needs in mind, we bring our work into line with theirs – and with the professional world that we share.

Bartram's "reflections reveal something about the devastation of our labor system," says Ballantyne.

Yes. And they also reveal something about the values of the research culture that socialized both her and everyone else that went through a doctoral program.

References

Bartam, Erin. "The Sublimated Grief of the Left Behind." *Erin Bartram* (personal blog), February 11, 2018. http://erinbartram.com/uncategorized/the-sublimated-grief-of-the-left-behind/

———. "Why Everybody Loses When Someone Leaves Academe." *Chron-*

7. Susan Basalla and Maggie Debelius, *"So What Are You Going to Do With That?": Finding Careers Outside Academia*, 3d ed. (Chicago: University of Chicago Press, 2015), 14.

icle of Higher Education, February 15, 2018. https://www.chronicle.com/article/why-everybody-loses-when-someone-leaves-academe/

Basalla, Susan, and Maggie Debelius. *"So What Are You Going to Do With That?": Finding Careers Outside Academia*. 3d ed. Chicago: University of Chicago Press, 2015.

Brown, Sarah. "She Wrote a Farewell Letter to Colleagues. Then 80,000 People Read It." *Chronicle of Higher Education*, February 15, 2018. https://www.chronicle.com/article/she-wrote-a-farewell-letter-to-colleagues-then-80-000-people-read-it/

Dunn, Sydni. "Why So Many Academics Quit and Tell." Chronicle Community, December 12, 2013. https://community.chronicle.com/news/216-why-so-many-academics-quit-and-tell

Lord, Alexandra. "Every PhD Needs a Plan B." *Chronicle of Higher Education*, March 16, 2009. https://www.chronicle.com/article/every-ph-d-needs-a-plan-b/

Schuman, Rebecca. "A Fine Rejection Season." *Chronicle of Higher Education*, February 7, 2018. https://www.chronicle.com/article/a-fine-rejection-season/

———. "Thesis Hatement." *Slate*, April 5, 2013. http://www.slate.com/articles/life/culturebox/2013/04/there_are_no_academic_jobs_and_getting_a_ph_d_will_make_you_into_a_horrible.html

They're Not Quitting! Reclaiming a Genre

Ian Saxine

Originally published in The Professor Is In, March 20, 2018
https://theprofessorisin.com/2018/03/20/theyre-not-quitting-reclaiming-a-genre-a-postac-guest-post/

THIS IS NOT a hot take on Erin Bartram's much read – and even more needed – essay, "Sublimated Grief of the Left Behind."[1] That essay stands wonderfully and poignantly on its own. I read it right before lecturing, and my students asked me who died. I suspect I'm not the only educator who had that experience.

Instead, this is a reflection on many of the responses to the piece, which I'd argue is revealing in a different way. I broke one of life's most important rules and read the comments, as well as other responses in other forums like *Inside Higher Ed* and *The Chronicle of Higher Ed.* And much of the response was thoughtful. What surprised me, though, even more than the fact that so many non-horrifying comments appeared on a thoughtful blog, was how so many writers from *Inside Higher Ed* on down have persisted in calling the piece "quit lit."

In fairness, the label is often accompanied by the qualifier "a new kind of" or something of that nature, but nevertheless the fact remains that many (presumably academic) readers keep resorting to that category for Bartram's piece.

[1] Erin Bartram, "The Sublimated Grief of the Left Behind," *Erin Bartram* (personal blog), February 11, 2018, http://erinbartram.com/uncategorized/the-sublimated-grief-of-the-left-behind/ [pp. 97-101 in the present volume].

But why do we (and by "we" I mean academics, and, speaking for myself, historians still on the visiting track, a year behind Bartram in the great junior academic life cycle) insist on labeling this genre of writing quit lit? Especially Bartram's, since she says herself, *she's not quitting.* Bartram wants to keep teaching and researching, but nobody will pay her a living wage to do it. Or if someone will, they want her to move to an unincorporated census tract in western Nebraska to teach a 4/4 load for 9 months, and then they're cutting her off.

So why again do we insist on calling this quit lit? (And now by "we" I especially mean historians?) Why can't we come up with a better shorthand for: *there are no jobs available that will pay Bartram and many more like her a living wage because they have been replaced by poorly paid adjunct positions.* They stopped paying her? I'm wedded to nothing, but we can do better than "quit lit."

Historians are far from the only scholars in this position, but we have the least excuse for the linguistic weasel words. Throughout graduate school we bang on about how words matter, and you don't use the passive voice because it obscures agency, and you don't say things like "racial tensions" to describe Jim Crow when "state-backed white supremacy" is more accurate. Then we spend our waking hours telling undergraduates the same thing. We also know what is happening. We teach and read and write about the series of decisions we as a society have made since the Second World War that have undermined labor and privatized so much of American life.

When I'm being charitable, I ask myself if we call this "quitting" because we think we're being nice to someone. "They didn't leave you, you broke up with them!" Or, maybe, this is a way of telling ourselves we still have "agency." (Historians love agency.) Bartram therefore made a choice to leave, rather than being forced out because no one will pay her money to do what she does best.

When I'm being uncharitable, which is often the case these days, I suspect that framing work — and experiences — like Bartram's as "quitting" is a way of deflecting responsibility. If Bartram quit, she just gave up. If she had only hung on for another year, or two, or three, she'd land that tenure-track job. Then no one has to talk about how there are many, many terribly paying teaching jobs out there, and that this isn't just about too many people and not enough chairs when the music stops.

Least charitably of all, labeling Bartram's piece as "quit lit" lets tenured scholars, sitting atop an exploitative system, off the hook for helping eliminate the possibility of her having a decently paying career to begin with. Yes, yes, I know, #notalltenuredscholars.

I don't have solutions to offer. (Historians are terrible at solutions.) But it seems to me that our collective mindset in which we insist on saying someone like Erin Bartram "quit" or "gave up" is one in which we've given up hope that we can make things better.

I don't judge Bartram for her decision to not play the exhausting and degrading game that is the visiting track for any longer. We all have to make that call when the time comes. But maybe if we stop calling her experience "quit lit," and what she's doing "quitting," and instead call it what it is: *driven out*, then maybe we'll make it easier for the people who are able and choose to stay and fight, to actually achieve something.

Bartram herself mentioned she worked to unionize her colleagues. And "collective bargaining" is not a term that I was able to find on the website of the American Historical Association, of which I am still a member in good standing. But maybe if the AHA and other scholarly organizations faced the reality openly said on a regular basis that people like Bartram are not merely choosing to "follow diverse career paths," in the words of Jim Grossman, our president, but are rather being replaced by minimum-wage level workers, that might pave the way for a more widespread mobilization of contingent faculty labor.

It's 2018. Lots of good people are upset and getting up to do something about grotesque excesses of a new Gilded Age in American life. The least we can do is admit, whenever we discuss it, that Bartram's (and mine, and your) situation is a part of that.

When you think about it, calling Bartram's piece "quit lit" is actually about encouraging more people to stop trying to fix the problems in front of us. Personally, I'm not ready for that yet.

References

Bartram, Erin. "The Sublimated Grief of the Left Behind." *Erin Bartram* (personal blog), February 11, 2018. http://erinbartram.com/uncategorized/the-sublimated-grief-of-the-left-behind/

Two Departures from the Professoriate: A World Apart

Howard Gardner

Originally published in *Howard Gardner* (personal blog), March 27, 2018; reposted at The Real World of College
https://www.therealworldofcollege.com/blog/two-departures-from-the-professoriate-a-world-apart

MATT WELSH was a highly talented assistant professor of computer science at Harvard University. Like some but by no means all junior professors, he was approved to become a full time, tenured professor – indeed, he was the occupant of a named chair, "The Gordon McKay Professor of Computer Science."

Just months after receiving tenure, Welsh resigned his professorship to become a fellow at Google. This decision caused quite a stir. Because so many were surprised, he decided to explain why.

In an article with the straightforward title "Why I'm Leaving Harvard," Welsh begins by saying that he did not have any major problems with his work at Harvard.[1] He liked his colleagues, said that the students were the best that he could ever hope for, and underscored that he had plenty of support for the research that he wanted to do.

But he went on to say, "There is one simple reason that I'm leaving academia: I simply love work I'm doing at Google. I get to hack all day, working on problems that are orders of magnitude larger and more interesting than I can work on at any university.... [W]orking at Google is realizing the dream

1. Matt Welsh, "Why I'm Leaving Harvard," *Matt Welsh* (personal blog), November 15, 2010, http://matt-welsh.blogspot.com/2010/11/why-im-leaving-harvard.html [pp. 19-22 in the present volume].

I've had of building big systems.... I can just sit down and write the code and deploy the system, on more machines than I will ever have access to at a university."

Let's take Welsh at his word – and assume that he did not leave Harvard simply (or primarily) to triple his salary or get a mortgage-free house or guaranteed scholarships for members of his family. In our country, few would say that Welsh should be deprived of the opportunity to fulfill his life's dream.

Yet as a fellow professor and as one who believes in educational institutions, I am disappointed – in him and/or in the system.

From the time of graduate school if not before, Welsh was supported in his pursuit of the doctorate and of post-doctorate work – on the tacit assumption that, if he had the opportunity, he would join the professoriate. Citizens (via their taxes) as well as private funding agencies put their faith in him. And now, he is working for private industry – admittedly having lots of fun, perhaps doing some good, but the more cynical would say that he has "gone over to the dark side."

Consider an entirely different case – that of Erin Bartram. Trained as an historian of nineteenth-century America, Bartram was an assistant professor at a much less prestigious school – the University of Hartford. After years of searching unsuccessfully for a tenure-track job, she decided to leave academe. She would have done so silently and without any public knowledge had she not decided to write an essay titled "The Sublimated Grief of the Left Behind" (an example of a genre apparently dubbed "quit lit").[2] In her soul-searching evocative piece, she notes, "We don't want to face how much knowledge [a] colleague has in their head that's just going to be *lost* to those who remain, and even worse, we don't want to face how much knowledge that colleague has in their head that's going to be utterly *useless* for the rest of their lives." To her surprise, the essay went viral, and as Bartram comments, subsequently and ruefully, had that not happened, "I would have been nobody."

Of course, and alas, Bartram's story is far more common than Welsh's. Every year, many hundreds of young scholars – primarily in the humanities and the "softer" social sciences – receive their doctorates and try, unsuccessfully, to find a full-time, tenure-track position. Some find a postdoc position for a year or two; some fill in for a professor who is on sabbatical; some moonlight on several campuses (so-called "taxi cab professors"); some end up teaching in high schools or for-profit institutions; and some, and one could even call them "lucky," end up teaching at a second- or third-tier school, or a

2. Erin Bartram, "The Sublimated Grief of the Left Behind," *Erin Bartram* (personal blog), February 11, 2018, http://erinbartram.com/uncategorized/the-sublimated-grief-of-the-left-behind/ [pp. 97-101 in the present volume].

community college, with a teaching (and perhaps also an advising) load so heavy that there is essentially no chance that they can carry out the scholarship that they were trained to do – and that they presumably want to do.

And many quit the academy altogether as Bartram has apparently done – sometimes trying to be "independent scholars," more often seeking and accepting positions that would have been more appropriate for those who have not spent years fulfilling the requirements for a doctoral degree.

Darting back to the words of Welsh, these less fortunate young scholars would not be soothed by his concession: "I also admire the professors who flourish in an academic setting, writing books, giving talks, mentoring students, sitting on government advisory boards, all that. I never found most of these things very satisfying, and all of that extra work only takes away from time spent building systems, which is what I really want to be doing."

I hope that readers of this [essay] join me in asking, "What's wrong with this picture?" or, more properly, "What's wrong with *these* pictures?" It's lamentable that Welsh does not appreciate many facets of the traditional professorship (which presumably he should have known about by the second year of doctoral training); it's tragic that Bartram is one of thousands of trained scholars who never get the opportunity to teach students who want to learn and to add their own bricks – small and not so small – to the edifice of knowledge in their chosen field of study.

At least in the United States, from pre-school to graduate school, education is no longer a public good; *it's become a private good.* The lucky few get to do just what they want to do – even if they never see another student or teach another class. A large majority of those with doctorates would give anything to take the place of the "leaver," but never gain the chance.

Other than remain with the unsatisfactory status quo, could this situation be handled differently?

One solution, with a long history in Europe, is to have two separate tracks – in practice, or at least in theory. For a fortunate few, there is a research track, wherein you join an institute, get to carry out the research that you want to, and never need to teach any students unless you so desire. For a vast majority, you either begin by teaching secondary students far from the metropolis, or you consign yourself to teaching huge lectures in the big universities, without having any contact with students, many of whom never show up in class and most of whom will never graduate. You are solely a teacher – not a teacher-researcher-scholar.

Another solution would be for the colleges and universities to cease graduate training altogether and let wealthy private companies set up their own schools. As I understand it, Google hires hundreds of postdocs, most trained at prestigious universities. Why not have Google, or Amazon, or

Microsoft, or "the next big tech company" train the next generation of in-house researchers? We'd have to decide (as a society) whether to award doctorates, doctorates with an asterisk (PhD, with a Twitter bird or Amazon shopping cart next to it), or some newfangled degree.

Yet another possibility. Perhaps students who elect to pursue a PhD would understand from the beginning that there is a respectable alternate lifestyle, called an independent scholar. After all, this option was in effect the tradition in much of Europe over the centuries. And of course, if you or your family are wealthy enough, this remains a viable pathway today. Not for Bartram, alas; she has to worry about how to pay next month's rent.

But there is a better way, though I have to admit it is no longer the American way: an agreed-upon bargain between our higher-degree-awarding institutions and our talented students who want to be teachers *and* scholars. If our institutions train you to be a skilled scholar and teacher, you commit to giving back – to staying within the professoriate, barring unusual circumstances. (Presumably Welsh could even come to like, to cherish his Harvard undergraduates.) Conversely, if we take you on as a student and you complete the requirements successfully, we commit to providing a job which makes use of your talents. If that means radically reducing the number of doctorates in history or in Romance languages, better to do so "up front" than to hold out the false hope of a job – and in the process, ensuring many repetitions of Erin Bartram's sad saga.

References

Bartram, Erin. "The Sublimated Grief of the Left Behind." *Erin Bartram* (personal blog), February 11, 2018. http://erinbartram.com/uncategorized/the-sublimated-grief-of-the-left-behind/

Welsh, Matt. "Why I'm Leaving Harvard." *Matt Welsh* (personal blog), November 15, 2010. http://matt-welsh.blogspot.com/2010/11/why-im-leaving-harvard.html

"Quit Lit" Then and Now

Grant Shreve

Originally published in *Inside Higher Ed*, April 4, 2018
https://www.insidehighered.com/views/2018/04/04/comparison-quit-lit-1970s-and-today-opinion

THE ACADEMIC JOB market is still collapsing, but academic "quit lit" is booming. The precipitous decline of tenure-track jobs in the humanities and social sciences over the past decade has meant that more early-career PhDs than ever are leaving academe and writing about their experiences.

As this genre has developed, it has come to be distinguished by its reliance on personal narrative and its authors' desire to publicly validate their private feelings at being shut out of a profession they've spent a significant portion of adulthood pursuing. Although the rise of quit lit feels unique to an era shaped by an epochal financial crisis and an unprecedented accessibility of publishing venues, this kind of writing by ex-academics is not quite as novel as it appears.

In fact, a form of "quit lit" (we might call it proto-quit lit) actually emerged in the 1970s, the first decade in which the number of new PhDs first outpaced the number of available academic jobs. By 1980, headlines like "The Plight of the PhDs," "PhD Equals 'Prospects Highly Depressing'," "Jobless PhDs Rack Brains to Live" and "Untenured Teachers Face Uncertain Futures" had become a familiar sight, and stock types like the itinerant scholar were often invoked alongside anecdotes of PhDs having to take second jobs as taxicab drivers, bartenders or bricklayers.

For all this public hand-wringing, the generation of PhDs who lived through this first wave of academic underemployment did not write essays with anywhere near the frequency or intensity of those of our own moment. Nevertheless, a few young academics were charting the course for the genre in newspapers, professional bulletins and academic journals.

One of the earliest examples is John T. Harwood's 1974 article for *AAUP Bulletin*, "Nonacademic Job Hunting."[1] More gently satiric than incisively critical of the academic profession, the essay peppers Harwood's eminently practical advice about how PhDs ought to go about securing non-academic employment with personal stories and a few winking literary references.

A more forceful and personal denunciation of the academic job market appears in "The New Academic Hustle: Marketing a PhD," a 1978 article by two sociology PhDs detailing the perils and grotesqueries of the academic hiring process. Despite their mostly measured tone, the authors manage to smuggle in a damning indictment of the academic job market in the form of an autobiographical note cleverly placed where an abstract would typically appear. "When we received our PhDs in 1976," it reads, "we knew we would have to look hard for the kinds of jobs we wanted. But we did not anticipate the often discourteous, unfeeling and degrading reception we were to encounter as job applicants."[2]

Perhaps the most instructive piece in this vein is a brief article written by a freshly minted sociology PhD in 1975 for *The Berkshire Eagle* and headlined, "Is a PhD Worth It?"[3] The author's list of complaints is all too familiar: the constriction of the labor market, the apathy of undergraduates, the consumer-centric focus of the modern university and the pressures to publish.

Yet his conclusion gestures toward wells of feeling yet untapped. "I have no regrets about my decision," he writes, but "this does not mean I am not bitter; trying to find work during these depressed times is no less anguishing for me than it is for most people." He hastens to add, however, "whatever anger I feel is not directed towards my seven years in graduate school." Unlike the quit lit of our current moment, this author explicitly diverts his anger away from his home institution in order to absolve it of any responsibility for his feelings.

1. John T. Harwood, "Nonacademic Job Hunting," *AAUP Bulletin* 60.3 (September 1974): 313-16.

2. Thomas A. Lyson and Gregory D. Squires, "The New Academic Hustle: Marketing a PhD," *American Sociologist* 13 (1978): 233.

3. Mitchell Garfield, "Is a PhD Worth It?" *Berkshire Eagle* (Pittsfield, MA), June 4, 1975, 23.

Notable in all these bygone essays is how reticent their authors are to give voice to their pain. When grief and anger surface, they are swiftly curtailed with pragmatic prescriptions for institutional change. They display a uniform resistance to soul-baring that stands in stark contrast to the recent wave of quit lit.

In light of the proto-quit lit of the 1970s, in the 2010s the genre's reliance on personal narratives that marshal intense feelings – of rage and grief and everything in between – to overturn a broken hiring system is indicative of how intractable the problem of academic underemployment has become. For so many of these authors, the very notion that institutional reforms will resolve this crisis seems absurd given its scope and duration.

There is no better or timelier example of this transformation than Erin Bartram's blog post, which led to a broad discussion in academe.[4]

Whereas a quit lit essay like Rebecca Schuman's 2013 barnburner for *Slate*, "Thesis Hatement,"[5] derives its rhetorical power from the righteous anger of its author, Bartram's piece appeals to collective grief and sympathy. In this way, it marks the genre's turn toward sentimentalism, by which I do not mean mere mawkishness but rather a philosophical and aesthetic paradigm – with a complicated legacy in American social history – that privileges feeling and leverages it to enact change.

In her essay, Bartram eloquently and movingly mobilizes her personal story to validate her private grief at having to leave the profession. "My feelings are, thankfully, not subject to peer review," she writes, snatching the legitimacy of her interior experience away from the profession's preferred methods of scrutiny and authorization.

The piece is far more than the story of one person's loss, however, as Bartram attempts to extend her grief to those "left behind" – the ones who have successfully secured jobs – urging them to recognize "not only the magnitude of the loss [of potential colleagues] but also that it was a loss at all."

Although the essay is more ethically than politically oriented, Bartram concludes it with a question that gestures in the direction of the latter. "What would happen," she asks, "if we actually grieved for those losses?" In this, she hints at the political possibilities that would inhere in the creation of a

4. Erin Bartram, "The Sublimated Grief of the Left Behind," *Erin Bartram* (personal blog), February 11, 2018, http://erinbartram.com/uncategorized/the-sublimated-grief-of-the-left-behind/ [pp. 97-101 in the present volume]; see Colleen Flaherty, "Calling Academe's Bluff," *Inside Higher Ed*, February 13, 2018, https://www.insidehighered.com/news/2018/02/13/historians-quit-lit-essay-rejects-notion-leaving-higher-ed-equals-personal-failure

5. Rebecca Schuman, "Thesis Hatement," *Slate*, April 5, 2013, http://www.slate.com/articles/life/culturebox/2013/04/there_are_no_academic_jobs_and_getting_a_ph_d_will_make_you_into_a_horrible.html [pp. 41-45 in the present volume].

community of mourners who grieve for those individuals chewed up and spit out by the academic job market.

There is much to admire in this vision, yet we should be cautious of relying on grief alone as a catalyst for change.

Ralph Waldo Emerson famously wrote, "I grieve that grief can teach me nothing, nor carry me one step into real nature." According to Georgetown University professor Dana Luciano, this sentence negates the "compelling cultural fantasy that grief can make one better."[6] Powerful though it may be, grief has as much potential to reinforce the status quo as to dismantle it. That some have already begun to repurpose Bartram's grief for political projects along precisely these lines is proof of this.[7]

A 1975 profile of an out-of-work professor concludes with her reflecting on a group of faculty recently ousted from a small, rural college where she previously taught. She implores her interviewer to "imagine how they feel." This imperative is a prescient anticipation of the guiding principle behind the most resonant academic quit lit of the 2010s. As we look to the genre's future, we ought to consider whether simply getting others to *feel right* is enough.

References

Bartam, Erin. "The Sublimated Grief of the Left Behind." *Erin Bartram* (personal blog), February 11, 2018. http://erinbartram.com/uncategorized/the-sublimated-grief-of-the-left-behind/

Cassuto, Leonard. "The Grief of the Ex-Academic." *Chronicle of Higher Education*, February 25, 2018. https://www.chronicle.com/article/the-grief-of-the-ex-academic

Flaherty, Colleen. "Calling Academe's Bluff." *Inside Higher Ed*, February 13, 2018. https://www.insidehighered.com/news/2018/02/13/historians-quit-lit-essay-rejects-notion-leaving-higher-ed-equals-personal-failure

Garfield, Mitchell. "Is a PhD Worth It?" *Berkshire Eagle* (Pittsfield, MA), June 4, 1975.

Harwood, John T. "Nonacademic Job Hunting." *AAUP Bulletin* 60.3 (September 1974): 313-16.

6. Dana Luciano, *Arranging Grief: Sacred Time and the Body in Nineteenth-Century America* (New York: New York University Press, 2007), 265.

7. See Leonard Cassuto, "The Grief of the Ex-Academic," *Chronicle of Higher Education*, February 25, 2018, https://www.chronicle.com/article/the-grief-of-the-ex-academic [pp. 149-53 in the present volume].

Luciano, Dana. *Arranging Grief: Sacred Time and the Body in Nineteenth-Century America.* New York: New York University Press, 2007.

Lyson, Thomas A., and Gregory D. Squires. "The New Academic Hustle: Marketing a PhD." *American Sociologist* 13 (1978): 233-38.

Schuman, Rebecca. "Thesis Hatement." *Slate*, April 5, 2013. http://www.slate.com/articles/life/culturebox/2013/04/there_are_no_academic_jobs_and_getting_a_ph_d_will_make_you_into_a_horrible.html

Quit Lit Is About Labor Conditions

Katie Rose Guest Pryal

Originally published in *Women in Higher Education*, June 7, 2018
https://www.wihe.com/article-details/74/quit-lit-is-about-labor-conditions/

THE DISMAL STATE of the academic labor market has been critiqued for years at this point. Those of us who began our doctorates before contingent labor became the norm, back when there were still jobs to be had, finished our doctorates with no hope for a career in sight. So, we took jobs in contingent positions under poor working conditions. Some of us – most of us – left. Some of us who left then wrote about it.

These essays about leaving academia became a genre, and the genre gained a name: "quit lit," which was, as far as I can tell, first coined in this context by higher education critic Dr. Rebecca Schuman in *Slate* in October 2013.

The Quit Lit Foremothers

Rebecca Schuman wrote an early piece of academic quit lit for *Slate* in April 2013. In "Thesis Hatement,"[1] Schuman does three main things. She warns readers not to go to graduate school: "Don't do it. Just don't." She tells them

1. Rebecca Schuman, "Thesis Hatement," *Slate*, April 5, 2013, http://www.slate.com/articles/life/culturebox/2013/04/there_are_no_academic_jobs_and_getting_a_ph_d_will_make_you_into_a_horrible.html [pp. 41-45 in the present volume].

why: "I now realize graduate school was a terrible idea because the full-time, tenure-track literature professorship is extinct." And she describes the pain she suffered as she trained for a career that was never going to manifest: "During graduate school, you will be broken down and reconfigured in the image of the academy.... Your academic self will be the culmination of your entire self, and thus you will believe, incomprehensibly, that not having a tenure-track job makes you worthless." These three arguments – warning, critique and description of suffering – comprise the genre of quit lit.

In her essay, Schuman doesn't hedge. She doesn't say there are "fewer" jobs. She says there are no jobs. Because, as she points out, in her discipline there are 150 applicants a year for six positions worldwide. With those numbers, the difference between few and none is no difference at all.

Despite its grimness, Schuman's essay is inspiring as well. She inspired me to write and publish my first nonacademic essay as I was inching toward the exit of higher ed. That essay was a litany of the small, daily humiliations of being a contingent faculty member. But in retrospect, that piece was also setting up the evidence I would use when I finally quit. That essay proved why life as contingent academic labor in the contemporary university is, for the most part, as untenable as Schuman described.

I quit, and I wrote about it. I also connected with other writers who wrote about quitting around the same time I did – with Schuman, Dr. Kelly J. Baker, Dr. Sarah Kendzior, Dr. Elizabeth Keenan and others I'm sure I'm forgetting here over the years. We wrote about the terrible experiences of academic labor. We were mocked for doing so, told to "stop complaining."

Over the years, my quit lit friends have gone their separate ways and found success in their new chosen fields: journalism, writing, editing, real estate (and writing!) and more. The fire that drove us away from the academy in the days of the rise of the academic precariat – and the attendant rise of quit lit – cooled to a slow burn. Because that's what drove quit lit in the beginning. Quit lit, at its heart, was a labor critique.

Insider Quit Lit

It's five years later, and something new has happened. In February2018, *The Chronicle of Higher Education* republished a blog essay by Dr. Erin Bartram, a historian, who wrote about leaving academia after years in a contingent faculty position and failure on the job market. Titled "Why Everybody Loses When Someone Leaves Academe,"[2] the essay opens with her final job rejec-

2. Erin Bartram, "Why Everybody Loses When Someone Leaves Academe," *Chronicle of Higher Education*, February 15, 2018, https://www.chronicle.com/article/why-everybody-loses-when-someone-leaves-academe/. This is a lightly revised version of her

tion. She leaves her office in her temporary department, described with all of the sentiment a professor can muster, including a drawer of fountain pen ink.

And then her essay takes a surprising turn. Her indictment is not one of the dismal labor market, but rather one of her field (history) that allows losses of colleagues to continue because their contributions to research will be lost forever. She writes, "Even in our supportive responses to those leaving, we don't want to face what's being lost, so we try to find ways to tell people it hasn't all been in vain." Later she writes, "We don't want these people to go, and we don't want to lose all the ideas floating around in their heads, so we say, 'Please give us those ideas, at least. Please stay with us just a little bit.'" And she's right; when I left academia, my former colleagues said similar things to me.

Like Schuman, Bartram talks about the pain of losing the part of her identity that she trained years to build: "I've lost a huge part of my identity, and all of my book-learning on identity construction can't help me now." And perhaps most poignantly: "I don't know what I'm going to do. I don't know what I'm good for."

The piece garnered a massive response. There were response essays in *CHE* itself, which noted that Bartram's piece "generated a vesuvian outpouring of responses" and that the original blog post was read at least 80,000 times.[3] By any metric, Bartram's piece struck a chord with readers.

Obviously, her essay appeals to outsiders who have quit academia. But Bartram's piece is radically unlike Schuman's and others in a particular way that makes it appealing to more than just those who have been forced out of the academy.

Bartram's essay also appeals to those who approve of the academic status quo because it maintains nostalgia for the academy itself. This nostalgia does not appear in Schuman's essay and other quit lit. Bartram doesn't speak to poor labor conditions and how working as contingent faculty can be back-breaking and poverty-inducing. She speaks to how much she'll miss her research and her chosen field. Bartram's essay doesn't provide a critique of the academic labor market, nor the poor working conditions.

---

personal blog post, "The Sublimated Grief of the Left Behind," February 11, 2018, http://erinbartram.com/uncategorized/the-sublimated-grief-of-the-left-behind/ [pp. 97-101 in the present volume].

3. Leonard Cassuto, "The Grief of the Ex-Academic," *Chronicle of Higher Education*, February 25, 2018, https://www.chronicle.com/article/The-Grief-of-the-Ex-Academic/242612 [pp. 149-53 in the present volume]; Sarah Brown, "She Wrote a Farewell Letter to Colleagues. Then 80,000 People Read It," *Chronicle of Higher Education*, February 15, 2018, https://www.chronicle.com/article/she-wrote-a-farewell-letter-to-colleagues-then-80-000-people-read-it

Indeed, she still speaks of her chosen field as though she were a part of it. She uses the first-person plural "we": "We don't want these people to go, and we don't want to lose all the ideas floating around in their heads." In this essay, Bartram herself is still an insider. No wonder it was so appealing to so many – even while forced out, Bartram still looks upon the field with love.

Although buried in her essay was a strong message of suffering, Bartram did not bring a labor critique: "What would happen if we, as a community, stopped saying 'he's gone to a better place,' bringing a casserole, and moving on. What would happen if we acknowledged the losses our discipline suffers every year? What would happen if we actually grieved for those losses?"

A Practical Labor Critique

If quit lit is about labor, then the best quit lit published in the last year wasn't about quitting at all.

In April 2018, *Chronicle Vitae* republished a blog post written by Dr. Annemarie Pérez on how an adjunct's current department can do material things to help that adjunct with her career – rather than continuing to exploit her.[4] It was one of the few recent pieces I've read on contingent issues that still burned with fire about the dismal academic job market and the attendant labor exploitation.

Quit lit does not tend to have the happy ending that Pérez's piece has – she landed a tenure-track job after many years of adjuncting and with the mentorship she found in her temporary department.

But don't be fooled: Pérez's piece is an indictment all the same. Titled "Instead of Gaslighting Adjuncts, We Could Help Them," the essay provides a practical guide for tenured faculty who work alongside adjuncts, and slams those who do not help. Pérez pulls no punches: "We don't have to just wring our hands about how terrible the situation is, or, worse still, say the job market has always been terrible and those who are adjuncts should never have started a PhD if they weren't willing to be exploited."

Bartram's piece has heart. But in the end, it maintains the status quo of academic life. Pérez's piece calls academics out for their gaslighting and provides concrete steps for fixing the problems we've been writing about for five years. But 80,000 people haven't read Pérez's piece because it isn't an encomium to the academy.

The academy doesn't need encomiums or casseroles. It needs practical labor critiques. Or there will be no insiders left.

4. Annemarie Pérez, "Instead of Gaslighting Adjuncts, We Could Help Them," *Chronicle Vitae*, April 16, 2018, https://chroniclevitae.com/news/2036-instead-of-gaslighting-adjuncts-we-could-help-them

References

Bartram, Erin. "Why Everybody Loses When Someone Leaves Academe." *Chronicle of Higher Education,* February 15, 2018. https://www.chronicle.com/article/why-everybody-loses-when-someone-leaves-academe/

Brown, Sarah. "She Wrote a Farewell Letter to Colleagues. Then 80,000 People Read It." *Chronicle of Higher Education*, February 15, 2018. https://www.chronicle.com/article/she-wrote-a-farewell-letter-to-colleagues-then-80-000-people-read-it

Cassuto, Leonard. "The Grief of the Ex-Academic." *Chronicle of Higher Education*, February 25, 2018. https://www.chronicle.com/article/The-Grief-of-the-Ex-Academic/ 242612

Pérez, Annemarie. "Instead of Gaslighting Adjuncts, We Could Help Them." *Chronicle Vitae,* April 16, 2018. https://chroniclevitae.com/news/2036-instead-of-gaslighting-adjuncts-we-could-help-them

Schuman, Rebecca. "Thesis Hatement." *Slate*, April 5, 2013. http://www.slate.com/articles/life/culturebox/2013/04/there_are_no_academic_jobs_and_getting_a_ph_d_will_make_you_into_a_horrible.html

Beyond the Beginnings of Ends: Quit Lit's Critique of the Academic-Industrial Complex and Its Legacy

Kristen Galvin

WHEN I THINK of quit lit, which is inflected by my own adventures on the academic job market and in contingent positions, I mash up two quotes from fictional and non-fictional moments of the late 1970s as a kind of pop-musical call and response.

The first phrase comes from the epic on-air speech of anchorman Howard Beale (played by the amazing Peter Finch) in the 1976 film *Network*. Naming various injustices of the time, and most centrally the degradation of values in his industry of network television news, he issues a wider call to action. Beale exclaims, *"I'm as mad as hell and I'm not going to take this anymore!"* encouraging home viewers to do the same, and yell out their windows in a collective primal scream. The full speech resonates more with the American quagmire that was 2020, the time of this essay's writing, and the rampant corporatization of higher education that is at the core of quit lit's critique, than I have space to address. Yet, while Beale's on-air meltdown is a moment of resistance and empowerment, it also divulges the character's emotional pain and instability.

The second is from John Lydon, better known as Johnny Rotten, front-man of the punk band, the Sex Pistols. He famously snarled to his audience, "Ever get the feeling you've been cheated?" at the exhausting end of the

Pistols' last show on a disastrous tour of the United States that resulted in Lydon's departure from the band. Compounding the sentiment, his famous words were uttered after he sang a cover of The Stooges' 1969 song, "No Fun."

In each performed moment, the legendary pop-cultural "quitter" stands and feels, as conduit and mirror, for the audience as angsty simpatico. They speak to and for their audience, and against the respective oppressive industrial systems that they struggle within.

While quit lit is often defined by personal narrative and affect, written from the perspectives of PhD candidate all the way "up the chain" to tenured professor, the genre also constitutes a vibrant, virally spreadable, collective critique of the academic-industrial complex. In her 2018 assessment, Katie Rose Guest Pryal succinctly claims, "quit lit, at its heart, was a labor critique."[1] Although not every work qualifies as an explicit labor critique, when laying bare one's soul, or soul searching, such expressions provide implicit commentary on the emotionally damaging impacts of the academic labor system and the prestige economy that it sustains, questioning who or what is really benefiting here.

As students have turned into customers, professors into gig workers, and deans into CEOs, the manifold abuses that quit lit denounces are deeply rooted in the widespread privatization of higher education – an industry whose problems and dubious ethics have only been further illuminated by questionable institutional responses to the COVID-19 pandemic. We can all admit out loud, in primal scream, that higher education is broken, flawed, and dysfunctional. Quit lit recognized academia's injustices and disservices and went "public" with them first on the Internet, before higher education's greater greed became weekly CNN news fodder and the subject of disgruntled student TikTok videos and Reddit posts in 2020.[2] Moreover, in

---

1. Katie Rose Guest Pryal, "Quit lit Is About Labor Conditions," *Women in Higher Education*, June 7, 2018, https://www.wihe.com/article-details/74/quit-lit-is-about-labor-conditions/ [pp. 169-73 in the present volume].

2. To clarify, there are certainly books and journal articles that discuss the problems of the neoliberalization and privatization of higher education. Quit lit is not "the first" to criticize higher education on this basis. My point is that quit lit's viral speed of sharing, dissemination, and response, due to the medium of the Internet, adds layers of personal narrative, connectivity, visibility, interactivity, immediacy, and urgency to its critique. A short list of titles critical of neoliberal higher education includes Martha Nussbaum, *Not for Profit: Why Democracy Needs the Humanities* (Princeton, NJ: Princeton University Press, 2010); Jeffrey R. Di Leo, *Corporate Humanities in Higher Education: Moving Beyond the Neoliberal Academy* (New York: Palgrave Macmillan, 2013); Almantas Samalavičius, ed., *Neoliberalism, Economism and Higher Education* (Newcastle upon Tyne: Cambridge Scholars Publishing, 2018); and Henry A. Giroux, *Neoliberalism's War on Higher Education* (Chicago: Haymarket, 2014).

hindsight, quit lit's legacy has evolved into a countermovement of books, blogs, and businesses determined to help other struggling academics transition out of the limited prospects of college-level teaching. Holding the system accountable for its exploitative practices, whether implicitly or explicitly, quit lit has morphed into a charge to change graduate education.

This essay parses the main issues that precipitated the flood of quit lit after the 2008 financial crisis, and traces how that impetus and advocacy (even if for oneself) can help PhD candidates, or those with a PhD, to better navigate a decision to enter the academic-industrial complex, post-pandemic. The term, "academic-industrial complex," was first popularized in a 2010 *New York Times* article by Graham Bowley. In the wake of higher education's response to the financial crisis, Bowley demonstrates the widespread convergence of corporation and college in the United States – mostly through the trend of top university presidents sitting on (multiple) corporate boards.[3] I use the term here to also name the exploitative labor practices caused by the corporatization of the academy. Its usage coincides with the rise of quit lit, which was in turn a response to the decimated academic job market alongside the casualization of academic labor in the 2010s. Unfortunately, what quit lit widely acknowledges is that a PhD is no longer a "license" to teach, research, and perform service responsibilities at the college level in the form of a tenure-track professorship.

The contentious national debate over issues such as tenure, fair academic labor practices, and doctoral cultural reform are briefly surveyed to etch out the field that quit lit operates in and comments upon. Importantly, the outpouring of quit lit that this anthology highlights is also connected to a new generation of thought leaders. Post-PhD, they all left a traditional academic path to forge new careers. They have gone on to write books and blogs, and to create businesses that not only perpetuate the foundational work of quit lit but constitute essential reading for current or future doctoral students. Not merely a final statement, the legacy of quit lit is as an urgent catalyst to re-energize, reframe, and sustain graduate education before institutions crush it in the name of financial exigency, or just "not letting a good pandemic go to waste."

My focus is on the quit lit of scholar-teachers that come out of the humanities and social sciences, which have been disproportionately impacted by the continued implosion of higher education. To be frank, these disciplines have long been on the chopping block as the "job-oriented" fields of STEM and business and management programs are prioritized in profit-

3. Graham Bowley, "The Academic-Industrial Complex," *New York Times*, July 31, 2010, https://www.nytimes.com/2010/08/01/business/01prez.html

oriented educational models (e.g., STEM's relationship to "Big Pharma").[4] The humanities and social sciences (along with the arts) are the first to be cut or consolidated due to sinking enrollments and thereby institutional priority and investment. Unsurprisingly, it is the humanities, arts, and social sciences that have produced the strongest critical voices within the genre and provide the backbone to its legacy. Humanities scholars are trained not only in writing, critical thinking, and interpretation, but also in the histories of oppression and theoretical frameworks that challenge power structures. This subset of once-excluded scholar-teachers voice the most poignant critiques, and some go on to support initiatives for career diversification.

The Golden (Plated) Tenure-Track Ticket

Whether it concerns the futile pursuit of a tenure-track position or the leaving of one, the status of academic tenure is at the thorny center of quit lit. I do not intend to undermine the vital importance of academic freedom and shared governance, which uphold tenure by advocating for fair academic labor practices. I have taught at a nonunionized, non-tenure-granting institution. Whatever you might presume that professional environment to be like, trust me when I say such toxicity, instability, and disempowerment exceeds your imagination. Instead, this essay calls attention to the timing of what I fear is the enforced extinction of tenure. The two key principles named above are increasingly under threat in the 2020s, while new tenure-track lines have all but evaporated. While there is a body of writing that debates the pros and cons of tenure, there are two truths that I believe both sides can agree on: 1) it has not adapted to or attempted to keep pace with the rapid changes in higher education in the twenty-first century, and 2) in softer terms, it is declining; in harsher, it is dying.

According to the American Association of University Professors' latest report, as of 2018, 22% of college-level faculty were tenured, while 78% were non-tenured in a variety of contractual configurations and titles (e.g., adjunct, visiting, non-tenure-track contracted instructors, graduate assistants, and instructors). To underscore the precarity, part-time instructors constituted 52% of faculty labor, and only 18% were in full-time, non-tenure-track positions. According to a research brief released in January 2020, 37% of tenure-track faculty are over age 55, while 13% are over 65: 50% of tenured faculty are over 55.[5] Half of tenured faculty are in danger of being forced into

4. However, STEM degrees, despite their perceived high-demand job status, are no longer impervious, and their programs are suffering from the same institutional pressures. Individual STEM departments as well as schools are calling for professional development initiatives for supporting career paths outside of the academy and of research more generally.

5. Jasper McChesney and Jacqueline Bichsel, *The Aging of Tenure-Track Faculty in*

early retirements within a decade, while the vast majority of adjunct and contingent instructors composing the actual "professoriate" will continue to desperately cling to increasingly unstable and undesirable jobs in a landscape with fewer and fewer institutions to teach in.

This is treacherous territory. Widening inequalities between classes of faculty, between the haves and have-nots, will only quicken the pace of academic-corporate cultural takeover. Moreover, the generational gap separating "aristocracy" from "precariat" is further exacerbated when other factors such as race and gender are considered, revealing the deep inequities of the tenure-track system when it comes to historically marginalized faculty achieving tenure. Any gains in diversifying faculty have unfortunately been made in non-tenured, contingent positions.[6]

The initial wave of quit lit in the 2010s came at a time when the system cracked under the pressures wrought by the financial crisis of 2008. For many disciplines, the job market was at its worst two to three years after the crash (and then ongoing). This created a movement to diversify career outcomes for PhD-holders, who were increasingly shut out of the tenure-track system — no matter the number of awards they received or the amount of teaching experience they had already gained. *Inside Higher Ed* reporter Colleen Flaherty repeatedly covered quit lit's rise as examples went viral in the age of social media.[7] However, it has also been noted that quit lit is not a new phenomenon in higher education; it has a precedent in another time of crisis, the economic downturn and "stagflation" of the 1970s.[8] The cruel irony of that historical connection in quit-lit production is that the current statistic of approximately three-quarters of faculty languishing in adjunct/contingent positions is the direct inverse of the ratio of tenure- to non-tenure-track faculty in the 1970s, fondly referred to as the "the golden age" of higher

Higher Education: Implications for Succession and Diversity, College and University Professional Association for Human Resources, January 2020, https://www.cupahr.org/wp-content/uploads/CUPA-HR-Brief-Aging-Faculty.pdf

6. Colleen Flaherty, "More Faculty Diversity, Not on Tenure Track," *Inside Higher Ed*, August 22, 2016, https://www.insidehighered.com/news/2016/08/22/study-finds-gains-faculty-diversity-not-tenure-track

7. Colleen Flaherty, "The Rise of 'Quit Lit'," *Slate*, September 11, 2015, https://slate.com/human-interest/2015/09/disgruntled-professors-and-the-rise-of-quit-lit-what-does-it-mean-for-academics.html, originally published as "Public Good-byes," *Inside Higher Ed*, September 9, 2015, https://www.insidehighered.com/news/2015/09/09/essays-academics-fed-higher-ed-mark-resurgence-quit-lit; Flaherty, "Calling Academe's Bluff," *Inside Higher Ed*, February 13, 2018, https://www.insidehighered.com/news/2018/02/13/historians-quit-lit-essay-rejects-notion-leaving-higher-ed-equals-personal-failure

8. Grant Shreve, "'Quit Lit' Then and Now," *Inside Higher Ed*, April 4, 2018, https://www.insidehighered.com/views/2018/04/04/comparison-quit-lit-1970s-and-today-opinion [pp. 163-67 in the present volume].

education.[9]

Historical antecedents and ironies aside, academics on the job market after 2008 could not be reabsorbed into the educational system that had funded and trained them as graduate students. As the dire cycle continued year after year, viable candidates piled up in extreme oversupply. In a buyer's market, job seekers had less and less power and room to negotiate, while teaching loads seemed to push toward a four-four normalization in any school outside of a Research I university, whether a visiting or tenure-track position. The academic "pipeline" was delivered a blow that it has never recuperated from, and unfortunately never will.

But, at this crucial turn in 2008, many PhD programs did not believe, anticipate, or convey such realities concerning job-market resurgence until "too late." Initially, the broad sentiment was to "wait out the storm" for a few years, giving institutions, and thereby the academic job market, time to convalesce. This of course, never happened. To make matters worse, as institutions failed to fully recover from the financial crisis, more questionable policies and practices were instituted as short-term solutions. Increasing numbers of adjunct/contingent faculty and decreasing tenure-track lines coincided with practices such as tuition hikes, building luxury facilities, spending less money per student, bloating administrative support, and raising executive salaries. In short, graduate education, as Leonard Cassuto aptly put it, was "a mess."[10]

Cassuto has been an important voice of solidarity as both a tenure-track faculty member and writer of the monthly column, "The Graduate Adviser," in *The Chronicle of Higher Education*, and now advocates for a more "student-centered, career-diverse, and public-facing" graduate education.[11] Hanging on for dear life, many of these "messy" PhD programs simply cannot afford to make the curricular adjustments, leading to cultural changes, needed to ready their students for the careers that they will actually end up in – meaning, not college-level teaching, the path that they will have apprenticed in for an average of six to seven years, with many earning stipends equating

9. Kristen Galvin and Christina M. Spiker, "The Cost of Precarity: Contingent Academic Labor in the Gig Economy," *Art Journal Open*, May 1, 2019, http://artjournal.collegeart.org/?p=11088

10. Leonard Cassuto, *The Graduate School Mess: What Caused It and How We Can Fix It* (Cambridge, MA: Harvard University Press, 2015).

11. Megan Zahneis, "What's Wrong With Graduate Education – and 2 Scholars' View on How to Fix It," *Chronicle of Higher Education*, January 15, 2021, https://www.chronicle.com/article/whats-wrong-with-graduate-education-and-2-scholars-view-on-how-to-fix-it. Although the writing of this essay predates Cassuto's new book, also see Leonard Cassuto and Robert Weisbuch, *The New PhD: How to Build a Better Graduate Education* (Baltimore: Johns Hopkins University Press, 2021).

to less than the aspirational minimum wage of $15 per hour.[12] What is even more upsetting, and what many PhD students still do not realize, is that the time of their graduate studies is likely the most stable in their academic teaching careers (with consistent pay and teaching appointments, health insurance, cheap gym membership, subsidized living costs, intellectual community, and so forth). While quit-lit production happens at a variety of career stages, many "quits" are called in the time after PhD completion, while working in an unsatisfying and/or temporary teaching position and waiting fruitlessly for an offer on the tenure-track job "market."

Expressions of quit-lit grievance center on tenure and a career path like those of one's dissertation committee – and the majority of their home department – as most PhD programs are at elite institutions with a lower contingent/adjunct to tenure-track/tenured faculty ratio. Therefore, a stable tenure-track teaching position is conceived of as a deserved prize or means to an end. Essentially, the career path that the "quitter" imagined, while grounded in the reality of their graduate faculty, exists for them only as an artifact. This is a kind of historical nostalgia, a yearning and mourning for a future that can only live in an imagined academic past – one not experienced firsthand but vicariously through one's professors. Marie-Alix Thouaille has applied cultural critic Lauren Berlant's theoretical term, "cruel optimism," to describe this predicament: students hold on tightly to a fantastic dream of an unattainable academic future, which simultaneously exploits them and damages their own livelihoods.[13]

This is especially true within graduate humanities programs that rely solely on an apprenticeship-style teaching model and have less of a connection to "industry" than do STEM fields, which often lead to and feed non academic careers in the private sector. While individual institutions vary in their percentages of non-tenured and tenured faculty, in general it is the most elite institutions that can afford to have the highest number of tenured faculty. However, these institutions also offload the most teaching responsibility onto their graduate students, because they *can* offer PhD-granting programs, resulting in another form of cheap, disposable, rotational labor – in the name of pedagogical training and professionalization for a career track that is all but nonexistent. Quit lit affirms that receiving a PhD is not the beginning of a traditional (tenure-track) academic career, but the culmination

12. Colleen Flaherty, "Grad Students' 'Fight for $15'," *Inside Higher Ed*, October 26, 2018, https://www.insidehighered.com/news/2018/10/26/graduate-student-assistants-campuses-across-us-are-pushing-15-hour-what-they-call

13. Marie-Alix Thouaille, "Is Pursuing an Academic Career a Form of 'Cruel Optimism'?" LSE Impact Blog, March 1, 2018, http://blogs.lse.ac.uk/impactofsocialsciences/2018/03/01/is-pursuing-an-academic-career-a-form-of-cruel-optimism/

and end of one.

Further, graduate students and faculty often fail to recognize that not all tenure-track jobs are the same, and in fact, many entail heavy teaching assignments, with few research opportunities or professional development support. If a PhD student miraculously secures a tenure-track job, it is likely very different from the "apprenticeship environment" of the student's teaching and research training. In retrospect, my first full-time teaching position was *nothing like* the pampered teaching experience that I gained during my doctoral education at a top public Research I university. Moreover, the cross-country hustle for temporary work while chasing the unicorn of a coveted tenure-track position is probably a marathon that most current PhD students' mentors never had to endure. Simply put, a path leading to nowhere, and one that is filled with stress, anxiety, and frustration (with many quitters reporting physical and mental health issues), is a path not worth taking. And yes, a handful do succeed each year in securing tenure-track positions, possibly even at top schools. But these are exceptions to the rule, as the vast majority remain in the academic purgatory of contingent/adjunct life if they choose to continue to teach in college.[14]

While I was on the academic job market from 2014 to 2019, it became increasingly rare to see a job call for a two-two tenure-track teaching assignment.[15] Soon, three-three teaching assignments were evaporating. Limited-term visiting professor positions carried three-three or four-four assignments, while "teaching-oriented" postdoctoral positions entailing two or three courses per semester became normalized, and would often last for just one year. To reiterate, most available positions are teaching intensive and contingent, and at institutions that are nothing like the elite schools housing PhD programs. If the golden achievement a tenure-track job is secured, it may be at an institution that is ideologically, culturally, and economically far from the environment in which the lucky recipient was trained. The position may be located far from a city, family, friends, or communities that the newly anointed faculty member identifies with.

As previously noted, cost of living is increasingly problematic for graduate students, as well as contingent/adjunct laborers, due to low wages and/or lack of benefits. As with most fields, academic salaries have stagnated since

14. Herb Childress, *The Adjunct Underclass: How America's Colleges Betrayed Their Faculty, Their Students, and Their Mission* (Chicago: University of Chicago Press, 2019).

15. Trained in the interdisciplinary field of visual cultural studies during the years 2014-2019, I would peruse and apply to relevant positions in film and media studies, art history (contemporary), and American studies, and occasionally performance studies and gender and sexuality studies. These are all disciplines and fields that are historically not in high demand, and generally have fewer and fewer positions available.

the 1980s while the cost of living has generally gone up, especially for housing. In 2019, graduate students in the University of California system went on strike for "cost of living adjustments" because they were spending most of their earnings on rent and could not afford other necessities. Some graduate students at the University of Santa Cruz were fired for their forms of protest, only to be rehired in the wake of COVID-19. According to a 2017 estimate, a quarter of adjuncts receive some type of public assistance.[16] Conversely, only a quarter of students in PhD programs will go on to any form of college-level teaching position, with those securing a tenure-track job hovering around 7% across all disciplines (and some fields lower still).[17] All these statistics predate the 2020 pandemic, widely projected to bring nothing short of utter devastation to higher education. Quit lit not only identifies the problems of the academic-industrial complex, but acts as a harbinger of much needed change if doctoral education is to survive.

Aside from the woes of quit lit, there are other stories of the negative impacts of the unfair and unethical practices of the academic labor system. These include a graduate student collecting fruit on the campus of Stanford University because she could not afford to buy food on her stipend; an adjunct instructor turning to sex work to supplement income; and tragic reports of untimely deaths due to adjuncts lacking health insurance.[18] Such stories surround non-tenured faculty in higher education, and this misery will only be compounded by hiring freezes, mass layoffs, consolidations, and closures in the coming years. Of added concern, instructors may be willing to endure even more risk in the time of COVID-19 to keep their jobs, with some teaching indoors, face to face, with poor ventilation and no health insurance.

These stories and statistics cut across other indicators, such as race, gender, sexuality, class, ability, and age, at a moment when higher education is under a great deal of pressure to rectify issues of inequality, and especially systemic racism. The accounts I refer to above concern the lives and

16. Alistair Gee, "Facing Poverty, Academics Turn to Sex Work and Sleeping in Cars," *The Guardian*, September 28, 2017, https://www.theguardian.com/us-news/2017/sep/28/adjunct-professors-homeless-sex-work-academia-poverty

17. Christopher L. Caterine, *Leaving Academia: A Practical Guide* (Princeton, NJ: Princeton University Press, 2020): 2.

18. See Childress, *Adjunct Underclass*; Gee, "Facing Poverty"; and Charlie Curnin, "'Every Day Was about Survival': Inside the Graduate Student Affordability Crisis," *Stanford Daily*, February 28, 2019, https://www.stanforddaily.com/2019/02/28/every-day-was-about-survival-inside-the-graduate-student-affordability-crisis/; Adam Harris, "Death of an Adjunct," *The Atlantic*, April 8, 2019, https://www.theatlantic.com/education/archive/2019/04/adjunct-professors-higher-education-thea-hunter/586168/

livelihoods of women and women of color. Quit lit is autobiographical, which differs from the newspaper articles and books that highlight the stories of these women. While it is absolutely vital to spread public awareness of these stories to advocate for change, quit lit, as self-reportage and representation, resists any accusation of sensationalism that might be leveled against media coverage of these issues. While at times sentimental in its indulgence of personal narrative, quit lit takes the academic-industrial complex to task and gives *direct* voice to the disenfranchised, non-tenured "faculty majority."

A National Movement and New Generation of Quit Lit 2.0 Thought Leaders

Importantly, quit lit demands systemic change, and with that comes doctoral and academic cultural/attitudinal reform. As a PhD student between the years of 2009 and 2015, I was someone who ducked into doctoral training in a time of crisis (yes, I am in *that* generation of graduate students). During my studies, I observed firsthand how institutional and national conversations shifted from relying on hopes of economic recovery to actively reconceiving notions of humanistic work and career pathways for PhD students. This shift was set against the backdrop of slashed state budgets, skyrocketing tuition, and student protest across the University of California System.[19] Since the time of my degree conferral, actions have been taken on a national scale, while individual programs have been enhanced by new initiatives, with others in development.

While there have been numerous efforts, I will consider some of the most impactful to date. I believe it is fair enough to call doctoral reform a national movement, which gained steam in the latter half of the 2010s. Foremost, in 2016 the National Endowment for the Humanities (NEH) Next Generation Humanities PhD program supported 28 institutions with a total of $1.65 billion to transform graduate education. From this, larger implementation grants were awarded to the University of Delaware, the University of Chicago, and Duke University. William D. Adams, NEH chair at the time, commented on the crucial stakes of doctoral reform: "The academic-focused future we're accustomed to training graduate students for is disappearing.... If graduate programs wish to make a case for the continuation of graduate education in the humanities, they're going to have to think about the professional futures of their students in entirely different

19. David Theo Goldberg, "The University We Are For?" *Huffpost*, November 28, 2011, updated January 28, 2012, https://www.huffpost.com/entry/university-california-protests_b_1106234

ways."[20] Adams recognized that the future of graduate education in the humanities is at risk if structural change is not enacted on a large scale.

In 2011, the American Historical Association (AHA) began its Career Diversity for Historians initiative with the publication of "No More Plan B: A Very Modest Proposal for Graduate Programs in History," co-authored by AHA president Anthony Grafton and executive director Jim Grossman.[21] In three phases and supported by three Andrew W. Mellon Foundation grants, the AHA has worked with a quarter of the nation's history departments to encourage career diversity. Approximately at the same time, and coming out of task force meetings in 2012, the Modern Language Association (MLA), also with support from the Mellon Foundation, developed the web-based career resource center Connected Academics. The MLA also supported career development programs at Arizona State University, Georgetown University, and the University of California Humanities Research Institute. However, many of the larger NEH- and Mellon Foundation-funded projects ended in 2019 and 2020. The important headway that was made as a result of those funding sources will only be challenged by graduate admissions moratoriums, as over 140 humanities and social sciences doctoral program suspensions have been reported for fall 2021, alongside additional budget cuts due to COVID-19.[22]

While some institutions have been internally working to enhance graduate education and provide more means of career support with diverse outcomes, "quitters" have also started entrepreneurial advising and professional development businesses assisting PhDs considering academic and non-academic career paths (and all of the gray areas in between). Karen Kelsky was a tenured professor and department head before leaving her 15-year career in academia to start her own business, The Professor Is In.[23] While services first catered to those pursuing academic jobs, the business has grown to meet market realities and supports more diverse career paths, with

20. National Endowment for the Humanities, "Press Release: NEH Announces $1.7 Million for 'Next Generation PhD'," August 9, 2016, http://www.neh.gov/news/press-release/2016-08-10

21. Anthony Grafton and Jim Grossman, "No More Plan B: A Very Modest Proposal for Graduate Programs in History," *Perspectives on History*, October 11, 2011, https://www.historians.org/publications-and-directories/perspectives-on-history/october-2011/no-more-plan-b-a-very-modest-proposal-for-graduate-programs-in-history

22. Melissa Korn, "Pandemic Leads Dozens of Universities to Pause Ph.D. Admissions," *Wall Street Journal*, updated December 29, 2020, https://www.wsj.com/articles/pandemic-leads-dozens-of-universities-to-pause-ph-d-admissions-11609261200

23. Karen Kelsky, "Death of a Soul (on Campus)," *Tech in Translation*, July 18, 2011, http://techintranslation.com/guest-post-death-of-a-soul-on-campus/ [pp. 23-28 in the present volume].

a subsection of the website declaring "It's OK to Quit."[24] L. Maren Wood stopped her pursuit of an academic job to found Beyond the Professoriate. She is now the organization's acting CEO and employs other ex-academics.[25] Beyond the Professoriate provides a range of services and resources to both institutions and individuals, with paid and free options available. To their credit, both Kelsky and Wood have rapidly adapted their content, services, and fees to accommodate students in the time of COVID-19.

Curiously, 2020 also happened to be the year that multiple books were published on subjects of career diversity and exploration for graduate students. I suggest that they are best understood as a direct outgrowth of quit lit, or "quit lit 2.0." Whether the authors self-identify as contributing to the canon of quit lit or not, I group them here because they discuss their struggles, suggest pathways for moving forward, and write to help others. The authors also successfully pursued alternative-academic (non-faculty university positions or scholarly positions outside of higher education) or non-academic careers (positions in industry or other non-academic sectors). The majority of the authors have doctorates in disciplines of the humanities, with one in education. This coterie of books can inform and empower graduate students to find rewarding career paths outside of collegiate teaching, with pathways of professional exploration tailored to individual interests and talents.

These "2.0" quit-lit legacy titles include Katina L. Rogers's *Putting the Humanities PhD to Work: Thriving in and Beyond the Classroom*; Christopher L. Caterine's *Leaving Academia: A Practical Guide*; Kathryn E. Linder, Kevin Kelly, and Thomas J. Tobin's *Going Alt-Ac: A Guide to Alternative Academic Careers*; and Chris Cornthwaite's *Doctoring: Building a Life after a PhD*. Three of these titles serve primarily as practical guides based on personal experience. Rogers's book is a slight outlier in that she speaks more to issues and constraints concerning humanities PhD programs, and addresses topics such as tenure; fair labor practices; definitions of scholarly merit; and diversity, equity, and inclusion in the academy. Perhaps a less obvious selection to include is Anne Helen Petersen's *Can't Even: How Millennials Became the Burnout Generation*. Petersen's work extends the challenges of the academic market and contingent/adjunct labor over the past ten years to the difficulties of millennials in general. Many quit-lit writers fall within this generation, including Petersen herself, who is also a well-

24. Karen Kelsky, "It's OK to Quit," The Professor Is In, n.d., https://theprofessorisin.com/its-ok-to-quit/

25. L. Maren Wood, "Walking Away From Academia When It Was Your Dream Job," Beyond the Professoriate, n.d., https://beyondprof.com/walking-away-from-academia-when-it-was-your-dream-job/

known academic "quitter."[26]

I view these books as continuing the legacy and labor of quit lit, but in the more substantial medium of a book, as opposed to the transient and more virality-dependent blog post or op-ed piece. It is notable that two titles are published by university presses, Duke's and Princeton's. These books represent the outgrowth and the productive future of quit lit. These academics, collectively publishing in the watershed moment of 2020, use their scholarly impulses and voices for good, to advise a new generation of graduate students (and in the case of Petersen, the broader categories of millennials and even Generation Z). They now implement their PhD training to guide graduate students through what often amounts to a very difficult five-to-ten-year transition out of graduate school life.

Quit Lit's Second Act: Mobilizing and Catalyzing Change

In his response to Erin Bartram's much-discussed piece, "The Sublimated Grief of the Left Behind," Ian Saxine suggests that the quit-lit genre is dangerously misnamed. He states that the genre is not about "quitting," but being "driven out."[27] For Saxine, the solitary agency and hopelessness connoted by the word *quit* may serve to absolve institutions and thereby discourage systemic change to "make things better." It implies that we simply can't effect change, or in the words of Petersen, "can't even."

To adopt Saxine's label, "driven-out" lit laments the misfortune that higher education has taken an ugly turn into a pyramid structure for faculty, and a Ponzi scheme for graduate students – that is, if a PhD is *only* about getting a tenure-track position (a question that is key to the future of graduate studies), an outcome hinged on luck, or being at the right place at the right time, and not on outright merit. For those in the know and on the ground (on the job market for multiple years in the 2010s), there are stories of

26. Anne Helen Petersen, "Leaving Academia For BuzzFeed: Six Months Later," *BuzzFeed News*, December 3, 2014, https://www.buzzfeednews.com/article/annehelenpetersen/leaving-academia-for-buzzfeed; and Jia Tolentino, "Talking to Anne Helen Petersen About Leaving Academia for BuzzFeed," *The Hairpin*, March 21, 2014, https://www.thehairpin.com/2014/03/talking-to-anne-helen-petersen-about-leaving-academia-for-buzzfeed/

27. Ian Saxine, "They're Not Quitting! Reclaiming a Genre," The Professor Is In (blog), March 20, 2018, https://theprofessorisin.com/2018/03/20/theyre-not-quitting-reclaiming-a-genre-a-postac-guest-post/ [pp. 155-57 in the present volume]; see Erin Bartram, "The Sublimated Grief of the Left Behind," *Erin Bartram* (personal blog), February 11, 2018, http://erinbartram.com/uncategorized/the-sublimated-grief-of-the-left-behind/ [pp. 97-101 in the present volume]. Leonard Cassuto uses the comparable term "pushed-out lit" in "The Grief of the Ex-Academic," *Chronicle of Higher Education*, February 25, 2018, https://www.chronicle.com/article/The-Grief-of-the-Ex-Academic/242612 [pp. 149-53 in the present volume].

candidates who published a book with an academic press coming up short after campus visits, while untested candidates with not one peer-reviewed journal article on their CVs (and little significant teaching experience) receive tenure-track offers. Such discrepancies, more often than not, are chalked up to "institutional fit." Those of us who have been lucky enough to receive campus visits on multiple occasions have bitten our tongues and smiled while being interrogated about our research by a committee of tenured professors who have not published any books, and in some cases lack PhDs. This absolutely happens for positions outside of the R1 solar system. And these are rather bland instances when it comes to the offenses, social unpleasantries, pain, sickness, and general extremes that candidates routinely endure on certain campus visits.[28] But the embarrassing riches of the "campus visit war story" make for another book to be written, no doubt in a vein reminiscent of Howard Beale and Johnny Rotten as quoted at the outset.

The academic-industrial system has been intentionally crafted over decades of unchecked greed, which will likely worsen in the wake of COVID-19. The question remains, whether it is *too late* to turn the ship of graduate education around. Perhaps the greatest legacy of quit lit is its timely relevance and resonance in the 2020s: it has already collectively identified systemic problems and provided a space to grieve over the state of higher education and its negative impacts. Quit lit 2.0 now provides a road map for cultural and structural change initiated by those who were "driven out" and went on to carve their own career pathways. They share their stories and insights to help programs, faculty, and students build a more sustainable future for

28. To share a personal campus visit story, a white male tenured faculty member driving me alone in his car to the selection committee dinner had a full-out temper tantrum when I politely refused to agree to order a "nice" bottle of wine for him at dinner. He made it very clear that if I ordered the bottle as the job candidate, it would force the school/committee to purchase a whole bottle, and not just individual glasses. Condescendingly, and assuming I had no wine knowledge, he insisted that he would choose the bottle. Apparently, he was very angry about the restaurant choice (not expensive enough for him) and felt that he was not being properly compensated. He deserved more — meaning a bottle to himself for all of the unpaid work he had already done on the search committee. This was all screamed in my face while I became increasingly anxious about getting into an accident. Soon, it turned into a tirade about how terrible the school and living in its town were. His behavior and conversation was insufferable at dinner (e.g., arguing that the SAT does not reflect systemic racism) as he downed cheap house red wine by the glass while the other committee members turned a blind eye. The uncomfortable strain of pulling it together to maintain a level of composure at the beginning of the meal quickly turned into hasty eating and get-me-out-of-here silence. I asked for someone else to drive me to my hotel after dinner. The sober committee member now driving me, trying to compensate for what just happened, proceeded to make excuses of academic stress and assured me that his colleague "was such a good father." I didn't get the job.

graduate studies. In 2020-2021, these authors are speaking at universities across the United States (albeit virtually), in a time when graduate students are under extreme duress. Recently minted PhDs will be hard pressed to find any kind of viable job opportunity, as multiple sectors struggle to recover economically and higher education remains in freefall with more faculty (both contingent and tenured) laid off.

Students, faculty, administrators, alumni, and allies must quickly begin to work collectively and creatively towards solutions that do not rely on futures and livelihoods based on the myths and greed of the academic-industrial complex. Instead, we must move forward as a coalition to enact positive change that ensures a future where academic work can be applied more broadly and meaningfully for the public good. Quit lit is not an end, but signals a beginning for the much-needed work that remains to be done together.

References

Bartram, Erin. "The Sublimated Grief of the Left Behind." *Erin Bartram* (personal blog), February 11, 2018. http://erinbartram.com/uncategorized/the-sublimated-grief-of-the-left-behind/ [pp. XXX in the present volume].

Bowley, Graham. "The Academic-Industrial Complex." *New York Times*, July 31, 2010. https://www.nytimes.com/2010/08/01/business/01prez.html

Cassuto, Leonard. *The Graduate School Mess: What Caused It and How We Can Fix It*. Cambridge, MA: Harvard University Press, 2015.

———. "The Grief of the Ex-Academic." *Chronicle of Higher Education*, February 25, 2018. https://www.chronicle.com/article/The-Grief-of-the-Ex-Academic/242612 [pp. XXX in the present volume].

Cassuto, Leonard, and Robert Weisbuch. *The New PhD: How to Build a Better Graduate Education*. Baltimore: Johns Hopkins University Press, 2021.

Caterine, Christopher L. *Leaving Academia: A Practical Guide*. Princeton, NJ: Princeton University Press, 2020.

Childress, Herb. *The Adjunct Underclass: How America's Colleges Betrayed Their Faculty, Their Students, and Their Mission*. Chicago: University of Chicago Press, 2019.

Cornthwaite, Chris. *Doctoring: Building a Life after a PhD*. N.p.: 2020.

Curnin, Charlie. "'Every Day Was about Survival': Inside the Graduate Student Affordability Crisis," *Stanford Daily*, February 28, 2019. https://www.stanforddaily.com/2019/02/28/every-day-was-about-survival-inside-the-graduate-student-affordability-crisis/

Di Leo, Jeffrey R. *Corporate Humanities in Higher Education: Moving Beyond the Neoliberal Academy*. New York: Palgrave Macmillan, 2013.

Flaherty, Colleen. "Calling Academe's Bluff." *Inside Higher Ed*, February 13, 2018. https://www.insidehighered.com/news/2018/02/13/historians-quit-lit-essay-rejects-notion-leaving-higher-ed-equals-personal-failure

———. "Grad Students' 'Fight for $15'." *Inside Higher Ed*, October 26, 2018. https://www.insidehighered.com/news/2018/10/26/graduate-student-assistants-campuses-across-us-are-pushing-15-hour-what-they-call

———. "More Faculty Diversity, Not on Tenure Track." *Inside Higher Ed*, August 22, 2016. https://www.insidehighered.com/news/2016/08/22/study-finds-gains-faculty-diversity-not-tenure-track

———. "Public Good-byes." *Inside Higher Ed*, September 9, 2015, https://www.insidehighered.com/news/2015/09/09/essays-academics-fed-higher-ed-mark-resurgence-quit-lit

———. "The Rise of 'Quit Lit'." *Slate* , September 11, 2015. https://slate.com/human-interest/2015/09/disgruntled-professors-and-the-rise-of-quit-lit-what-does-it-mean-for-academics.html

Galvin, Kristen, and Christina M. Spiker. "The Cost of Precarity: Contingent Academic Labor in the Gig Economy." *Art Journal Open*, May 1, 2019. http://artjournal.collegeart.org/?p=11088

Gee, Alistair. "Facing Poverty, Academics Turn to Sex Work and Sleeping in Cars." *The Guardian*, September 28, 2017. https://www.theguardian.com/us-news/2017/sep/28/adjunct-professors-homeless-sex-work-academia-poverty

Giroux, Henry A. *Neoliberalism's War on Higher Education*. Chicago: Haymarket Books, 2014.

Goldberg, David Theo. "The University We Are For?" *Huffpost*, November 28, 2011, updated January 28, 2012. https://www.huffpost.com/entry/university-california-protests_b_1106234

Grafton, Anthony, and Jim Grossman. "No More Plan B: A Very Modest

Proposal for Graduate Programs in History." *Perspectives on History*, October 11, 2011. https://www.historians.org/publications-and-directories/perspectives-on-history/october-2011/no-more-plan-b-a-very-modest-proposal-for-graduate-programs-in-history

Guest Pryal, Katie Rose. "Quit lit Is About Labor Conditions." *Women in Higher Education*, June 7, 2018. https://www.wihe.com/article-details/74/quit-lit-is-about-labor-conditions/

Harris, Adam. "Death of an Adjunct." *The Atlantic*, April 8, 2019. https://www.theatlantic.com/education/archive/2019/04/adjunct-professors-higher-education-thea-hunter/586168/

Kelsky, Karen. "Death of a Soul (on Campus)." *Tech in Translation*, July 18, 2011. http://techintranslation.com/guest-post-death-of-a-soul-on-campus/

———. "It's OK to Quit." The Professor Is In, n.d. https://theprofessorisin.com/its-ok-to-quit/

Korn, Melissa. "Pandemic Leads Dozens of Universities to Pause Ph.D. Admissions." *Wall Street Journal*, updated December 29, 2020. https://www.wsj.com/articles/pandemic-leads-dozens-of-universities-to-pause-ph-d-admissions-11609261200

Linder, Kathryn E., Kevin Kelly, and Thomas J. Tobin. *Going Alt-Ac: A Guide to Alternative Academic Careers*. Sterling, VA: Stylus, 2020.

McChesney, Jasper, and Jacqueline Bichsel. *The Aging of Tenure-Track Faculty in Higher Education: Implications for Succession and Diversity*. College and University Professional Association for Human Resources, January 2020. https://www.cupahr.org/wp-content/uploads/CUPA-HR-Brief-Aging-Faculty.pdf

Nussbaum, Martha. *Not for Profit: Why Democracy Needs the Humanities*. Princeton, NJ: Princeton University Press, 2010.

Petersen, Anne Helen. *Can't Even: How Millennials Became the Burnout Generation*. Boston: Houghton Mifflin, 2020.

———. "Leaving Academia For BuzzFeed: Six Months Later." *BuzzFeed News*, December 3, 2014. https://www. buzzfeednews.com/article/annehelenpetersen/leaving-academia-for-buzzfeed

Rogers, Katina L. *Putting the Humanities PhD to Work: Thriving in and Beyond the Classroom*. Durham, NC: Duke University Press, 2020.

Samalavičius, Almantas, ed. *Neoliberalism, Economism and Higher Education*. Newcastle upon Tyne: Cambridge Scholars Publishing, 2018.

Saxine, Ian. "They're Not Quitting! Reclaiming a Genre." The Professor Is In (blog), March 20, 2018. https://theprofessorisin.com/2018/03/20/theyre-not-quitting-reclaiming-a-genre-a-postac-guest-post/

Shreve, Grant. "'Quit Lit' Then and Now." *Inside Higher Ed*, April 4, 2018. https://www.insidehighered.com/views/2018/04/04/comparison-quit-lit-1970s-and-today-opinion

Thouaille, Marie-Alix. "Is Pursuing an Academic Career a Form of 'Cruel Optimism'?" LSE Impact Blog, March 1, 2018. http://blogs.lse.ac.uk/impactofsocialsciences/2018/03/01/is-pursuing-an-academic-career-a-form-of-cruel-optimism/

Tolentino, Jia. "Talking to Anne Helen Petersen About Leaving Academia for BuzzFeed." *The Hairpin*, March 21, 2014, https://www.thehairpin.com/2014/03/talking-to-anne-helen-petersen-about-leaving-academia-for-buzzfeed/

Wood, L. Maren. "Walking Away From Academia When It Was Your Dream Job." Beyond the Professoriate, n.d. https://beyondprof.com/walking-away-from-academia-when-it-was-your-dream-job/

Zahneis, Megan. "What's Wrong With Graduate Education — and 2 Scholars' View on How to Fix It." *Chronicle of Higher Education*, January 15, 2021. https://www.chronicle.com/article/whats-wrong-with-graduate-education-and-2-scholars-view-on-how-to-fix-it.

It's Systemic: Leaving Academia and the Politics of Withdrawal

Pepita Hesselberth

Originally published in expanded form as Chapter 10, "On Leaving Academia and the Need to Take Refuge," in *Politics of Withdrawal: Media, Arts, Theory*, ed. Pepita Hesselberth and Joost de Bloois (Lanham, MD: Rowman and Littlefield, 2020), pp. 147-60.

Why People Leave

In the early 2010s a surge of articles began appearing in Anglophone (online) magazines and newspapers such as *Inside Higher Ed*, *The Chronicle of Higher Education*, *Times Higher Education*, even *The Guardian*, *Vox*, *Slate Magazine*, and *Nature*, as well as on numerous personal blogs, on the topic of "leaving academia." In unison, or so it seemed, (soon-to-be) former academics – from PhDs and postdocs to adjuncts and tenure-tracked professors – began to report on why they felt compelled to leave a profession to which, in general, they nonetheless felt committed. Indeed, by the mid-2010s, the raucous subgenre had become so commonplace in the US that Rebecca Schuman, an academic turned freelance writer, dubbed it "quit lit,"[1] a term that – although still trending – is as problematic as it is catchy. The precipitous collapse of the academic job market, and the changing landscape of higher education in response to neoliberal reforms, have continued to sustain this outpouring of reflections about leaving academia. And I am one of the genre's riveted

1. Rebecca Schuman, "'I Quit Academia,' An Important, Growing Subgenre of American Essays," *Slate*, October 24, 2013, https://slate.com/culture/2013/10/quitting-academic-jobs-professor-zachary-ernst-and-other-leaving-tenure-and-tenure-track-jobs-why.html [pp. 137-40 in the present volume].

readers.

The reasons reported for leaving are manifold and often vary, but certain themes suffuse these essays. First, there are the working conditions: the precarity, the humiliating succession of temporary contracts, the low pay, the lack of career-development support, the insane working hours, the continual demand for relocation, the overall dearth of future prospects in the field. Second, there is the changing landscape of higher education itself: its ever increasing bureaucracy, its audit-culture, the erosion of resources devoted to scholarship, its management by metrics, its orientation towards research grants, and the general privileging of economic over academic values, along with the consumerism and grade inflation that now seem to lie at the heart of the academic enterprise. Third, there are the incentives within the university system itself that are seen to challenge the declared principles of equality, autonomy, and self-determination for its participants, as well as the norms of appropriate assessment and behavior. Here I would count the failures to properly address (sexual) harassment and to guarantee academic freedom in the face of financialized targets and the assertion of corporate interests. Fourth, and finally, the issues of mental health and general well-being are repeatedly brought up: the liminal experience,[2] the absence of a healthful work-life balance, and the constant stress and anxiety relating to everything I've outlined above; the pressure to publish, the competitive atmosphere, the often acutely felt imposter syndrome, the fear of failure, and (especially, though not solely, upon leaving) the loss of identity and of peers, both individual colleagues as well as the sense of belonging to a group.

To be sure, there are also individuals for whom leaving is not so much about diverging from a once-chosen path or opting-out but rather about opting-in to something new, something (more) exciting, something to look forward to: a new job, a change of environment, a different lifestyle. Even as many feel pushed away from academia, others feel pulled towards some other, presumably better livelihood. As Anne Trubek remarks, contemplating giving up her tenured position in order to expand her career as a freelance writer: "It is a job, being a tenured professor. Just a job."[3] So indeed: "Why not leave?" At times one can, as Trubek observes, detect a sense of self-importance in academics, and "a certain exceptionalism and a tinge of arro-

2. See Herminia Ibarra and Otilia Obodaru, "Betwixt and between Identities: Liminal Experience in Contemporary Careers," *Research in Organizational Behavior* 36 (2016): 47-64.

3. Anne Trubek, "Giving Up Tenure? Who Does That?" *Chronicle of Higher Education*, April 8, 2013, https://www.chronicle.com/article/Giving-Up-Tenure-Who-Does/138345

gance" in some of the essays of those who have left. Some of these frustrated academics depart in silence (in fact, most of the leaving still occurs quietly), others leave with a bang. And then there are those who leave one privileged position for another and still feel compelled to make a huge statement about it at the expense of those who are left behind: students, colleagues, peers.[4] Not everyone has that kind of privilege. That, at least in part, is precisely the point. Overwhelmingly, though, for those who leave and end up writing about it, their departures are neither instigated nor followed by openings and opportunities. Rather, they are a form of retreat or withdrawal.

Combining incisive criticism with a strong reliance on personal narratives, today's essays on leaving academia, Grant Shreve observes, contrary to those of the 1970s, often "marshal intense feelings – of rage and grief and everything in between."[5] Indeed, they often are a testimony to the "author's desire to publicly validate their private feelings at being shut out of a profession they have spent a significant portion of adulthood pursuing." The centrality of such needs explains why, as Shreve and others have pointed out, the term "quit lit" is so misleading. "I do not know one person with a PhD who is a quitter," writes Ellen Kirkpatrick in a recent post in *Times Higher Education*. She therefore proposes to call the genre "exit lit": "People are leaving academia not because they are quitters but because the system is broken."[6] Indeed, the real problem, the ongoing outpouring of articles seems to suggest, is systemic. And it is precisely because the affective has become intertwined with the institutional, I contend, that the essays take on the shape of testimonials.

Speaking Out

"This is my story," writes Sarah Ahmed, announcing her public resignation from Goldsmith College, UCL, in protest against "sexual harassment as institutional culture."

4. E.g., Michael Edwards, "I Quit! Why I Am Leaving UK Academia," *Times Higher Education*, July 25, 2017, https://www.timeshighereducation.com/cn/blog/uk-academia-has-gone-hell-handcart-and-i-quit; Oliver Lee [Bateman], "I Have One of the Best Jobs in Academia. Here's Why I'm Walking Away," *Vox*, September 8, 2015, https://www.vox.com/2015/9/8/9261531/professor-quitting-job [pp. 77-86 in the present volume].

5. Grant Shreve, "'Quit Lit' Then and Now," *Inside Higher Ed*, April 4, 2018, https://www.insidehighered.com/views/2018/04/04/comparison-quit-lit-1970s-and-today-opinion [pp. 163-67 in the present volume].

6. Ellen Kirkpatrick, "The Academy I Dreamed of for 20 Years No Longer Exists, and I Am Waking Up," *Times Higher Education*, May 23, 2019, https://www.timeshighereducation.com/features/academy-i-dreamed-20-years-no-longer-exists-and-i-am-waking

It is personal.
The personal is institutional.[7]

Tapping into what Heidi Hartmann has referred to as the "great thrust of radical feminist writing"[8] – i.e., the thinking coalescing around the 1960s' consciousness-raising slogan "the personal is political" as well as its rephrasing as "the institutional is political" by Gillies and Lucey in the mid-2000s to call attention to the "everyday processes of negotiating institutional power relations" that generally remain invisible[9] – Ahmed's resignation draws on a long tradition of feminist activist writing in which the personal is leveraged as a catalyst for social change.[10] "To resign," Ahmed writes, "is a tipping point, a gesture that becomes necessary because of what the previous actions did not accomplish.... *Resigning was speaking out.* It was saying: this is serious enough that I have had enough." For Ahmed, then, "resignation is a feminist issue." And in this she is not alone. For Liz Morrish, the emergent audit-culture was what triggered the "feminist snap – the moment at which your faith in academia finally yields to terminal antipathy."[11] Like Ahmed and some of the other prominent voices within the leaving-academia debate, Morrish continues her activist work outside of academia, writing (and

7. Sarah Ahmed, "Resignation Is a Feminist Issue," *Feministkilljoys* (blog), August 27, 2016, https://feministkilljoys.com/2016/08/27/resignation-is-a-feminist-issue/ [emphasis in original].

8. Heidi Hartmann, "The Unhappy Marriage of Marxism and Feminism: Towards a More Progressive Union," in *Feminist Theory Reader: Local and Global Perspectives*, ed. Carole McCann and Seung-kyung Kim, 3d ed. (London: Routledge, 2013), 191.

9. Val Gillies and Helen Lucey, eds., *Power, Knowledge and the Academy: The Institutional Is Political* (Basingstoke, UK: Palgrave Macmillan, 2007), 2. On "the personal is political," see Carol Hanisch, "The Personal Is Political: The Women's Liberation Movement Classic with a New Explanatory Introduction," in *Carol Hanisch: Women of the World, Unite!* (2009 [1969]), http://www.carolhanisch.org/CHwritings/PIP.html

10. See, for example, Sara Ahmed, *The Cultural Politics of Emotion* (New York: Routledge, 2004); Donna Haraway, "Situated Knowledges: The Science Question in Feminism and the Privilege of Partial Perspective," *Feminist Studies* 14 (1988): 575-99; Nancy K. Miller, *Getting Personal: Feminist Occasions and Other Autobiographical Acts* (New York: Routledge, 1991); Diane P. Freedman, Olivia Frey, and Frances Murphy Zauhar, eds., *The Intimate Critique: Autobiographical Literary Criticism* (Durham, NC: Duke University Press, 1993); Jane Gallop, *Anecdotal Theory* (Durham, NC: Duke University Press, 2002); Marianne Hirsch and Valerie Smith, "Feminism and Cultural Memory: An Introduction," *Signs* 28 (2002): 1-19; Hirsch, *Family Frames: Photography, Narrative and Postmemory* (Cambridge, MA: Harvard University Press, 2007).

11. Liz Morrish, "Why the Audit Culture Made Me Quit," *Times Higher Education*, March 2, 2017, https://www.timeshighereducation.com/features/why-audit-culture-made-me-quit [pp. 87-96 in the present volume].

earning her living writing) on, among other topics, the state of higher education today.[12] Indeed, one cannot help but note that, unlike in the scholarly discourse on exiting – where, Sarah Sharma has rightly pointed out, contemplations regarding exiting or exodus as a form of "engaged withdrawal (or founding leave-taking)" are dominated by men[13] – most of these essays about *actually leaving* academia (with the odd exception – yes, there are a few) have been written by women.

In what is perhaps one of the most often read, quoted, and indeed echoed contributions within the leaving-academia debate, eloquently entitled "The Sublimated Grief of the Left Behind," Erin Bartram strikes a somewhat different chord.[14] Adhering to the same tradition of feminist activist writing discussed above, the essay opens with Bartram's final job rejection. Contemplating the "abundance of quit-lit out there," she observes that "[t]he genre is almost universally written by those leaving, not those left behind, a reflection of the way we insulate ourselves from grappling with what it means for dozens, hundreds, thousands of our colleagues to leave the field."

Situating herself as someone who, despite her imminent departure, is still an insider in the world of higher education, Bartram invokes here the grief of the leaving and the left behind – a rhetorical choice that clearly plucked the heartstrings of many readers, judging by the massive outpouring of responses, of the leaving and the left behind alike, after the essay's publication.[15] Bartram's essay is conspicuous in its acknowledgment of the "disavowed work of mourning" that comes with exiting. With Bartram, then, the "leaving academia" debate quickly went from "it's ok to quit" (no, you are not a failure) to "it's ok to grieve" (and if you are not grieving, perhaps you should be). Yet the essay also warrants some caution, powerful though it may be. Critics have pointed out that its undergirding grief, nostalgia, or melancholy

12. See, for example, Morrish, "Pressure Vessels: The Epidemic of Poor Mental Health among Higher Education Staff," *Academic Irregularities* (blog), May 23, 2019, https://academicirregularities.wordpress.com/2019/05/23/pressure-vessels-the- epidemic-of-poor-mental-health-among-higher-education-staff/

13. Sarah Sharma, "Exit and the Extensions of Man," *Transmediale: Art and Digital Culture*, April, 2017, https://transmediale.de/content/exit-and-the-extensions-of-man; the quoted phrase is from Paolo Virno, "Virtuosity and Revolution: The Political Theory of Exodus," trans. Ed Emery, in *Generation Online*, n.d., http://www.generation-online.org/c/fcmultitude2.html

14. Erin Bartram, "The Sublimated Grief of the Left Behind," *Erin Bartram* (personal blog), February 11, 2018, https://erinbartram.com/uncategorized/the-sublimated-grief-of-the-left-behind [pp. 97-101 in the present volume].

15. See Sarah Brown, "She Wrote a Farewell Letter to Colleagues. Then 80,000 People Read It," *Chronicle of Higher Education*, February 15, 2018, https://www.chronicle.com/article/She-Wrote-a-Farewell-Letter-to/242564

reveals Bartram's inability to detach herself from the object of loss in the present, i.e., the myth of the academic good life (once a potential, now lost). "No wonder [the essay] was so appealing to so many," writes Katie Pryal, author of *The Freelance Academic*: "even while forced out, Bartram still looks upon the field with love."[16] "This," Wendy Brown suggests in "Resisting Left Melancholy," "is what renders melancholia a persistent condition, a state, indeed, a structure of desire, rather than a transient response to death or loss."[17] As such, Bartram's calling upon the grief of the left behind, Shreve points out, possesses as great a potential to reinforce as to dismantle the (academic) status quo.[18]

Yet it would be a mistake to accuse Bartram, as Pryal does, of failing to provide a genuine critique of academic labor. Quite the contrary. In Bartram, I argue, labor precarity, perhaps for the first time, takes on the form we fear the most: the exhaustion and annihilation of our productive labor powers, and the (feared) reality of no future, no identity, and — above all — no wage. Resignation here still features not as a last instrument of empowerment but rather as the ultimate sign, and materialization, of disempowerment: her surrender. "Buy me a cup of tea," reads the essay's final, uncomfortable words.

Hidden Injuries

If the "leaving academia" debate strikes deep chords of recognition, I suspect it does so because it speaks to affective embodied experiences that impinge on the leaving and the left behind alike: all those feelings of exhaustion, precarity, stress, anxiety, overload, anger, shame, competitiveness, grief, guilt, and so on — experiences which the sociologist and feminist cultural theorist Rosalind Gill calls the "hidden injuries of neoliberal academia."[19] What Gill's ruminations suggest is that the "leaving academia" debate reflects more than an upwelling of the wretched or courageous few, i.e., the departing — rather,

16. Katie Rose Guest Pryal, "Quit Lit Is About Labor Conditions," *Women in Higher Education*, June 7, 2018, https://www.wihe.com/article-details/74/quit-lit-is-about-labor-conditions/ [pp. 169-73 in the present volume].

17. Wendy Brown, "Resisting Left Melancholy," *Boundary 2* 26 (1999): 2.

18. Shreve, "'Quit Lit' Then and Now." Indeed, as Shreve points out, the essay has already been repurposed along these lines. See, for example, Leonard Cassuto, "The Grief of the Ex-Academic," *Chronicle of Higher Education*, February 25, 2018, https://www.chronicle.com/article/The-Grief-of-the-Ex-Academic/242612 [pp. 149-53 in the present volume].

19. Rosalind Gill, "Breaking the Silence: The Hidden Injuries of Neoliberal Academia," in *Secrecy and Silence in the Research Process: Feminist Reflections*, ed. Roisin Ryan-Flood and Rosalind Gill (London and New York: Routledge, 2010), 228-44.

it points to a permanent state or condition. While, for those working in academia, such experiences are "at once ordinary and everyday," Gill observes, "at the same time [they] remain largely secret and silenced in the public spaces of the academy," where they lack "'proper channels' of communication." Indeed, Gill writes, "[f]or all the interest in reflexivity in recent decades, the *experiences of academics* have somehow largely escaped critical attention." Instead,

> [t]hey are spoken in a different, less privileged register; they are the stuff of the chat in the corridor, coffee-break conversations and intimate exchanges between friends, but not, it would seem, the keynote speech or the journal publication, or even the departmental meeting.

The "leaving academia" debate is so compelling precisely because it unveils some of these "hidden injuries" and "gives voice" to affective embodied experiences that hitherto were hearable only as "a 'moan', as an expression of complaint or unhappiness, rather than being formulated as an analysis or a (political) demand for change."[20]

What Gill's reflections on the "hidden injuries" of working in academia further make clear is that the very predicament that makes people leave academia and then write about it is practically indistinguishable from what enables them to work and *survive* working in Higher Education during times of radical uncertainty in the first place – in a nutshell, our passionate attachment to the work on the one hand, and, on the other and often simultaneously, our attuned withdrawal from it through various forms of resignation (fatigued, triumphant, defeated, infuriated, subdued, and so on). Such, writes Lauren Berlant, is the "cruel optimism" of the (academic) good-life fantasy: it is what enables us to endure all the uncertainty and (self-) exhaustion, and what binds us ever more tightly into the neoliberal regime.[21] Significantly, the myth of the academic good life is not monolithic but

20. Gill, "Breaking the Silence," 229-31. Since the time of her writing, things have slowly started to shift, not least due to Gill's own critical interventions. See, for example, "Academics, Cultural Workers and Critical Labour Studies," *Journal of Cultural Economy* 7 (2014): 12-30; and (with Ngaire Donaghue) "Resilience, Apps and Reluctant Individualism: Technologies of Self in the Neoliberal Academy," *Women's Studies International Forum* 54 (2016): 91. Other notable examples include, to name but a few, Maggie Berg and Barbara K. Seeber, *The Slow Professor: Challenging the Culture of Speed in the Academy* (Toronto: University of Toronto Press, 2016), and Marjan De Coster and Patrizia Zononi, "Governing Through Accountability: Gendered Moral Selves and the (Im)possibilities of Resistance in the Neoliberal University," *Gender, Work and Organization* 26 (2019): 411-29.

21. Lauren Berlant, *Cruel Optimism* (Durham, NC: Duke University Press, 2011).

manifold: it entails a patchwork of different, at times competing flights of the imagination, varying from dreams of fame and respect (or just the security provided by tenure), to the aspiration to engage in intellectual exchange or escape from the straightjacket of 9-to-5 waged labor. The sanity of most academics, indeed, seems to rely on their faith that their "moment" is (still) to come.

Well acquainted as I am with the various forms of enervation and uncertainty that come with working in academia, and no stranger to the need to take refuge, what has always struck me most powerfully about the "leaving academia" debate is its call to action. This rallying cry at once invigorates me (indeed, to the extreme) even as it ultimately tends more to exhaust me than to give me strength. For if invigoration leads to the realization that the only logical conclusion to mounting concerns over precarity (in academia) is to resign, or else become complacent toward a system that is broken, then, it seems to me, we are trapped in a political double-bind. I have often wondered, therefore, what a less precarious take on the need to take refuge, or withdrawal, in academia might entail, other than, say, "speaking out" by quitting – which for many of us (academics) still boils down to depriving oneself of one's source of (joy and) livelihood. Moreover, I wonder if a "politics of withdrawal" is (still) even possible *within* an academic context (and if so, to what extent),[22] if *writing* about withdrawal, politically, is so clearly at odds with *acting out* the gesture of withdrawing itself, here understood as opting-out of the neoliberal university's "pressure vessel,"[23] where the only way to "elude control" and evade some the aforementioned pressures and uncertainties may be, to speak with Deleuze, the creation of little "gaps of silence" and "vacuoles of non-communication."[24]

To the point: my intention here is not to downplay or trivialize the importance of "speaking out" or "breaking the silence" but rather to call attention to the differences *and* congruity among various gestures of withdrawal, as well as between, on the one hand, our attachment to academic work and, on the other, our need to withdraw from it, so as to underscore the political weight of the latter.

22. On what the "politics of withdrawal" might entail, see Pepita Hesselberth and Joost de Bloois, "Introduction: Towards a Politics of Withdrawal?" in *Politics of Withdrawal: Media, Arts, Theory*, ed. Hesselberth and de Bloois, 1-12 (Lanham, MD: Rowman and Littlefield, 2020).

23. Morrish, "Pressure Vessels."

24. Gilles Deleuze, "Control and Becoming: A Conversation between Toni Negri and Gilles Deleuze," trans. Martin Joughin, *The Funambulist Magazine*, February 22, 2011 [1990], https://thefunambulist.net/law/philosophy-control-and-becoming-a-conversation-between-toni-negri-and-gilles-deleuze

Cruel Optimism and the Politics of Withdrawal

As Berlant writes in *Cruel Optimism*, "all attachments are optimistic," if we understand optimism to be a structure of relationality or bonding that is invested "in one's own or the world's continuity."[25] Optimistic relations are "not inherently cruel," Berlant insists, but rather "become cruel only when the object that draws your attachment actively impedes the aim that brought you to it initially"[26] – as with, in our case, the promises of upward mobility, of autonomy and personal growth, of societal relevance, and so on. For Berlant, more important than the *experience* of such optimistic attachment (whatever its content) is its *affective* structure: the continuity of the form is what "provides something of the continuity of the subject's sense of what it means to keep on living on and to look forward to being in the world."[27] The condition of cruel optimism, then, differs from melancholia in that it is not "backward looking" but is rather invested in the historical present, is bound to the here and now.[28]

Both the "leaving academia" debate's call to action and Gill's demand that we "break the silence," I argue, are driven by optimistic attachments. But – and this is important – so are complaints and moans about the "hidden injuries" of working in neoliberal academia. These gestures converge in that they can all be seen as forms and modes of surviving the affective labor of cruel optimism in our present moment, which – Berlant insists – is a time of ongoing crisis (a crisis of the ordinary). Although the cruelty of these attachments usually remains unstated, Berlant observes, it is experienced when we are faced with "a sudden incapacity to manage startling situations" – as occurs when driven out of the university or during *any* situation producing the aforementioned "hidden injuries" or "reasons for leaving" cited above. What we fear, then, is that "the loss of the scene of optimism" (here: the academic good-life fantasy) "itself will defeat the capacity to have any hope about anything," at which point the fantasy starts disciplining us to keep on investing, as Gill asserts, "with ever growing costs, not least to ourselves."[29]

As an affective structure, Berlant points out, cruel optimism "involves a sustaining inclination to return to the scene of fantasy."[30] Significantly, the scene of fantasy to which the "leaving academia" debate's call to action and

25. Berlant, *Cruel Optimism*, 23, 13.

26. Berlant, *Cruel Optimism*, 1.

27. Berlant, *Cruel Optimism*, 24.

28. Brown, "Resisting Left Melancholy," 22.

29. Berlant, *Cruel Optimism*, 24.

30. Berlant, *Cruel Optimism*, 2.

Gill's plea to "break the silence" time and again returns, I contend, is twofold: it entails both the academic good-life fantasy and the fantasy of a particular model of political action, one that is rooted in dialectics. It is the latter that holds my attention here. For, as Darin Barney points out in a somewhat different context, it is in upholding dialectics as a model of political action that the "leaving academia" debate's call to action and Gill's plea to "break the silence" risk to "reproduce a set of normative expectations about politics – i.e., that it consists of willed, intentional public actions" that *must* be outspoken to be recognized as such. This necessity, in my view, raises the question, precisely, of what transpires in silence and in what is silenced: in "the rolling everyday" of academia, the chats in the corridor, the intimate exchanges; the moan, the complaint, the unhappiness; the quiet departure and silent surrender; the retreat to recompose – that is, in all those (little) gestures of withdrawal understood as "resignation, directed nowhere" that arguably *precede* resignation as "event"– for some, *ad infinitum*.[31]

The Impasse

If I make a point of being explicit here I do so because of the sense of envy and at times (unspoken) guilt one can detect in the "leaving academia" debate, where the online comment sections, Ian Saxine observes, tend to be remarkably thoughtful and un-horrifying (even if gloomy).[32] Indeed, Anne Trubek remarks, the news of people leaving their tenured jobs is commonly "received with congratulations and, often, envy," both in real life and in the online echo chambers.[33] Guilt, another one of Gill's "hidden injuries," also figures – not just the kind that is often said to "guilt-trip" especially young academics into staying (i.e., the kind of guilt Lobo calls "academic guilt": the sense of failure to get work done and/or appreciate the opportunities one is given),[34] but more specifically the kind of guilt that Sally Racket, using

31. Darin Barney, "Withdrawal Symptoms: Refusal, Sabotage, Suspension," in *Politics of Withdrawal: Media, Arts, Theory*, ed. Pepita Hesselberth and Joost de Bloois (Lanham, MA: Rowman and Littlefield, 2020), 122.

32. Ian Saxine, "They're Not Quitting! Reclaiming a Genre," The Professor Is In (blog), March 20, 2018, https://theprofessorisin.com/2018/03/20/theyre-not-quitting-reclaiming-a-genre-a-postac-guest-post/ [pp. 155-57 in the present volume].

33. Trubek, "Giving Up Tenure?"

34. Guiseppina Iacono Lobo, "Academic Guilt," in *How to Build a Life in the Humanities: Meditations on the Academic Work-Life Balance*, ed. Greg Colón Semanza and Garrett A. Sullivan Jr. (New York: Palgrave Macmillan, 2015), 83-90. On being guilt-tripped into staying, see, for example, Elizabeth Keenan, "Leaving Academia? It's Time to Have 'The Talk'," *Chronicle Vitae*, April 9, 2014, https://chroniclevitae.com/news/434-leaving-academia-it-s-time-to-have-the-talk; Mike Dwyer, "The Hidden Guilt of Leaving Academia,"

another war metaphor, calls "survivor's guilt": the sort of guilt that comes from *not leaving* and obtaining that tenured job that others didn't get, as well as from the fear (and reality) of being or becoming complacent toward a system from which one nonetheless feels progressively alienated and within which one is in fact struggling to survive.[35]

From the point of view of cruel optimism, no matter what the gesture of withdrawal — to leave, to write, to speak out, to resign, to remain in silence, to complain or to moan, to feel disheartened or depressed, to retreat or seek refuge: it always signals fissures in the world that once was, a world organized and disrupted by the neoliberal capitalist regime, as prior phantasmatic structures continue to exhaust and restructure our sensorium, with no genuine alternative to speak of. Cruel optimism's activity, its work so to speak, Berlant indeed reminds us, is one of (self- or world-) maintenance, not of making; its temporal structure that of the impasse, the cul-de-sac. "In a cul-de-sac," she writes, "one keeps moving, but one moves paradoxically, in the *same space*."[36] Berlant is worth quoting at some length here:

> Whatever else it is, and however one enters it, the historical present — as an impasse ... — is a middle without boundaries, edges, a shape.... It is the name for the space where the urgencies of livelihood are worked out all over again, without assurances of futurity, but nevertheless proceeding via durable norms of adaptation. People are destroyed in it, or discouraged but maintaining, or happily managing things, or playful and enthralled.[37]

Framing academia's hidden injuries and the overall leaving-academia debate in terms of Berlant's reflections on cruel optimism is illuminating, then, because to do so helps shed light on why we remain attached to something that is not working, as well as on our need to protect such optimism in the

Ordinary Times (blog), May 14, 2015, https://ordinary-times.com/2015/05/14/the-hidden-guilt-of-leaving-academia/; Gayatri Phadke, "Guilty as Charged: On Leaving Academia," *Medium*, June 20, 2017, https://medium.com/@gayatriphadke/guilty-as-charged-on-leaving-academia-d85c3294f652; Alison Green, "'My Boss Keeps Guilt-Tripping Me for Leaving My Job!'" *The Cut*, October 15, 2019, https://www.thecut.com/article/my-boss-is-mad-that-im-quitting.html; r/LadiesofScience, "Guilty for Wanting to Leave Academia," Reddit, October 29, 2013, https://www.reddit.com/r/LadiesofScience/comments/1pgc01/guilty_for_wanting_to_leave_academia/

35. Sally Racket,"Survivor's Guilt," *Chronicle of Higher Education*, March 15, 2011, https://www.chronicle.com/article/Survivors-Guilt/126710

36. Berlant, *Cruel Optimism*, 199.

37. Berlant, *Cruel Optimism*, 200.

face of being defeated.

What the "leaving academia" debate and Gill's "hidden injuries" also make clear, however, is that the myth of the academic good life, itself, entails a fantasy of retreat: it *is*, in many ways, a gesture of withdrawal. Take, for example, Ahmed's "resignation": well before it becomes "a giving of notice," it involves first and foremost a vision (an idea and an ideal) of "the university" as a counter-normative, utopic, feminist, indeed a queer space – a place of safety into which one can withdraw to investigate, contemplate, resist, and challenge the normative identity politics and overall logics of neoliberal capitalism and its dominant modes of governance. Only when this fantasy of the university as a place of withdrawal starts to break down does Ahmed decide to retreat, once again, by giving notice, so as to continue her work outside of academia.

It is perhaps no coincidence, then, that the leaving-academia debate for the most part seems to unfold on personal blogs, an intermediate form *par excellence*, situated between an "intimate" and a public discourse. The *academic* blog is preeminently an "intimate" public space. As such, it is as much a response to the problem (i.e., the evaporation of the boundary between public and private, work and leisure) as it is one of its symptoms. Consisting of "discrete, often informal diary-style text entries"[38] written "for fun," the genre *at once* figures as a stage for the continuous self-promotion of the academic, which is necessitated by the conditions of labor precarity, *and* yet at the same time makes it possible for (former) academics to criticize the intimate intertwining of the personal and the institutional. The latter "preaching to the choir," Berlant insists in a somewhat different context, should not be undervalued, for as "as a world-confirming strategy of address that performs solidarity and asserts righteousness, it is absolutely necessary to do."[39] But, and this is important, the same holds true for the complaint and the moan, and all the other gestures of ordinary withdrawal instilled by the hidden injuries Gill speaks of. Together, these gestures signal a collective disidentification with the state of higher education today, a search for a new "scene for being together in the political" beyond normative politics, in a community bound (as it formerly had been) through critique. To complain (or moan, or just to be unhappy), in this context, is a way of "bargaining with what is there," a performative plea that "implicitly holds no hope for change in the conditions ... apart from whatever response the complaint itself might elicit."[40] In times of radical uncertainty, which is how Berlant describes our

38. Wikipedia, s.v. "Blog," last modified April 9, 2021, https://en.wikipedia. org/wiki/Blog

39. Berlant, *Cruel Optimism*, 238.

40. Berlant, *The Female Complaint: The Unfinished Business of Sentimentality in*

present times, the personal is a collective rather than an individual experience. "The personal is the general," she writes in *The Female Complaint*: "publics presume intimacy."[41]

References

Ahmed, Sara. *The Cultural Politics of Emotion*. New York: Routledge, 2004.

———. "Resignation Is a Feminist Issue." *Feministkilljoys* (blog), August 27, 2016. https://feministkilljoys.com/2016/08/27/resignation-is-a-feminist-issue/.

Barney, Darin. "Withdrawal Symptoms: Refusal, Sabotage, Suspension." In *Politics of Withdrawal: Media, Arts, Theory*, edited by Pepita Hesselberth and Joost de Bloois, 115-32. Lanham, MA: Rowman and Littlefield, 2020.

Bartram, Erin. "The Sublimated Grief of the Left Behind." *Erin Bartram* (personal blog), February 11, 2018. https://erinbartram.com/uncategorized/the-sublimated-grief-of-the-left-behind/

Berg, Maggie, and Barbara K. Seeber. *The Slow Professor: Challenging the Culture of Speed in the Academy*. Toronto: University of Toronto Press, 2016.

Berlant, Lauren. *Cruel Optimism*. Durham, NC: Duke University Press, 2011.

———. *The Female Complaint: The Unfinished Business of Sentimentality in American Culture*. Durham, NC: Duke University Press, 2008.

Brown, Sarah. "She Wrote a Farewell Letter to Colleagues. Then 80,000 People Read It." *Chronicle of Higher Education*, February 15, 2018. https://www.chronicle.com/article/She-Wrote-a-Farewell-Letter-to/242564

Brown, Wendy. "Resisting Left Melancholy." *Boundary 2* 26 (1999): 19-27.

Cassuto, Leonard. "The Grief of the Ex-Academic." *Chronicle of Higher Education*, February 25, 2018. https://www.chronicle.com/article/The-Grief-of-the-Ex-Academic/242612

De Coster, Marjan, and Patrizia Zanoni. 2019. "Governing through Accountability: Gendered Moral Selves and the (Im)Possibilities of Resistance in

American Culture (Durham, NC: Duke University Press, 2008), 243.

41. Berlant, *Female Complaint*, vii.

the Neoliberal University." *Gender, Work and Organization* 26 (4): 411-29.

Deleuze, Gilles. "Control and Becoming: A Conversation between Toni Negri and Gilles Deleuze." Translated by Martin Joughin. *The Funambulist Magazine*. February 22, 2011 [1990]. https://thefunambulist.net/law/philosophy-control-and-becoming-a-conversation-between-toni-negri-and-gilles-deleuze

Dwyer, Mike. "The Hidden Guilt of Leaving Academia." *Ordinary Times* (blog), May 14, 2015. https://ordinary-times.com/2015/05/14/the-hidden-guilt-of-leaving-academia/

Edwards, Michael. "I Quit! Why I Am Leaving UK Academia." *Times Higher Education*, July 25, 2017. https://www.timeshighereducation.com/cn/blog/uk-academia-has-gone-hell-handcart-and-i-quit

Freedman, Diane P., Olivia Frey, and Frances Murphy Zauhar, eds. *The Intimate Critique: Autobiographical Literary Criticism*. Durham, NC: Duke University Press, 1993.

Gallop, Jane. *Anecdotal Theory*. Durham, NC: Duke University Press, 2002.

Gill, Rosalind. "Academics, Cultural Workers and Critical Labour Studies." *Journal of Cultural Economy* 7 (2014): 12-30.

———. "Breaking the Silence: The Hidden Injuries of Neoliberal Academia." In *Secrecy and Silence in the Research Process: Feminist Reflections*, edited by Roisin Ryan-Flood and Rosalind Gill, 228-44. London and New York: Routledge, 2010.

Gill, Rosalind, and Ngaire Donaghue. "Resilience, Apps and Reluctant Individualism: Technologies of Self in the Neoliberal Academy." *Women's Studies International Forum* 54 (2016): 91-99.

Gillies, Val, and Helen Lucey, eds. *Power, Knowledge and the Academy: The Institutional Is Political*. Basingstoke, UK: Palgrave Macmillan, 2007.

Green, Alison. "'My Boss Keeps Guilt-Tripping Me for Leaving My Job!'" *The Cut*, October 15, 2019. https://www.thecut.com/article/my-boss-is-mad-that-im-quitting.html

Guest Pryal, Katie Rose. *The Freelance Academic: Transform Your Creative Life and Career*. Chapel Hill, NC: Snowraven Books, 2019.

Hanisch, Carol. 2009. "The Personal Is Political: The Women's Liberation Movement Classic with a New Explanatory Introduction." *Carol*

Hanisch: Women of the World, Unite! 2009 [1969]. http://www.carolhanisch.org/CHwritings/PIP.html

Haraway, Donna. "Situated Knowledges: The Science Question in Feminism and the Privilege of Partial Perspective." *Feminist Studies* 14 (1988): 575-99.

Hartmann, Heidi. "The Unhappy Marriage of Marxism and Feminism: Towards a More Progressive Union." In *Feminist Theory Reader: Local and Global Perspectives*, edited by Carole McCann and Seung-Kyung Kim, 3d ed., 187-201. London and New York: Routledge, 2013.

Hesselberth, Pepita, and Joost de Bloois. "Introduction: Towards a Politics of Withdrawal?" In *Politics of Withdrawal: Media, Arts, Theory*, edited by Hesselberth and de Bloois, 1-12. Lanham, MA: Rowman and Littlefield, 2020.

Hirsch, Marianne. *Family Frames: Photography, Narrative and Postmemory*. Cambridge, MA.: Harvard University Press, 2007.

Hirsch, Marianne, and Valerie Smith. "Feminism and Cultural Memory: An Introduction." *Signs* 28 (2002): 1-19.

Ibarra, Herminia, and Otilia Obodaru. "Betwixt and between Identities: Liminal Experience in Contemporary Careers." *Research in Organizational Behavior* 36 (2016): 47-64.

Keenan, Elizabeth. "Leaving Academia? It's Time to Have 'The Talk'." *Chronicle Vitae*, April 9, 2014. https://chroniclevitae.com/news/434-leaving-academia-it-s-time-to-have-the-talk

Kirkpatrick, Ellen. "The Academy I Dreamed of for 20 Years No Longer Exists, and I Am Waking Up." *Times Higher Education*, May 23, 2019. https://www.timeshighereducation.com/features/academy-i-dreamed-20-years-no-longer-exists-and-i-am-waking

Lee [Bateman], Oliver. "I Have One of the Best Jobs in Academia. Here's Why I'm Walking Away." *Vox*, September 8, 2015. https://www.vox.com/2015/9/8/9261531/professor-quitting-job

Lobo, Guiseppina Iacono. "Academic Guilt." In *How to Build a Life in the Humanities: Meditations on the Academic Work-Life Balance*, edited by Greg Colón Semanza and Garrett A. Sullivan Jr., 83-90. New York: Palgrave Macmillan, 2015..

Miller, Nancy K. *Getting Personal: Feminist Occasions and Other Autobio-*

graphical Acts. New York: Routledge, 1991.

Morrish, Liz. "Pressure Vessels: The Epidemic of Poor Mental Health among Higher Education Staff." *Academic Irregularities* (blog), May 23, 2019. https://academicirregularities.wordpress.com/2019/05/23/pressure-vessels-the-epidemic-of-poor-mental-health-among-higher-education-staff/

———. "Why the Audit Culture Made Me Quit." *Times Higher Education*, March 2, 2017. https://www.timeshighereducation.com/features/why-audit-culture-made-me-quit

Phadke, Gayatri. "Guilty as Charged: On Leaving Academia." *Medium*, June 20, 2017. https://medium.com/@gayatriphadke/guilty-as-charged-on-leaving-academia-d85c3294f652

———. "Quit Lit Is about Labor Conditions." *Women in Higher Education*, June 7, 2018. https://www.wihe.com/article-details/74/quit-lit-is-about-labor-conditions/

Racket, Sally. "Survivor's Guilt." *Chronicle of Higher Education*, March 15, 2011. https://www.chronicle.com/article/Survivors-Guilt/126710

r/LadiesofScience. "Guilty for Wanting to Leave Academia." Reddit, October 29, 2013. https://www.reddit.com/r/LadiesofScience/comments/1pgc01/guilty_for_wanting_to_leave_academia/

Saxine, Ian. "They're Not Quitting! Reclaiming a Genre." *The Professor Is In* (blog), March 20, 2018. https://theprofessorisin.com/2018/03/20/theyre-not-quitting-reclaiming-a-genre-a-postac-guest-post/

Schuman, Rebecca. "'I Quit Academia,' an Important, Growing Subgenre of American Essays." *Slate*, October 24, 2013. https://slate.com/culture/2013/10/quitting-academic-jobs-professor-zachary-ernst-and-other-leaving-tenure-and-tenure-track-jobs-why.html

Sharma, Sarah. "Exit and the Extensions of Man." *Transmediale: Art and Digital Culture*, April 2017. https://transmediale.de/content/exit-and-the-extensions-of-man

Shreve, Grant. "'Quit Lit' Then and Now." *Inside Higher Ed*, April 4, 2018. https://www.insidehighercom/views/2018/04/04/comparison-quit-lit-1970s-and-today-opinion

Trubek, Anne. "Giving Up Tenure? Who Does That?" *Chronicle of Higher Education*, April 8, 2013. https://www.chronicle.com/article/Giving-Up-Tenure-Who-Does/138345

Virno, Paolo. "Virtuosity and Revolution: The Political Theory of Exodus." Translated by Ed Emery. *Generation Online*. N.d. http://www.generation-online.org/c/fcmultitude2.html

"Toward the Love of Life and a Life of Love": Quit Lit, Consciousness-Raising, and the Pursuit of Reforms in Graduate Education

Christine Kelly

IN THE WINTER of 2011, with equal measures of duty and anxiety, I set out to draft a statement of purpose for a fellowship application. In the throes of applications to doctoral programs in a humanities field, the fellowship was aimed at supporting future faculty members who wished to teach at religiously affiliated colleges and universities. I interpreted the required statement as an opportunity to air the high-minded idealism and deeply embedded sense of purpose that guided my pursuit of a life in academia, one I referred to as nothing other than a *vocation*, with all of the implications of a transcendent calling that the term implies.[1] As I later discovered, the material and emotional sacrifices involved would render vocational language misguided if not dangerous.[2] Nevertheless, my early impressions of life as a professional academic were informed by at least as many "platitudes and untruths," in the words of quit-lit author Melissa

1. See Mark Schwehn, *Exiles from Eden: Religion and the Academic Vocation in America* (New York: Oxford University Press, 2005), and more recently, David Cunningham, "The Importance of a Return to a More Profound Meaning of Vocational Education," *Inside Higher Ed*, January 7, 2019, https://www.insidehighered.com/views/2019/01/07/importance-return-more-profound-meaning-vocational-education-opinion

2. Karen Kelsky and Kellee Weinhold, "Going Post-Ac: The Non-Academic Job Search," lecture, Fordham University, New York, March 1, 2018.

Dalgleish.[3] In my fellowship application, these impressions shaped my aspirations for a life that, channeling a beloved historian, I described in the following way:

> Through this [fellowship], years of graduate training, and a subsequent profession of teaching and research, I hope to devote myself to what John Gaddis, among my favorite historians, says about academic pursuits. When done well, he believes them to lead us all toward "wisdom, maturity, the love of life and a life of love."[4]

Years later, in the summer of 2017, I sat in the frosty and silent stacks of my university library. An advanced doctoral student, I cracked open the preface to *Leaving the Ivory Tower*, sociologist Barbara Lovitts's seminal study on doctoral student attrition in the US.[5] By now, the routine rejections, humiliations, and disappointments that formed my socialization in the academy had eroded a good deal of my earlier idealism. That afternoon, I considered the recent collapse of a professional opportunity I had hung too many hopes on. As I was then certain that I would no longer aim for a tenure-track job after graduate school, this recent rejection signaled the demise of what I considered my only meaningful chance at diversifying my skill set and exposing me to needed professional networks. In contrast to the hopes I articulated over a half-decade earlier, I now more closely related to Lovitts's unusually candid articulation of the fear and disappointment that marked the twilight of her graduate career. I was, moreover, struck by her resolve to do something about it: "During my last semester as a graduate student," Lovitts recalled, "I woke with tears streaming down my cheeks, wondering where to find the book that would tell me my life was going to be okay. I knew such a book didn't exist and resolved to write it."[6]

I observed Lovitts's careful examination of the implications of the "high and persistent rate of attrition" among doctoral programs in the US, and the attention she drew to the affective dimensions of leaving the academy; the author fielded what "quitting" *feels* like.[7] She echoed voices that, time and

3. Melissa Dalgleish, "My 'I Quit' Letter," *Hook and Eye* (blog), November 7, 2013, https://hookandeye.ca/2013/11/07/my-i-quit-letter/ [pp. 55-60 in the present volume].

4. Quote from John Gaddis, *The Landscape of History: How Historians Map the Past* (Oxford, UK: Oxford University Press, 2002), 151.

5. Barbara Lovitts, *Leaving the Ivory Tower: The Causes and Consequences of Departure from Doctoral Study* (Lanham, MD: Rowman and Littlefield, 2001), x.

6. Lovitts, *Leaving the Ivory Tower*, x.

7. Lovitts, *Leaving the Ivory Tower*, 31.

again, I turned to when seeking strength, resolve, and hope amid the tumultuous ebbs and flows of my graduate school career – "quit-lit" authors. Wholly unexpectedly, their voices – often beyond the traditional voices of authority in my program – guided my own professional development. That year, though not yet knowing it, I began what would become a gradual transition from graduate student to academic administrator, specializing in the support and professionalization of Master's and doctoral students on a university campus. A historian of second-wave feminism, I now see my immersion in quit lit while a graduate student as resembling the effects of feminist consciousness-raising circles in the mid-twentieth century. The candid, in many cases autobiographical, essays of quit-lit authors reflect on the limits of the normative configurations of power, hierarchy, and authority they navigated throughout their academic training. In this way, they run parallel to those nascent feminists who voiced their experiences as women just beginning to recognize the unselfconscious patriarchy that shaped their lives.[8] Beginning with awareness, consciousness-raising ended with agency.[9] In a similar vein, my own journey has been shaped by quit-lit essays whose authors acknowledged the challenges of academic life while modeling new professional possibilities and life priorities for graduate students and faculty members who opt to leave the academy some time during their careers.

Although quit lit and related genres, such as what author Lenny Cassuto labels the "'don't go to graduate school' genre," have captured the attention of major publications in the higher education industry for at least a generation, the raw expressiveness of many quit-lit pieces, and the places where they often sprout – on Reddit forums, personal blogs, YouTube channels, and other corners of informal sharing and community-building over the Internet – smack of subversion and reinforce the outsider status of "quitters."[10] Now working from within a university institution, I strive to extend the discourse of honest expression, empowerment, and the exploration of options that one finds in quit-lit pieces to spaces inside the academy,

8. Kirsten Swinth, *Feminism's Forgotten Fight: The Unfinished Struggle for Work and Family* (Cambridge, MA: Harvard University Press, 2018), 31.

9. Ruth Rosen, *The World Split Open: How the Modern Women's Movement Changed America*, rev. ed. (New York: Penguin, 2006), 18, 201.

10. Leonard Cassuto, *The Graduate School Mess: What Caused It and How We Can Fix It* (Cambridge, MA: Harvard University Press, 2015), 94. See Sydni Dunn, "Why So Many Academics Quit and Tell," Chronicle Community, December 12, 2013, https://community.chronicle.com/news/216-why-so-many-academics-quit-and-tell [pp. 141-47 in the present volume]; and Colleen Flaherty, "Public Good-byes," *Inside Higher Ed*, September 9, 2015, https://www.insidehighered.com/news/2015/09/09/essays-academics-fed-higher-ed-mark-resurgence-quit-lit

and am grateful to those fellow colleagues who are actively making a similar commitment. I am convinced that the rigors of the academy do not have to come with long-lasting emotional bruises, and that a well-trained scholar and professional is still capable of throwing herself into "the love of life and a life of love." This is my story.

"Doubting My Decisions, Doubting Myself, Is What I Am an Expert At": Navigating the Turbulent Terrain of the Terminal Master's Degree in the Humanities

In 2010, a commentator who joined a roundtable discussion facilitated by *The Chronicle Review* asked a question about humanities Master's degree programs. "How many master's programs," she wondered, "are thinly disguised cash cows or providers of cheap labor for their departments rather than an organic part of them?"[11] The commentator's language, in the words of Lenny Cassuto, "demands close reading," and points out the "respect problem" endemic to Master's degree training, especially in humanities fields.[12] One piece of the dialogue that rarely emerges in forums that broach rethinking or reforming the Master's degree is the lived experience of Master's candidates, who often find themselves lacking a road map to navigate the special complexities of the MA degree – a degree that lacks a streamlined professional purpose across colleges and universities, and whose training, as the commentator acknowledged, varies dramatically from one program to another.[13] Confused and overwhelmed by my own experience in a terminal MA degree, I drew solace and gained perspective from quit-lit authors and other informal commentators on the graduate student experience.

It was not long after I enrolled in a terminal Master's degree program in a humanities field that I came to understand, thanks to the gratuitous remarks of graduate student peers, that I was numbered among the program's "cash cows." Unfunded, I learned quickly about the heart-throbbing and insomnia-provoking anxiety that accompanies a degree financed entirely on debt, an enterprise that, however problematic, has been on the rise among candidates for Master's degrees.[14] I soon noticed that what I lacked in economic capital

11. "Graduate Humanities Education: What Should Be Done?" (forum), *Chronicle of Higher Education*, April 4, 2010, https://www.chronicle.com/article/graduate-humanities-education-what-should-be-done/

12. Cassuto, *Graduate School Mess*, 154.

13. See Cassuto, *Graduate School Mess*, 151; and Robert Peters, *Getting What You Came For: The Smart Student's Guide to Earning a Master's or Ph.D.* (New York: Noonday Press, 1992), 6-7, 81.

14. According to the National Center for Education Statistics, in the years 1999-2000

was compounded by equally limited reserves of social and cultural capital. I had no idea then that I was a "first-generation" graduate student, and that some of my more confident peers were brought up in and around academic families and other social networks relevant to their professional aspirations.[15] In the words of quit-lit author Viola Allo, I concluded that "doubting my decisions, doubting myself, is what I am an expert at."[16]

I found the graduate seminar experience especially challenging for reasons that, years later, I recognized were not – as a trusted undergraduate mentor explained – "entirely normal." I began coursework in the seminar of a professor who has been lauded for his incisive mentorship of generations of graduate students, even if his capricious temper and frequent insults of students and colleagues became an open secret among those who related to him professionally. I vividly remember watching him lean across a narrow seminar table, marveling in a loud voice at how "absolutely wrong" students were in their analysis of weekly readings, and threatening "B's," which can "ruin a career," if more students were to trouble him with their inexperienced approach to the assigned texts. His impatience notwithstanding, I don't recall him ever offering strategies to guide our approach to reading and discussion. In retrospect, he possessed little by way of a discernable pedagogical strategy. In *The Graduate School Mess*, Lenny Cassuto remarks on the minimal commitment to pedagogical craft that one finds among some faculty members who teach graduate seminars. He explains that hardworking and committed graduate students will try to "carry the load" of apathetic instructors in the classroom, but that their performance will be "uneven," since "they're not experienced pros."[17] When this instructor reluctantly agreed to supervise a research project – but only on the condition that I did not become a nuisance to him (the language he used was, in point of fact, much more colorful) – this most memorable interaction with him also became my last.

The advice that I received from informal mentors, peers, and friends

and 2015-2016, student debt increased by an average of 57% among those who complete Master's degree programs, with an average loan balance in 2015-2016 of $72,800 for a Master of Arts degree. See "Spotlights: Trends in Student Loan Debt for Graduate School Completers," *The Condition of Education 2018* (Washington, DC: US Department of Education, National Center for Education Statistics), 3, 5, https://nces.ed.gov/programs/coe/pdf/coe_tub.pdf

15. Bailey B. Smolarek, "The Hidden Challenges for Successful First-Generation Ph.D.s," *Inside Higher Ed*, October 9, 2019, https://www.insidehighered.com/advice/2019/10/09/first-generation-phd-student-describes-her-struggles-opinion

16. Viola Allo, "Leaving: A Personal Narrative of Graduate School," *Michigan Discussions in Anthropology* 18.1 (2010): 112-47, http://hdl.handle.net/2027/spo.0522508.0018.104

17. Cassuto, *Graduate School Mess*, 57-59.

inside the academy pushed me to accept what, in a recent "don't go to graduate school" piece, author Hannah Alpert-Abrams describes as "very particular cruelties" that "are given names like 'mentorship' and 'pedagogy' and 'academic rigor.'"[18] Recently, in coordination with university administrators throughout North America, the Council of Graduate Schools has opened up arenas for dialogue on faculty members who operate as "anti-mentors" in the lives of their students, pointing out the damaging professional and mental health effects that anti-mentors can have on their students.[19] But in this period, I lacked colleagues from within respectable academic circles who would offer a critical perspective on my experience. Consequently, I found it outside of them. Posts on a then new blog, "From Grad School to Happiness," reminded me to take this challenging new experience a step a time, and offered a dose of pragmatism to offset my romanticized hopes for academic life: "Just get through each day," the author advised, "and keep in mind that you have options. You can choose to leave if you want. Academia is a job ... nothing more, nothing less."[20]

On more melancholy days I turned to the macabre humor of the blog "100 Reasons Not to Go to Graduate School," where an anonymous author dissected the disadvantages of almost every aspect of the graduate school experience in the humanities and social sciences.[21] When the author declared that "graduate seminars can be unbearable," remarking on the pressure of the experience, followed by an abrupt conclusion ("after three hours, you will go your separate ways"), I felt less isolated in the fears that mounted prior to attending class, and the lonely evenings that followed. My consumption of "don't go to graduate school" lit, and quit lit, was not always healthy; the "100 Reasons" blog, for example, can fill readers in graduate programs with regret, and the dialogue that unfolds on the site can be long on vitriol and short on substance. These concerns notwithstanding, the author validated the pain points of my experience in a way that those in my academic social

18. Hannah Alpert-Abrams, "Open Letter to My Friend, Who I Love, Who Wants to Get a PhD in Literature," *Noteworthy: The Journal Blog*, July 19, 2020, https://blog.usejournal.com/open-letter-to-my-friend-who-i-love-who-wants-to-get-a-phd-in-literature-87392dabec16; Cassuto, *Graduate School Mess*, 94. See also James Van Wyck, "Managing Your Adviser," *Inside Higher Ed*, May 2, 2016, https://www.insidehighered.com/advice/2016/05/02/career-preparation-and-graduate-adviser-advisee-relationship-essay

19. Karen Colley and Sherri Irvin, "Dealing with the Anti-Mentor," panel presentation, Council of Graduate Schools annual meeting, Nashville, TN, December 5, 2019.

20. JC, "Good Luck!" *From Grad School to Happiness* (blog), August 29, 2011, http://leavingacademia.blogspot.com/2011/

21. "Graduate Seminars Can Be Unbearable," *100 Reasons NOT to Go to Graduate School* (blog), October 14, 2010, http://100rsns.blogspot.com/2010/10/21-graduate-seminars- can-be-unbearable.html

circles would not.

The "Death" – and Resurrection – of "A Soul (On Campus)": From Conformity to Consciousness-Raising in Academic Life

In her 2011 quit-lit essay, "Death of a Soul (On Campus)," Karen Kelsky, author of the influential book and website *The Professor Is In*, reflected on the isolating and competitive environment that she encountered as a newly hired, tenured faculty member at a major research university.[22] Describing her colleagues as possessing an air of self-importance while perpetually preoccupied with rigorous research and writing obligations, Kelsky recalled that "human connection was virtually impossible," attaching this problem to a broader climate issue on her university campus.[23] As an early-career doctoral student, I encountered similar experiences with alienation, and one-upmanship, in what I had hoped would be a congenial academic space. At this time, I became fascinated with trends in critical theory across humanities and social science disciplines for two reasons that, in retrospect, contradicted each other. On the one hand, I was proud of the dedication it took to master the academic jargon that has become an informal hallmark of theoretical essays in academic circles; I had sweated out this learning curve over many long days and nights in silent library stacks. On the other hand, I was struck by a basic impulse among critical theorists to interrogate the systems of power and hierarchy that, for cultures and societies throughout history, have constituted everyday life; power, they explain, is hidden behind its very ordinariness. That I had to scale what Christopher Schaberg calls "theory as a wall" to arrive at a thoughtful skepticism of hierarchy was something I left unquestioned at the time.[24]

But later I spent a summer studying theory and criticism with a group of colleagues, an experience that threw the contradictions of the manner in which critical theory is sometimes taught and discussed into stark relief. Dedicated theorists derided and laughed at colleagues who introduced concepts beyond the most authoritative or fashionable into the room. Rigidly

---

22. Karen Kelsky, "Death of a Soul (On Campus)," *Tech in Translation* (blog), July 18, 2011, http://techintranslation.com/guest-post-death-of-a-soul-on-campus/ [pp. 23-28 in the present volume]. See also Kelsky, *The Professor Is In: The Essential Guide to Turning Your Ph.D. into a Job* (New York: Three Rivers Press, 2015); and "Getting You through Graduate School, the Job Market and Tenure," The Professor Is In (blog), 2020, http://theprofessorisin.com/

23. Kelsky, "Death of a Soul."

24. Christopher Schaberg, "Teaching Critical Theory Today," *Inside Higher Ed*, February 13, 2019, https://www.insidehighered.com/views/2019/02/13/professors-should-teach-critical-theory-healthy-dose-self-awareness-opinion

loyal to "approved methods of knowing," as Jack Halberstam explains, they did "not allow for ... flights of fancy," or any suggestions that went beyond "the well-lit territories" of accepted theoretical interventions to be given meaningful consideration, much less a modicum of respect.[25] I understood these modalities of knowledge as intended, at least in part, to undermine arbitrarily acquired power by exposing its very genealogy.[26] But here, instead, I found the language of critical interventions mobilized, time and again, to establish one's superiority, often at the immediate and public expense of one's colleagues. As Schaberg claims, "theory had started to reproduce the very patterns and habits that it was supposed to help us think about and change."[27]

In the winter of 2017, my experience with incivility among academic colleagues extended to the arena of academic publishing, when the first article I submitted to an academic journal was rejected. The rejection itself was, in retrospect, unsurprising and unproblematic. In many cases, rejections point to the value of the peer-review refereeing process that assures the quality of research that goes into print.[28] Moreover, the feedback that I received from two of three reviewers offered thoughtful and generous guidance on where and how to improve. When I glanced at the remarks of a third reviewer, however, the ground shifted from under me. The short, pungent review did not address any aspect of the paper in detail, but instead dismissed the whole through a string of clever zingers, later declaring the work better off as "a parody of itself."

Devastated, but striving for resilience, I gave myself 14 days to swallow my pride and move on. Meanwhile, I drew comfort from a flurry of online articles that console scholars reeling from harsh and, more precisely, inappropriate reviews. I laughed, through tears, at posts accompanied by the Twitter handle, "#Reviewer2," that commiserated regarding especially mean-spirited or otherwise unprofessional feedback.[29] Still, a new fog of sadness and self-doubt crept in; it lasted well over 14 days. I doubted my abilities now more than ever, a reaction that science journalist Jason Murugesu explains is espec-

25. J. Jack Halberstam, *The Queer Art of Failure* (Durham, NC: Duke University Press, 2011), 6. See also Maggie Berg and Barbara Seeber, *The Slow Professor: Challenging the Culture of Speed in the Academy* (Toronto: University of Toronto Press, 2016), 71-72.

26. Michel Foucault, *The Archaeology of Knowledge* and *The Discourse on Language* (New York: Vintage, 1982), 231-32.

27. Schaberg, "Teaching Critical Theory Today."

28. Frank Gannon, "The Essential Role of Peer Review," *EMBO Reports* 2, no. 9 (September 15, 2001): 743, https://doi.org/10.1093/embo-reports/kve188

29. Reviewer2 (@GrumpyReviewer2), Twitter, https://twitter.com/GrumpyReviewer2?ref_src=twsrc%5Egoogle%7Ctwcamp%5Eserp%7Ctwgr%5Eauthor

ially common in women (like myself). According to Murugesu, in a recent survey of 1,106 researchers across 14 STEM disciplines, "women were 2.3 times as likely as white men to say they fully doubted their scientific abilities after receiving unprofessional peer review comments."[30] These findings are no doubt revealing and equally applicable to my experience as a student in the humanities. This was, as I recall, a hazy and preoccupied time. Unsure of what to do next, night after night I began to look up articles, videos, and resources developed by graduate students who left the academy.

"I Quit Graduate School, and It's OK": Quit Lit as Consciousness-Raising

Staring at my computer screen, I sat, engrossed, listening to "Wanda" tell her story. Wanda – whose YouTube channel is aptly named "Wanda the Brave" – breathed out a long sigh. "Hi, my name's Wanda," she began. In "November of 2016 I made a very difficult and important decision ... I quit graduate school." In a Superman T-shirt, which Wanda claimed that she donned "any time I'm really afraid to talk about something," she described this exit as her life's most challenging, and most rewarding, decision. Frequently pausing to maintain her composure, Wanda spoke of leaving to "pursue the things that I love again," and to devote more of her time to "people that made me want to live again."[31] At her story's end, through deep breaths, Wanda proclaimed: "I quit graduate school, and it's OK."

The popular video-streaming web platform YouTube, which has popularized individual vlogging in the last decade, houses scores of recordings by former students speaking about their decisions to leave graduate programs.[32] The explosive growth of these videos extends the form and, as their many thousands of views attest, the influence of quit lit beyond the printed word. Like their print counterparts, these videos often capture the raw emotions of those who leave, and many, even if they contain tragic elements, end on notes of empowerment. I smiled when "Amanda," who in

30. Jason Murugesu, "Harsh Peer Reviewer Comments Disproportionately Affect Minorities," *New Scientist*, January 27, 2020, https://www.newscientist.com/article/2231559-harsh-peer-reviewer-comments-disproportionately-affect-minorities/; see also Jeff C. Clements, "Don't Be a Prig in Peer Review," *Nature*, September 1, 2020, https://doi.org/10.1038/d41586-020-02512-0

31. Wanda the Brave, "I Dropped Out of Graduate School," YouTube video, 14:49, March 15, 2017, https://www.youtube.com/watch?v=P2GSQ7NTtNk&t=527s

32. On the rise of the vlogging, see Jean Burgess and Joshua Green, "The Entrepreneurial Vlogger: Participatory Culture Beyond the Professional-Amateur Divide," in Patrick Vonderau and Pelle Snickars, eds., *The YouTube Reader*, illustrated ed. (Stockholm: National Library of Sweden, 2010), 94.

sharing her decision to leave a PhD program, plainly stated that "I believe in doing what you love, creating a life you love, believing in yourself, believing in your gifts [and] believing your gifts are enough."[33] "Quitters," I found, whether they left academic life before or after obtaining the PhD, embraced the unexpected. They told their audiences that professional pathways were often nonlinear, while urging aspiring academics to prioritize their needs over what L. Maren Wood, founder of Beyond the Professoriate, describes as "a system that has no room for us."[34]

Wood, who references the limitations of a broader system in her personal quit-lit narrative, "Walking Away from Academia When It was Your Dream Job," resonated.[35] As my immersion in quit lit deepened, so also did my immersion in dissertation research. My alienation from graduate school notwithstanding, I continued to dissertate on a topic that connected with the rise of second-wave feminism in the US. Quit lit bears a surprising resemblance to an early strategy of mid-twentieth century feminists seeking to uncover the patriarchal assumptions that shaped their lives: consciousness-raising circles.[36] Historian of second-wave feminism Ruth Rosen explains that consciousness-raising relied on personal revelations told to small groups of listeners, and later sprouted in "novels, position papers, essays, and new forms of artistic expression [that] also raised a woman's consciousness."[37] Rosen claims that these shared reflections enabled budding feminists to recognize the cultural, legal, political, and economic assumptions that pigeon-holed women into stereotypical and limiting roles in areas that included family life, work, sex, health, and education.[38] Self-reflective narratives shared from individual experience became a source of awareness-raising about systemic issues. Later, these narratives buttressed organized efforts to address inequities no longer regarded as norms.[39] The quitters who, like

33. Amanda Frances, "Why I Quit My PhD Program," YouTube video, 5:01, May 2, 2014, https://www.youtube.com/watch?v=BdLucqNPanM

34. L. Maren Wood, "Walking Away from Academia When It Was Your Dream Job," Beyond the Professoriate, n.d., https://beyondprof.com/walking-away-from-academia-when-it-was-your-dream-job. See also Wood, "After the PhD: Interview with L. Maren Wood," Beyond the Professoriate, https://beyondprof.com/after-the-phd-interview-with-l-maren-wood-phd-and-jennifer-polk-phd/; Tibees, "I Quit My PhD," YouTube video, 18:19, February 8, 2019, https://www.youtube.com/watch?v=e3Heip-2jYQ; and Frances, "Why I Quit My PhD Program."

35. Wood, "Walking Away from Academia."

36. Swinth, *Feminism's Forgotten Fight*, 31.

37. Ruth Rosen, *The World Split Open: How the Modern Women's Movement Changed America* (New York: Penguin, 2000), 197.

38. Rosen, *World Split Open*, 197.

39. Rosen, *World Split Open*, 201.

these feminists, laid bare their experiences with honesty and vulnerability wedged some badly needed critical distance between myself and my experiences as a graduate student. They gave me permission not only "to make another choice," in Karen Kelsky's words, but to more fully address systemic issues in the academy when the opportunity – at my lowest point – emerged.[40]

"And So, I Quit. Though Not as Completely as Some": From Despondency to Agency

In "They're Not Quitting! Reclaiming a Genre," historian Ian Saxine questions the nomenclature of "quit lit" as a genre.[41] Foregrounding the word "quit," Saxine worries that readers will dismiss the affecting stories of ex-academics as the embittered tales of those who failed to "make it" in the academy.[42] Saxine urges more apt language for the genre. Using the example of Erin Bartram's narrative "Sublimated Grief of the Left Behind," Saxine urges readers to stop calling what Bartram is doing "quitting" and instead "call it what it is: *driven out*."[43] Saxine raises an important point about quit lit's role in shining a light on systemic issues, though one can take the concerns he raises about the genre a step further. Not only do quit-lit narratives undermine the experiences of their authors as fragmented or occurring in a vacuum; they also routinely challenge the binary divide that casts "quitters" in direct opposition to those who follow traditional academic pathways. My own story more closely mirrors the narrative of Melissa Dalgleish, in that I quit, though "not as completely as some."[44]

Ten days after news arrived of the rejection I mentioned earlier – for a fellowship opportunity I considered my last immediate hope at landing a position in a robust, non-academic industry – I was contacted to interview for a position in a dean's office at my university. After one rejection upon another, I was stunned to be selected for a part-time role that tasked me with maintaining, and enhancing, the school's professional development initiatives for graduate students. Supplied a humble budget but plenty of latitude

40. Karen Kelsky, "It's OK to Quit," *The Professor Is In* (blog), http://theprofessorisin.com/its-ok-to-quit/

41. Ian Saxine, "They're Not Quitting! Reclaiming a Genre," The Professor Is In (blog), n.d., https://theprofessorisin.com/2018/03/20/theyre-not-quitting-reclaiming-a-genre-a-postac-guest-post/ [pp. 155-57 in the present volume].

42. Saxine, "They're Not Quitting!"

43. Saxine, "They're Not Quitting!" See Erin Bartram, "The Sublimated Grief of the Left Behind," *Erin Bartram* (personal blog), February 11, 2018, https://erinbartram.com/uncategorized/the-sublimated-grief-of-the-left-behind/ [pp. 97-101 in the present volume].

44. Dalgleish, "My 'I Quit' Letter."

to explore and propose new opportunities and resources, I threw myself into this job with an enthusiasm I had not known in years. Having been a student at my university for four years, but blinded by a siloed perspective, only now did I really get to know the campus community that surrounded me. I met with staff members that specialized in student support services, like career services or counseling and psychological services, and shared my experiences. I felt safe in the company of these people. They were members of the university, but removed from the immediacy of my academic program and social circle. It seemed on the whole less risky to share my shortcomings and hardships with them. I began networking with "quitters," too, joining conversations with former academics who built influential professional development and coaching organizations, including Beyond the Professoriate, The Professor Is In, and Versatile PhD.[45]

With the help of the new colleagues and friends who listened to my account with empathy and generosity, I began organizing panel discussions and networking events that dealt with topics seldom discussed, but central to the lives and success of many graduate students. These topics included parenting while in graduate school, developing healthy coping mechanisms for managing failure, networking strategies in graduate school, managing time, and recognizing and responding to "stereotype threat" among high achievers.[46] Telling became doing on many levels; as these initiatives grew, so also did my investment in my dissertation research. The collaborative nature of the work broke the isolation and discouragement that bred inertia in my degree progress. And so, I finished. Three days after graduating from my doctoral program, I began a full-time role at the same university, in the area of graduate student support and professional development. Together, a dedicated team — many of whom are current students — and I make it our daily business to identify the pain points of the graduate student experience, and to build out new avenues of professional development and support. These efforts by no means provide perfect or all-encompassing solutions to complex and historically ingrained problems. But they are a start. Between this role and regular stints as an adjunct professor in my academic field, I feel that I hardly left the academy; I only detached from the experiences I found wounding and depleting, in hopes of contributing some small effort, day by day, to denaturalizing and mitigating them.

At the beginning of each fall semester, at a new student orientation event, I encourage a room full of new graduate students — at once anxious and

45. See the websites Beyond the Professoriate (https://beyondprof.com), The Professor Is In (http://theprofessorisin.com), and The Versatile PhD (https://versatilephd.com).

46. On "stereotype threat," see Claude Steele, *Whistling Vivaldi: And Other Clues to How Stereotypes Affect Us* (New York: Norton, 2010).

hopeful — to recognize that their intended paths may be less linear than they assume; as they navigate their programs, they are likely to experience personal and professional highs and lows that they cannot now fathom. By the expressions that register on their faces, I can tell that at least some are surprised to be hearing about failure, adversity, or even the unexpected in the first formal hour of their graduate school careers. But I am convinced that, at the very moment we welcome students into the life of the university, it is important to share the "quitters'" truths. Here I think of "Tibees," who in a homemade YouTube video on leaving her PhD program describes her decision to abandon the "straight trajectory ... from student to professor" that once characterized her professional self-concept.[47] Like Tibees, and many quit-lit authors and content creators besides, I believe that circuitous paths lead toward "the love of life and a life of love," if only we have the encouragement and support we need to find them, wherever they may lie.

References

Allo, Viola. "Leaving: A Personal Narrative of Graduate School." *Michigan Discussions in Anthropology* 18, no. 1 (2010): 112-47. http://hdl.hndle.net/2027/spo.0522508.0018.104

Alpert-Abrams, Hannah. "Open Letter to My Friend, Who I Love, Who Wants to Get a PhD in Literature." *Noteworthy: The Journal Blog*, July 19, 2020. https://blog.usejournal.com/open-letter-to-my-friend-who-i-love-who-wants-to-get-a-phd-in-literature-87392dabec16

Bartram, Erin. "The Sublimated Grief of the Left Behind." *Erin Bartram* (personal blog), February 11, 2018. https://erinbartram.com/uncategorized/the-sublimated-grief-of-the-left-behind/

Berg, Maggie, and Barbara Seeber. *The Slow Professor: Challenging the Culture of Speed in the Academy*. Toronto: University of Toronto Press, 2016.

Burgess, Jean, and Joshua Green. "The Entrepreneurial Vlogger: Participatory Culture Beyond the Professional-Amateur Divide." in *The YouTube Reader*, edited by Patrick Vonderau and Pelle Snickars, 89-107. Stockholm: National Library of Sweden, 2010.

Cassuto, Leonard. *The Graduate School Mess: What Caused It and How We Can Fix It*. Cambridge, MA: Harvard University Press, 2015.

47. Tibees, "I Quit My PhD."

Colley, Karen, and Sherri Irvin. "Dealing with the Anti-Mentor." Panel presentation at the annual meeting of the Council of Graduate Schools. Nashville, TN, December 5, 2019.

Clements, Jeff C. "Don't Be a Prig in Peer Review." *Nature*, September 1, 2020. https://doi.org/10.1038/d41586-020-02512-0

Cunningham, David. "The Importance of a Return to a More Profound Meaning of Vocational Education." *Inside Higher Ed*, January 7, 2019. https://www.insidehighered.com/views/2019/01/07/importance-return-more-profound-meaning-vocational-education-opinion

Dalgleish, Melissa. "My 'I Quit' Letter." *Hook and Eye* (blog), November 7, 2013. https://hookandeye.ca/2013/11/07/my-i-quit-letterb/

Dunn, Sydni. "Why So Many Academics Quit and Tell." Chronicle Community, December 12, 2013. https://community.chronicle.com/news/216-why-so-many-academics-quit-and-tell

Flaherty, Colleen. "Public Good-byes." *Inside Higher Ed*, September 9, 2015. https://www.insidehighered.com/news/2015/09/09/essays-academics-fed-higher-ed-mark-resurgence-quit-lit

Foucault, Michel. *The Archaeology of Knowledge* and *The Discourse on Language*. New York: Vintage, 1982.

Frances, Amanda. "Why I Quit My Ph.D. Program." YouTube video, 5:01. May 2, 2014. https://www.youtube.com/watch?v=BdLucqNPanM

Gaddis, John. *The Landscape of History: How Historians Map the Past*. Oxford: Oxford University Press, 2002.

Gannon, Frank. "The Essential Role of Peer Review." *EMBO Reports* 2, no. 9 (2001): 743. https://doi.org/10.1093/embo-reports/kve188

"Graduate Humanities Education: What Should Be Done?" (forum). *Chronicle of Higher Education*, April 4, 2010. https://www.chronicle.com/article/graduate-humanities-education-what-should-be-done/

Halberstam, Jack J. *The Queer Art of Failure*. Durham, NC: Duke University Press, 2011.

JC. "Good Luck!" *From Grad School to Happiness* (Blog). August 29, 2011. http://leavingacademia.blogspot.com/2011/

Kelsky, Karen. "Death of a Soul (On Campus)." *Tech in Translation* (blog), July 18, 2011. http://techintranslation.com/guest-post-death-of-a-soul-on-campus/

———. "It's OK to Quit." *The Professor Is In* (blog), n.d. http://theprofessorisin.com/its-ok-to-quit/

———. *The Professor Is In: The Essential Guide to Turning Your Ph.D. into a Job.* New York: Three Rivers Press, 2015.

Kelsky, Karen, and Kellee Weinhold. "Going Post-Ac: The Non-Academic Job Search." Lecture, Fordham University, New York. March 1, 2018.

Lovitts, Barbara. *Leaving the Ivory Tower: The Causes and Consequences of Departure from Doctoral Study.* Lanham, MD: Rowman and Littlefield, 2001.

Murugesu, Jason. "Harsh Peer Reviewer Comments Disproportionately Affect Minorities." *New Scientist*, January 27, 2020. https://www.newscientist.com/article/2231559-harsh-peer-reviewer-comments-disproportionately-affect-minorities/

Peters, Robert. *Getting What You Came For: The Smart Student's Guide to Earning a Master's or Ph.D.* New York: Noonday Press, 1992.

Rosen, Ruth. *The World Split Open: How the Modern Women's Movement Changed America.* Revised edition. New York: Penguin, 2006.

Saxine, Ian. "They're Not Quitting! Reclaiming a Genre." The Professor Is In (blog). https://theprofessorisin.com/2018/03/20/theyre-not-quitting-reclaiming-a-genre-a-postac-guest-post/

Schaberg, Christopher. "Teaching Critical Theory Today." *Inside Higher Ed*, February 13, 2019. https://www.insidehighered.com/views/2019/02/13/professors-should-teach-critical-theory-healthy-dose-self-awareness-opinion

Schwehn, Mark. *Exiles from Eden: Religion and the Academic Vocation in America.* New York: Oxford University Press, 2005.

Smolarek, Bailey B. "The Hidden Challenges for Successful First-Generation Ph.D.s." *Inside Higher Ed*, October 9, 2019. https://www.insidehighered.com/advice/2019/10/09/first-generation-phd-student-describes-her-struggles-opinion

"Spotlights: Trends in Student Loan Debt for Graduate School Completers." *The Condition of Education 2018.* Washington, DC: US Department of Education, National Center for Education Statistics, 2018. https://nces.ed.gov/programs/coe/pdf/coe_tub.pdf

Steele, Claude. *Whistling Vivaldi: And Other Clues to How Stereotypes Affect Us.* New York: Norton, 2010.

Swinth, Kirsten. *Feminism's Forgotten Fight: The Unfinished Struggle for Work and Family*. Cambridge, MA: Harvard University Press, 2018.

Tibees. "I Quit My PhD." YouTube video, 18:19. February 8, 2019. https://www.youtube.com/watch?v=e3Heip-2jYQ

Van Wyck, James. "Managing Your Adviser." *Inside Higher Ed*. May 2, 2016. https://www.insidehighered.com/advice/2016/05/02/career-preparation-and-graduate-adviser-advisee-relationship-essay

Wanda the Brave. "I Dropped Out of Graduate School." YouTube video, 14:49. March 15, 2017. https://www.youtube.com/watch?v=P2GSQ7NTtNk&t=527s

Wood, L. Maren. "After the PhD: Interview with L. Maren Wood." Beyond the Professoriate. N.d. https://beyondprof.com/after-the-phd-interview-with-l-maren-wood-phd-and-jennifer-polk-phd/

———. "Walking Away from Academia When It Was Your Dream Job." Beyond the Professoriate, November 20, 2018. https://beyondprof.com/walking-away-from-academia-when-it-was-your-dream-job/

“What We May Be”: Quit Lit and Academic Identity

Jennifer Vannette

QUIT LIT GIVES voice to a Shakespearean level of tragedy. While a great many characters could make us feel seen, *Hamlet*’s Ophelia seems the epitome of the broken academic grasping to hold on to all she thought was real, and the madness and uncertainty of it all, when she says, “we know what we are but not what we may be.” This is what quit lit does: it speaks about the academic identity — what we are — and acknowledges the changes in how to view that identity — what we may be.

The essays attempt to do many different things: challenge the academy’s failures, debunk the myths about cushy academic life, warn unsuspecting (or denialist) grad and prospective grad students about the dwindling job market and toxic culture, and expose unsustainable labor conditions and subsistence wages. Quit lit also feels like commentary on a new trend, but the current model, where laborers are overworked and student-customers no longer believe in the value of their investment, is the result of decades of efforts to undermine the academy. Economic downturns contributed to the effect, but those were not the only factors, which means we also have to look at the larger cultural and political narrative. By the 1960s, many Americans viewed higher education as a path for upward mobility, yet some Americans sought to undercut this advancement in order to maintain the status quo. Hiding in plain sight, political and business leaders waged a decades-long assault on academe's institutional identity. This successful impairment of a collective academic identity shifted into threats toward personal identity by the 2000s, coinciding with the adjunctification of the academy. To understand how the current state of academia is not an anomaly or a result of personal failures, we need to look at the quit-lit genre as a product of historical events.

Within three years of Matt Welsh kicking off the quit-lit trend, the writings were prolific enough that Rebecca Schuman pinpointed it as a specific genre. And that is not due to the success of its labor critiques or solutions to course-correct the academy. It is because quit lit models a coping response. When our identity is threatened, and that includes our expectation of future identity, the resulting instability can harm our self-worth. The identity threat also produces coping responses in order to facilitate stability and search for continuity. Quit lit embodies the process of transforming the internalized values of the professional academic identity into a new identity still being formed.[1] Ophelia could not guide herself through a transformation in circumstance, but by understanding the historical processes which made and unmade collective and personal academic identities, we can better navigate how to hold and revise our identities. Perhaps we can even cope with what we are yet to become.

There has been perennial debate about who should have access to college and just how wide open the collegiate hall doors should be thrown. Although the reality is more complicated, Americans perceived the post-WWII G.I. Bill as the moment those halls were open to the masses.[2] The latter half of the twentieth century produced a sense of opportunity related to higher education, as more and more youth were encouraged to consider a college track. The Cold War, with its emphasis on science and expertise in global cultures, histories, and languages, increased the perceived value of academia so much that when President Lyndon Johnson proclaimed college "a necessity" in 1965, it did not seem out of place to do so.

It appeared as if the climbing enrollments and greater access to higher education would continue without impediment, because Americans viewed academia as a path to stability and advancement. Rising affluence coupled with extended adolescence produced a new youth culture, and those youth, who were initially "rebels without a cause ... not a mass movement mobilized around a programme of civil actions," as anthropologist Marshall Sahlins

---

1. Jennifer Louise Petriglieri, "Under Threat: Responses to and the Consequences of Threats to Individuals' Identities," *Academy of Management Review* 36.4 (2011): 642-45, https://www.jstor.org/stable/41318089

2. Keith W. Olson, "The G.I. Bill and Higher Education: Success and Surprise," *American Quarterly* 25.5 (1973): 597-98; Sidney Burrell, "The G.I. Bill and the Great American Transformation, 1945-1967," *Boston University Graduate Journal*, 15 (1967): 3.

characterized them,[3] became active in participatory democratic action. The young rebels who found their causes learned civil disobedience and other nonviolent tactics from Black student leaders who organized lunch counter sit-ins, registered voters in the South, and engaged in other civil rights demonstrations. By the end of the decade, universities were fending off attacks about coddled students and ivory-tower elitist faculty, all of whom were disconnected from reality, and this laid the groundwork for the devaluation of academia that we see today. Two stories highlight the transition: the student-led Free Speech Movement at Berkeley and the faculty-led University of Michigan Teach-in.

The Free Speech Movement, although not yet named, began at the start of the fall semester in 1964, when UC Berkeley administrators told students they were no longer allowed to share political information at the traditional gathering place on the corner of Bancroft and Telegraph. As sociologist Nathan Glazer, then a new professor at Berkeley, explained for *Commentary*, the corner had long been the gathering place for students to advocate for various political activities. The space served as the main pedestrian entrance to campus. While on campus, free speech had long been deemed acceptable, *advocacy and organization* had not. The tenuous distinctions had bumped along for years in relative harmony until the University of California Regents decided to ban political tabling because the space, although viewed by most as being acceptably off-campus, was in fact university property.[4]

Already well versed in civil rights tactics, hundreds of students were primed and ready to protest when administrators decided to discipline them for ignoring the ban. Events continued to escalate during the fall semester, making activists like Jack Weinberg and Mario Savio household names. Anger on both the students' and administrators' sides culminated in a mass demonstration on December 2, 1964, in front of Sproul Hall, that soon became a sit-in when 800 students entered and took over the building. As if to underscore that students had learned civil disobedience tactics from the civil rights movement, Joan Baez sang "We Shall Overcome" on the steps of Sproul Hall.

Police broke through and arrested hundreds of protestors, leading to a strike by the Graduate Teaching Assistants that effectively cancelled many classes. Glazer prophetically said that the emphasis on administration, increase on grant-funded research, and reliance on graduate students would

3. Marshall Sahlins, "The Teach-Ins: Anti-War Protest in the Old Stoned Age," *Anthropology Today* 25.1 (2009): 3, 4.

4. Nathan Glazer, "What Happened at Berkeley," *Commentary*, February 1965, https://www.commentarymagazine.com/articles/nathan-glazer-2/what-happened-at-berkeley/

one day have a catastrophic effect on academia.[5]

The general public overwhelmingly disapproved of the students' disruptive actions, and rising Republican darling Ronald Reagan would soon capitalize on their frustration in California. Unaware of future consequences, Berkeley calmed, but student protests – for civil rights, free speech, and anti-war – spread across campuses nationwide.

Faculty also earned scorn and negatively changed American perceptions about the value of higher education when in mid-March 1965 a group of University of Michigan faculty organized an anti-war "teach-in," calling for a "work moratorium" to protest the escalation of the Vietnam War. Criticism quickly came from the general public, newspaper editorial boards, state government officials, university administrators, and even other faculty. Some claimed that the professors were lazy and looking for an excuse to avoid teaching. Newspaper editorials agreed, calling the faculty an "unpatriotic band of ivory tower intellectual troublemakers." Governor George Romney wrote to one of the organizers, philosophy professor Arnold Kaufman, "you are inviting anarchy in saying that you, or any other person or group, have the right to decide when an issue is important enough to halt the regular activity of a public institution." The state senate introduced and passed a censure calling the work moratorium a "totally ill-advised [and] clear violation of their duties as instructors," and many of the Michigan faculty worried over what might transpire during the annual budget review in Lansing if they supported political action.

The Michigan organizing group saw that the backlash against the work moratorium took attention away from anti-war messaging. A solution came from faculty member Marshall Sahlins, who reportedly said, "I've got it. They say we're neglecting our responsibilities as teachers. Let's show them how responsible we feel. Instead of teaching out, we'll teach in – all night."[6] Advertised as "An Appeal to Our Students," the first teach-in took place in Angell Hall March 24-25, 1965. About 3,000 students attended.

Even though Romney grudgingly accepted the merits of a teach-in, the general public still labeled the professors as "radicals," "discontents," "kooks," and "subversives," and as protests spread across the nation, so too did public

5. Glazer, "What Happened at Berkeley."

6. Footnote in the US Senate Committee on the Judiciary, Subcommittee to Investigate the Administration of the Internal Security Act and other Internal Security Laws, "The Anti-Vietnam Agitation and the Teach-In Movement: The Problem of Communist Infiltration and Exploitation," staff report, Washington, DC: US Government Printing Office, 1965, as quoted in Sahlins, "Teach-Ins," 5; Jack Rothman, "The Radical Liberal Strategy in Action: Arnold Kaufman and the First Teach-In," *Social Theory and Practice* 2.1 (1972): 33-45, http://www.jstor.org/stable/23556667

scorn. Conservatives happily jumped on the narrative that universities and their faculties were simultaneously instigators of and captives to the rabble-rousers. In 1969 then-Vice President Spiro Agnew, with the help of speechwriter Pat Buchanan, uttered words that still echo today, saying that the academy was an "effete corps of impudent snobs who characterize themselves as intellectuals."[7] Romney may have been more measured in his word choice, but essentially, the conservative political admonishment to university faculty was the same: don't think too highly of yourselves.

In California, gubernatorial candidate Ronald Reagan tapped into the constituency's discontent about campus upheaval and campaigned against Berkeley's "radicals." Once in office, Reagan proved that his attacks on the academy were more than a campaign ploy; he succeded in raising California state tuition by convincing the public that making higher education more expensive would "weed out the non-serious student and promote respect for school property."[8]

Many faculty members at Berkeley, Michigan, and beyond voiced concerns in 1965 that states would reduce funding for universities unless they managed to quell the unrest. They proved prophetic when, under Reagan's leadership, California voters rejected a higher education funding bond in November 1968. This action offered a glimpse of what was to come on the national level with a Reagan presidency in 1981.

As the protests roiled and only a few paid full attention to the financial precarity that loomed, some professors attacked their politically active colleagues. New York University's Sidney Hook proved especially influential in his accusation that faculty were tacitly approving the student behaviors. He argued, "it is the faculties who are responsible for the present state of American universities — responsible because of their apathy for what has developed in the past, and for missed educational opportunities."[9] In reality, most faculty simply wanted whatever would calm the turbulence. Maybe because attacks came both from right-wing politicians and from liberal university faculties fearing the loss of prestige and funding, by the end of the 1960s, higher education had already become a declension story. We just didn't know it yet.

While the protests of the 1960s produced rhetorical attacks on the

7. Ellen Schrecker, "The Roots of the Right-Wing Attack on Higher Education," *Thought and Action* 26 (2010): 73.

8. Ronald Reagan, quoted in Schrecker, "Roots of the Right-Wing Attack," 73.

9. Sidney Hook, *Academic Freedom and Academic Anarchy* (New York: Cowles, 1970), quoted in O. Lawrence Burnett, Jr., review of *Academic Freedom and Academic Anarchy*, *AAUP Bulletin* 56.3 (1970): 335.

academy, the stagflation of the 1970s further damaged its credibility, as academic "experts" struggled to address the economic woes. Naturally, stagflation also hurt graduates entering a crumbling job market. In 1978, sociologists Thomas A. Lyson and Gregory D. Squires shared their experiences on the job market, using humor to soften the "tragedy of being in grad school in a boom only to finish in a bust."[10] They noted the dismal transition from more jobs than candidates in 1970, to about double the number of new PhDs to available jobs by mid-decade in their field. Only a few others published essays about their experiences, and they are not nearly as blunt, frustrated, or angry as today's producers of quit lit. In fact, the writers Grant Shreve labeled as "proto-quit lit" tended not to direct frustration at their own programs or institutions, but at the overall situation and job market.[11]

Quit lit feels like a response to a new situation, but proto-quit lit demonstrates that the cultural criticism was a problem long in the making. If the purpose was to warn other academics, then 1970s grad students would have listened to Nathan Glazer who warned that the administration-faculty imbalance and economic concerns portended crisis.[12] The proto-quit lit writers found themselves surprised at their circumstances, and like today's quit lit essayists, they worked through the process of reimagining their identity as they found employment outside of academia. John T. Harwood even challenged the notion that academic work was better than industry, arguing that academics are, "as petty, venal, and tiresome as the stereotype of businessmen in [Sinclair Lewis's satirical novel] *Babbit*."[13] Willingly criticizing academia showed his transition to a new identity.

Although the economy recovered and even boomed in the early 1990s, the ideological transformation of academe, which began in the 1960s with the bombastic rhetoric of those like Spiro Agnew, continued. It became a more sophisticated and slow-moving devaluation in the 1970s and following decades, when corporations, or rather the people who ran them, began to take a more active interest in higher education to promote conservative thinking. As student enrollment increased, suspicions arose that colleges must be reducing standards. Many bemoaned the decentering of men and whiteness as an effort lacking "intellectual seriousness." In order to correct the "imbalance of many faculties," as they saw it, corporate leaders began to

10. Thomas A. Lyson and Gregory D. Squires, "The New Academic Hustle: Marketing a PhD," *American Sociologist* 13 (1978): 233.

11. Grant Shreve, "'Quit Lit' Then and Now," *Inside Higher Ed*, April 4, 2018, https://www.insidehighered.com/views/2018/04/04/comparison-quit-lit-1970s-and-today-opinion [pp. 163-67 in the present volume].

12. Glazer, "What Happened at Berkeley."

13. John T. Harwood, "Nonacademic Job Hunting," *AAUP Bulletin* 60.3 (1974): 313.

endow professorships and chairs, a process that grew pronounced in the decade 1969-1979. They also established special programs in law and economics at many prestigious schools, including Harvard and Yale, while the Walton family (Walmart) focused on transforming universities along business-friendly models by funding free enterprise business programs from the Rust Belt to the Sun Belt.[14]

Conservative think tanks worked to undermine the perception that academia held value by advocating for a "return" to "traditional" education – meaning education that disregarded strides in global and transnational studies, critical race theory, women and gender studies, and history that decentered Western civilization. These think tanks accused university faculties of acting as "thought police" who demanded conformity to liberal ideas. According to historian Ellen Schrecker, by the mid-1980s, "this network of conservative institutions and individuals was furnishing the media ... with an alternative source of expertise that looked, at least superficially, like scholarship."[15] They achieved results. The false accusations had staying power even though they were "highly exaggerated ... [and] this demonized portrayal of American universities and their faculties [became] entrenched in the popular mind."[16] After the frustrations over the 1960s turbulence, Americans were primed for this narrative.

Faculties and administrators failed to effectively counter the attacks and have perpetually played defense since. These slings and arrows helped to justify continued reduction in public funding. Several current quit-lit essayists have noted this reputational damage, and how it has affected work life in higher education. Terran Lane offered one of the more insightful summaries when she wrote in 2012, "There is a terrifying trend in this country right now of attacking academe, specifically, and free thought and intellectualism, generally. Free thought is painted as subversive, dangerous, elitist, and (strangely) conspiratorial."[17] However, what contemporary writers like Lane have missed is that the trend is not new.

In her analysis essay, Sarah Kendzior argued that the average American will be – if they are not already – barred from academic pursuits because of cost. That will effectively make higher education the province of the elite

14. Schrecker, "Roots of the Right-Wing Attack," 79; Bethany Moreton, *To Serve God and Wal-Mart: The Making of Christian Free Enterprise* (Cambridge, MA: Harvard University Press, 2009), 142, 145-48.

15. Schrecker, "Roots of the Right-Wing Attack," 79.

16. Schrecker, "Roots of the Right-Wing Attack," 78.

17. Terran Lane, "On Leaving Academe," *Chronicle of Higher Education,* August 19, 2012, https://www.chronicle.com/article/on-leaving-academe/ [pp. 29-34 in the present volume].

once again.[18] The ideological devaluation of the past several decades has worked effectively. Grad students struggle to justify years of training they cannot use due to the lack of available jobs, which means they must give up who they thought they would become. Undergrads cannot afford school, limiting their options. Consider that in 1971 students attending a four-year public colleges or universities paid $1,405 on average for tuition, fees, and room and board.[19] By 2019 the average reached $21,950.[20] Wages have not kept pace with rising tuition, so students have few choices other than taking on debt. These limitations create precarity at all levels of academia and produce a continued assault on identity.[21] This in turn has caused Americans to question the value of both academia and academics, while bitterness over the system continues to be directed at colleges and universities rather than corporations or government policies.

Corporations used bachelor's degrees as a gatekeeping mechanism, ensuring continued enrollments, and universities began an arms race of amenities to attract students. Everyone – administrators, politicians, and the public – became invested in the corporate model of education, wherein students are customers and everyone is a stakeholder. Although universities have long provided amenities to attract students, the 1990s saw an uptick in a demand-model focus.[22] In order to compete for customers, universities spent large sums creating a "university experience" by providing amenities such as high-end suites instead of traditional dorms, state-of-the-art fitness centers, multi-million-dollar athletic programs, and ever more extensive dining options. To manage all of this, administrations continue to balloon.

If state governments and the public valued the educational mission of

18. Sarah Kendzior, "The Closing of American Academia," *Al Jazeera*, August 20, 2012, https://www.aljazeera.com/opinions/2012/8/20/the-closing-of-american-academia/ [pp. 133-36 in the present volume]

19. Marshall Sahlins, "The Teach-Ins Helped Galvanize Student Activism in the 1960s. They Can Do So Again Today," *The Nation*, April 6, 2017, https://www.thenation.com/article/archive/teach-ins-helped-galvanize-student-activism-in-the-1960s-they-can-do-so-again-today/

20. Jennifer Ma et al., "Trends in College Pricing, 2019," Trends in Higher Education series (New York: College Board, 2019), 3.

21. Petriglieri, "Under Threat," 643-45.

22. Researchers found a consistent average ratio of amenity (student services and auxiliaries) to academic (instruction and academic support) spending of 0.51 in the years 1992-2007. All students, they found, place emphasis on amenities when choosing a school, whereas only the academically gifted place priority on instruction and academic support. See Brian Jacob, Brian McCall, and Kevin M. Stange, "College as Country Club: Do Colleges Cater to Students' Preferences for Consumption?" Working Paper 18745, National Bureau of Economic Research, January 2013, https://www.nber.org/papers/w18745

colleges and universities, then it seems faculty compensation would be a main priority. It is not. While tuition dollars flow unquestioned toward administration, athletic programs, and building projects, academic departments struggle to get approval for new or replacement faculty lines.

Enter the adjuncts. Once a means to fill short-term gaps, adjuncts have become standard in most departments. In 2012, 67% of all university teaching positions were temporary fixed-term or adjunct positions, and now that number is closer to 75%.[23] In the last decade, quit-lit writers have instigated conversations about the instability of the system, particularly its imbalance between expected credentials and compensation. The COVID-19 pandemic has further exposed academia's participation in the gig economy.

Understanding the decades-long cultural and political attacks allows us to place the current precarity into context, but it also reveals a shift from an assault on collective or institutional identity toward an assault on personal identity as well. The adjunctification of academia devalues people not just financially, but in terms of self-worth and societal worth. It also devalues the academy, because adjuncts do not have the luxury of time and resources to cultivate relationships within their departments with colleagues or students. Far too many faculty have accepted the system without examining its failures, and therefore perpetuate the myth that those who adjunct are somehow less qualified than those who land on the tenure track. This is despite so much evidence to the contrary, including the fact that the prestige of the degree-conferring university is a better indicator of job placement success than any other metric.[24]

Adjuncts devote long hours and energy to their colleges or universities while navigating these problematic hierarchies, and when they commit to that work, the institution becomes an integral part of their personal identities. We sustain our self-worth through our identities, but when there are persistent experiences that devalue our work, our personal identities become threatened. Then we must find ways to negotiate those threats.[25]

The systemic failures of academia created greater demands on graduate students as well. No longer is it sufficient to succeed in your program and

23. Trevor Griffey, "Decline of Tenure for Higher Education Faculty: An Introduction," Labor and Working-Class History Association, September 2, 2016, https://www.lawcha.org/2016/09/02/decline-tenure-higher-education-faculty-introduction/; Todd Wallis, "The Rise of Adjunct Faculty: A Brief History," *Inside Scholar*, April 11, 2018, https://insidescholar.org/the-rise-of-adjunct-faculty/; "Background Facts on Contingent Faculty," American Association of University Professors, https://www.aaup.org/issues/contingency/background-facts

24. Aaron Clauset, Samuel Arbesman, and Daniel B. Larremore, "Systematic Inequality and Hierarchy in Faculty Hiring Networks," *Science*, February 12, 2015, 1 .

25. Petriglieri "Under Threat," 643.

produce a promising dissertation. Instead of *doing* work, academics *become* their work, as Rebecca Schuman argues is really the goal: "During graduate school, you will be broken down and reconfigured in the image of the academy."[26] Generally, one is expected to leave a PhD program with several years of teaching experience and excellent student evaluations (despite these being a meaningless metric),[27] several conference presentations, a good publication record, and preferably at least a book contract in hand. And all of that is on top of needing to produce a dissertation with depth and expansiveness far exceeding what was required of doctoral candidates 20 years ago.[28] If the standards sound impossible, it is because they basically are. But as more PhDs are produced to enter ever-dwindling job markets, the gatekeeping becomes more elaborate, and the threat to one's identity increases.

If you secure a tenure-track job, it is likely to come with a high teaching load, the expectation to publish, and mountains of "university service" necessary to achieve tenure. Once again, your teaching evaluations must be stellar, your publication record must be impeccable, and you need to volunteer your time in any number of time-consuming university initiatives. After all, you are part of the team.

Although the corporatizing influences on academia have increased in the last decade, clearly this is the result of a long cultural trend. In the post-WWII era, American higher education was celebrated for the opportunities it yielded. That narrative shifted under the strain of mid-century protest movements, which in turn allowed space for conservatives to paint a worrisome picture about indoctrination. Funding has decreased as questions about the value of academia and academics have increased, and the long view helps us recognize that the combination of cultural forces and economic change has led us to this moment of deep uncertainty. Therefore, a better economy alone will not provide salvation, nor will we be able to address labor conditions without a deeper conversation about academic identity.

In psychological terms, the writers of quit lit have expressed identity threat, or the sense that the experiences and values that gave meaning to their

---

26. Rebecca Schuman, "Thesis Hatement," *Slate*, April 5, 2013, http://www.slate.com/articles/life/culturebox/2013/04/there_are_no_academic_jobs_and_getting_a_ph_d_will_make _you_into_a_horrible.html [pp. 41-45 in the present volume].

27. See, among other studies, Kristina M. W. Mitchell and Jonathan Martin, "Gender Bias in Student Evaluations," *PS: Political Science and Politics* 51.3 (2018): 648-52, doi:10.1017/S104909651800001X.

28. Sidonie Smith, *Manifesto for the Humanities: Transforming Doctoral Education in Good Enough Times* (Ann Arbor: University of Michigan Press, 2016), 131-36; Erik D. Curren, "No Openings at This Time: Job Market Collapse and Graduate Education," *Profession* 94 (1994): 57-61.

identity can no longer be maintained. Their group identity as academics has become unstable. Therefore, they react with coping responses such as efforts to "actively [educate] others about the value of the threatened identity" and to restructure their own identities.[29] Quit lit models these responses.

Some of the earliest writers of quit lit were faculty who had, in the eyes of the academic world, "made it," and yet left to pursue interests and work outside of academia. These writers highlighted the difficult expectations placed on academics, including the need to move away from family and other support networks to secure a job. This uprooting is simply part of the academic world. Matt Welsh talked about seeking joy and creativity in his work. He, and other early writers like Karen Kelsky and Alexandra Lord, felt compelled to justify their decisions and remind readers that academia can be very isolating and wholly work-centric. Those who wanted a more balanced life found themselves out of sync with academic demands.[30]

Others spent many hiring cycles as adjuncts before walking away, and still others found themselves disillusioned with the system before trying to land an academic job. Unsurprisingly, given the job market, many of the latest quit lit authors did not so much quit – how can you quit a job you don't have? – but rather just stopped trying to be part of the system. Again, it is important to note that the level of personal identification embedded in academics is such the act of looking for work outside of academia, even if unemployed within it, implies "giving up" on the profession. Leonard Cassuto labels these essays a subgenre called "pushed-out lit."[31]

Those who were "pushed out" express grief, anger, and bitterness. Joe Fruscione memorably compared academia to a game of "Calvinball": the only constant is that the rules always change in favor of those in power.[32] The power system is maintained through the academic hierarchy, with tenured and tenure-track academics most highly valued, then non-tenure-track

---

29. Petriglieri, "Under Threat," 647.

30. Matt Welsh, "Why I'm Leaving Harvard," *Matt Welsh* (personal blog), November 15, 2010, http://matt-welsh.blogspot.com/2010/11/why-im-leaving-harvard.html [pp. 19-22 in the present volume]; Alexandra M. Lord, "Location, Location, Location," *Chronicle of Higher Education*, September 12, 2012, https://www.chronicle.com/article/Location-Location-Location/ 134264/ [pp. 35-40 in the present volume]; Karen Kelsky, "Death of a Soul (on Campus)," *Tech in Translation*, July 18, 2011, http://techintranslation.com/guest-post-death-of-a-soul-on-campus/ [pp. 23-28 in the present volume].

31. Leonard Cassuto, "The Grief of the Ex-Academic," *Chronicle of Higher Education*, February 25, 2018, https://www.chronicle.com/article/The-Grief-of-the-Ex-Academic/242612 [pp. 149-53 in the present volume].

32. Joe Fruscione, "New Game, New Rules," *Chronicle Vitae*, February 12, 2014, https://chroniclevitae.com/news/330-new-game-new-rules?cid=vem [pp. 63-66 in the present volume].

lecturers or researchers, and finally adjuncts. Kelly Baker wrote about how this hierarchy determines worth. Her publication and teaching records were not acknowledged simply because of her position as an adjunct, further limiting her opportunities to advance in the profession.[33] Baker recognized her personal need to step away, to reassess her place and identity within and apart from the system.

While some writers have attempted to offer concrete solutions to the labor crisis,[34] most only offer anecdotal criticism. Rebecca Schuman begged readers not to go to grad school in the first place, while Katie Rose Guest Pryal chastised those who embrace lamentation rather than substantive critique: "The academy doesn't need encomiums or casseroles. It needs practical labor critiques. Or there will be no insiders left."[35] Pryal's exhortation is necessary, but it misses the purpose and need for quit lit.

As a genre, quit lit captures a transitional moment of deep anxiety. It offers a way not just to address individual identity shifts, but to redefine a broader academic identity — perhaps even as one with no need of an academy per se. As demonstrated, the value Americans placed on the opportunities higher education afforded were challenged by the campus turmoil of the 1960s. Powerful politicians and business leaders capitalized on that uncertainty to push a cultural narrative that devalued the academy and its faculties. Funding reductions, even during times of economic recovery, created systems that devalued those within it. Historical context may not provide exacting answers, but it can help negotiate the identity response, particularly by demonstrating that this moment is not a result of personal mistakes. As scholars continue to leave, we pour out words of grief over the lost possibilities for individuals and for academe. Maybe, in the end, we are still left with a Shakespearean tragedy, but possibly, through shared lamentations and hopeful transitions, we can (unlike Ophelia) find what we may be.

---

33. Kelly J. Baker, "My Post-Academic Grace Period," *Chronicle Vitae*, November 3, 2013, https://chroniclevitae.com/news/95-my-post-academic-grace-period [pp. 53-54 in the present volume].

34. One such is Howard Gardner, "Two Departures from the Professorate: A World Apart," personal blog, March 27, 2018, https://howardgardner.com/2018/03/27/two-departures-from-the-professoriate-a-world-apart/ [pp. 159-62 in the present volume]. For a critique of Gardner's prescription, see James Van Wyck, "Academia is an Ecosystem, Not a Container: Rethinking (with) Quit Lit," pp. 243-62 in the present volume.

35. Schuman, "Thesis Hatement"; Katie Rose Guest Pryal, "Quit Lit Is about Labor Conditions," *Women in Higher Education*, June 7, 2018, https://www.wihe.com/article-details/74/quit-lit-is-about-labor-conditions/ [pp. 169-73 in the present volume].

References

"Background Facts on Contingent Faculty Positions." American Association of University Professors. https://www.aaup.org/issues/contingency/background-facts

Baker, Kelly. "My Post-Academic Grace Period." *Chronicle Vitae*, November 3, 2013. https://chroniclevitae.com/news/95-my-post-academic-grace-period

Burnett, Jr., O. Lawrence. Review of *Academic Freedom and Academic Anarchy*, by Sidney Hook. *AAUP Bulletin* 56.3 (1970): 334-35.

Burrell, Sidney. "The G.I. Bill and the Great American Transformation, 1945-1967." *Boston University Graduate Journal* 15 (1967): n.p.

Cassuto, Leonard. "The Grief of the Ex-Academic." *Chronicle of Higher Education*, February 25, 2018. https://www.chronicle.com/article/The-Grief-of-the-Ex-Academic/242612

Clauset, Aaron, Samuel Arbesman, and Daniel B. Larremore. "Systematic Inequality and Hierarchy in Faculty Hiring Networks." *Science*, February 12, 2015. https://advances.sciencemag.org/content/advances/1/1/e1400005.full.pdf

Curren, Erik D. "No Openings at This Time: Job Market Collapse and Graduate Education." *Profession* 94 (1994): 57-61.

Fruscione, Joe. "New Game, New Rules." *Chronicle Vitae*, February 12, 2014. https://chroniclevitae.com/news/330-new-game-new-rules?cid=vem

Gardner, Howard. "Two Departures from the Professorate: A World Apart." *Howard Gardner* (personal blog), March 27, 2018. Reposted at The Real World of College, https://www.therealworldofcollege.com/blog/two-departures-from-the-professoriate-a-world-apart

Glazer, Nathan. "What Happened at Berkeley." *Commentary*, February 1965, https://www.commentarymagazine.com/articles/nathan-glazer-2/what-happened-at-berkeley/

Griffey, Trevor. "Decline of Tenure for Higher Education Faculty." Labor and Working-Class History Association, September 2, 2016. https://www.lawcha.org/2016/09/02/decline-tenure-higher-education-faculty-introduction/

Guest Pryal, Katie Rose. "Quit Lit Is about Labor Conditions." *Women in Higher Education*, June 7, 2018. https://www.wihe.com/article-details/74/quit-lit-is-about-labor-conditions/

Harwood, John T. "Nonacademic Job Hunting." *AAUP Bulletin* 60.3 (1974): 313-16.

Hook, Sidney. *Academic Freedom and Academic Anarchy*. New York: Cowles, 1970.

Jacob, Brian, Brian McCall, and Kevin M. Stange. "College as Country Club: Do Colleges Cater to Students' Preferences for Consumption?" Working Paper 18745, National Bureau of Economic Research, January 2013. https://www.nber.org/papers/w18745

Kelsky, Karen. "Death of a Soul (on Campus)." *Tech in Translation*, July 18, 2011. http://techintranslation.com/guest-post-death-of-a-soul-on-campus/

Kendzior, Sarah. "The Closing of American Academia." *Al Jazeera*, August 20, 2012. https://www.aljazeera.com/opinions/2012/8/20/the-closing-of-american-academia/

Lane, Terran. "On Leaving Academe." *Chronicle of Higher Education*, August 19, 2012. https://www.chronicle.com/article/on-leaving-academe/

Lord, Alexandra M. "Location, Location, Location." *Chronicle of Higher Education*, September 12, 2012. https://www.chronicle.com/article/Location-Location-Location/134264/

Lyson, Thomas A., and Gregory D. Squires. "The New Academic Hustle: Marketing a PhD." *American Sociologist* 13 (1978): 233-38.

Ma, Jennifer, Sandy Baum, Matea Pender, and C. J. Libassi. "Trends in College Pricing, 2019." Trends in Higher Education Series. New York: College Board, 2019. https://research.collegeboard.org/pdf/trends-college-pricing-2019-full-report.pdf

Mitchell, Kristina M. W., and Jonathan Martin. "Gender Bias in Student Evaluations." *PS: Political Science and Politics* 51.3 (2018): 648-52.

Moreton, Bethany. *To Serve God and Wal-Mart: The Making of Christian Free Enterprise*. Cambridge, MA: Harvard University Press, 2009.

Olson, Keith W. "The G.I. Bill and Higher Education: Success and Surprise." *American Quarterly* 25.5 (1973): 596-610.

Petriglieri, Jennifer Louise. "Under Threat: Responses to and the Consequences of Threats to Individuals' Identities." *Academy of Management Review* 36.4 (2011): 641-62. https://www.jstor.org/stable/ 41318089

Rothman, Jack. "The Radical Liberal Strategy in Action: Arnold Kaufman and the First Teach-In." *Social Theory and Practice* 2.1 (1972): 33-45, http://www.jstor.org/stable/23556667

Sahlins, Marshall. "The Teach-Ins: Anti-War Protest in the Old Stoned Age." *Anthropology Today* 25.1 (2009): 3-5.

———. "The Teach-Ins Helped Galvanize Student Activism in the 1960s. They Can Do So Again Today." *The Nation*, April 6, 2017. https://www.thenation.com/article/archive/teach-ins-helped-galvanize-student-activism-in-the-1960s-they-can-do-so-again-today/

Schrecker, Ellen. "The Root of the Right-Wing Attack on Higher Education." *Thought and Action* 26 (2010): 71-82.

Schuman, Rebecca. "Thesis Hatement." *Slate*, April 5, 2013. http://www.slate.com/articles/life/culturebox/2013/04/there_are_no_academic_jobs_and_getting_a_ph_d_will_make_you_into_a_horrible.html

Shreve, Grant. "'Quit Lit' Then and Now." *Inside Higher Ed*, April 4, 2018. https://www.insidehighered.com/views/2018/04/04/comparison-quit-lit-1970s-and-today-opinion

Smith, Sidonie. *Manifesto for the Humanities*. Ann Arbor: University of Michigan Press, 2016.

US Senate Committee on the Judiciary, Subcommittee to Investigate the Administration of the Internal Security Act and other Internal Security Laws. "The Anti-Vietnam Agitation and the Teach-In Movement: The Problem of Communist Infiltration and Exploitation." Staff report. Washington, DC: US Government Printing Office, 1965.

Wallis, Todd. "The Rise of Adjunct Faculty: A Brief History." *Inside Scholar*, April 11, 2018. https://insidescholar.org/the-rise-of-adjunct-faculty/

Welsh, Matt. "Why I'm Leaving Harvard." *Matt Welsh* (personal blog), November 15, 2010. http://matt-welsh.blogspot.com/2010/11/why-im-leaving-harvard.html

Academia Is an Ecosystem, Not a Container: Rethinking (with) Quit Lit

James M. Van Wyck

Originally published in earlier form as "Academia is Not a Container," in *Inside Higher Ed*, November 2, 2020

https://www.insidehighered.com/advice/2020/11/02/academia-must-reconsider-its-binary-thinking-and-be-open-new-metaphors-lead-new

WHY IS ACADEMIA persistently described as a space that one can either remain in or else leave, totally and forever? Why are people either in academia or out of it?

First of all, we imagine the academy as a space from force of habit. For most of us, academia started out as a space: a campus. It was a place to go, a place to be, a place to work. Not for nothing do colleges celebrate their campuses as catalysts for community.

Now let's look at the campus space: in its classical form, it's enclosed. So it's something to be in or out of. Our habit of thinking about academia as a space derives from the nature of the physical space it so often occupies. Why does this matter? Because when we talk about higher education in spatial terms, our habitual descriptions – beginning with choices as simple as the prepositional phrases we use – reflect and perpetuate many of our current problems with doctoral preparation.

Like the physical campus, the figurative space of academia is enclosed. Sometimes it's even walled off entirely. One tightly closed-off area of academia is the academic job market, whose terms and practices are rife with spatially oriented language. The academic job market's guiding job term is the "tenure track," which someone is either on or off.

We're also prone to describe academia in ways that create space between the academy and other arenas. There are careers *in* academia and those *outside* academia. People *leave* academia, or *remain in* academia. Still others are *beyond* the tenure track or academia itself – which is a better, more positive descriptor, but still a spatially bound concept.

We're also prone – especially in the humanities and humanistic social sciences – to describe research contributions in terms of "the field," as in "Professor Jones retires after changing the way we see the field." The authors of the bitingly funny *Keywords; : For Further Consideration and Particularly Relevant to Academic Life, &c.* note that in

> the wonderland of Academia, a *field* is a veritable Alice, which is to say, an entity with variable dimensions when measured against subjects and disciplines.... The coded assumption of territoriality reinforces speculation that, in fact, an academic field is a deceptively hospitable habitat for competitive gazelles engaged in eternal inter- and intra-generational conflict over circumscribed tracts of grassland.[1]

Spatially bound metaphors and language persist in the quit-lit genre, too, including essays in this volume. Here are a few examples.

When we think spatially, we often do so in ways that restrict rather than free. In "Jailbreaking My Academic Career," Jessica Collier writes about "breaking out once you're in."[2] If you're like me, maybe you last used the term "jailbreaking" when talking about reprogramming a cell phone to allow it to do more than the manufacturer wanted – in short, to expand its capabilities rather than exchange them for a completely different set. That seems like a great way to describe a PhD's relationship to academia. But the idea of "breaking out once you're in" seems more focused on the idea of physical escape. Collier later describes it as "breaking from academia." In general, the tendency is to describe academic worlds as decidedly and spatially different from worlds beyond the academy. Joseph Conley describes a "transition into the 'real' world," as well as "life on the other side" and finally describes a place called "adjunct purgatory."[3]

---

1. A Community of Inquiry, *Keywords; : For Further Consideration and Particularly Relevant to Academic Life, &c.* (Princeton, NJ: Princeton University Press, 2018), 29-30 (emphasis mine).

2. Jessica Collier, "Jailbreaking My Academic Career," *Medium*, April 23, 2013, https://medium.com/altac-chronicles/jailbreaking-my-academic-career-3ec7b0fe1671 [pp. 47-51 in the present volume].

3. Joseph Conley, "Just Another Piece of Quit Lit," *Chronicle of Higher Education*, March 8, 2018, https://www.chronicle.com/article/Just-Another-Piece-of-Quit-Lit/242756 [pp. 103-6 in the present volume].

The spatial imagery often operates in very personal ways. In "My Post-Academic Grace Period," Kelly J. Baker (who is editor of "Women *in* Higher Education," emphasis mine) writes first of "walk[ing] away from academia" but later revises this to a "year hiatus from the academy" after which she "can decide to walk away."[4] In between these two spatially driven conceptions of the academy comes much different – and more fruitful – language: "I can decide if there is anything that I will miss about academic life. I can decide to take the parts I like (research and writing) and apply them to other careers." It is this modular thinking that seems to have led to Baker's blended career.

Our usage of spatial imagery often has personal and psychological dimensions. Constantina Katsari, for example, describes her "decision to leave" as a struggle that lasted for quite some time before she "took the first step towards freedom." Later, she describes "escap[ing] the ivory tower." Joe Fruscione writes about "fe[eling] wistful about the prospect of leaving the profession I worked so hard – and spent so much money – to enter." L. Maren Wood writes compellingly about the moment when "we decide we can no longer afford – financially or psychologically – to stay in a system that has no room for us." Erin Bartram writes that quit lit reflects "the way we insulate ourselves from grappling with what it means for dozens, hundreds, thousands of our colleagues to leave the field.... Those left behind ... don't often write about what it means to lose friends and colleagues."[5]

At the outset of this chapter, I listed a few ways that we're inclined to use spatial imagery when describing the academy—and work that somehow occurs "within" academe. Writing in response to Bartram's essay (as well as that of Matt Welsh), Howard Gardner calls it "tragic" that "Bartram is one of thousands of trained scholars who never get the opportunity to teach students who want to learn and to add their own bricks – small and not so small – to the edifice of knowledge in their chosen field of study."[6] Of Matt

4. Kelly J. Baker, "My Post-Academic Grace Period," *Chronicle Vitae*, November 5, 2013, https://chroniclevitae.com/news/95-my-post-academic-grace-period [pp. 53-54 in the present volume].

5. Constantina Katsari, "Leaving Academia: 'I Can Offer More to the Public Outside University System'," *Guardian*, November 22, 2013, https://www.theguardian.com/higher-education-network/blog/2013/nov/22/leaving-academia-life-beyond-university [pp. 61-62 in the present volume]; Joe Fruscione, "New Game, New Rules," *Chronicle Vitae*, February 12, 2014, https://chroniclevitae.com/news/330-new-game-new-rules [pp. 63-66 in the present volume]; L. Maren Wood, "Walking Away from Academia When It Was Your Dream Job," Beyond the Professoriate, n.d., https://beyondprof.com/walking-away-from-academia-when-it-was-your-dream-job; Erin Bartram, "The Sublimated Grief of the Left Behind," *Erin Bartram* (personal blog), February 11, 2018, http://erinbartram.com/uncategorized/the-sublimated-grief-of-the-left-behind [pp. 97-101 in the present volume].

6. Howard Gardner, "Two Departures from the Professoriate: A World Apart," *Howard*

Welsh, Gardner writes: "he is [now] working for private industry – admittedly having lots of fun, perhaps doing some good, but the more cynical would say that he has 'gone over to the dark side.'" If Gardner isn't cynical, he's at least skeptical, and his language here suggests he finds "having lots of fun" something that is viewed as a kind of confession, rather than a positive benefit of a workplace environment. (More about Gardner below.)

When we describe academia – and the work scholars do – using spatial imagery, we endorse an imagined separation of worlds. That separation is a pernicious construct: it creates a world within opposed to a world outside. Or to put it more bluntly, it leads to separatism: us and them.

This binary thinking separates academia from society at large and hinders us from imagining ourselves in a productive relation to that wider society. We need to exchange this binary for new, more capacious metaphors. New metaphors will liberate us to think about new practices. Academia is not one world but many intersecting and overlapping ones – and we need new ways to inhabit them together.

I propose that we examine carefully the ways we describe academia – and our relationships with it. In the next section of this essay, I argue that spatially derived metaphors have stunted the ways we imagine ourselves to connect with academia. Then I look in the following section to the boldest, most imaginative quit-lit essays for how we might exchange well-worn metaphors for new terms, new metaphors, and new practices and ways of inhabiting the complex, intersecting worlds that make up academia – and more important, the lived experiences of those in graduate school. Their experiences require new language, and new policies and procedures with it.

Academia Is Not a Container

I quoted Howard Gardner's response to Erin Bertram and Matt Welsh in the previous section. Let's look a bit more at his reaction.

Gardner asks, apparently sincerely, what is to be done? Gardner puts forward a suggestion for solving the problems of people either quitting the professoriate, or not making it in at all. One way? Adopt the European model of separating research and pedagogy through the institute and lectureship model:

> But there is a better way, though I have to admit it is no longer the American way: an agreed-upon bargain between our higher-degree-awarding institutions and our talented students who want to be

Gardner (personal blog), March 27, 2018, https://howardgardner.com/2018/03/27/two-departures-from-the-professoriate-a-world-apart [pp. 159-62 in the present volume].

> teachers *and* scholars. If our institutions train you to be a skilled scholar and teacher, you commit to giving back—to staying within the professoriate, barring unusual circumstances. (Presumably Welsh could even come to like, to cherish his Harvard undergraduates.) Conversely, if we take you on as a student and you complete the requirements successfully, we commit to providing a job which makes use of your talents. If that means radically reducing the number of doctorates in history or in Romance languages, better to do so "up front" than to hold out the false hope of a job – and in the process, ensuring many repetitions of Erin Bartram's sad saga.

Let's focus on a few phrases from the "better way" Gardner proposes. The first is his implied definition of "the professoriate" that PhDs would somehow have to solemnly covenant not to leave. But earlier in his essay he writes about "hundreds of young scholars – primarily in the humanities and the 'softer' social sciences" who cannot find "a full-time tenure-track position."

In a list of potential outcomes, Gardner ends with this doozy of a descriptor:

> some, and one could even call them "lucky," end up teaching at a second- or third-tier school, or a community college, with a teaching (and perhaps also an advising) load so heavy that there is essentially no chance that they can carry out the scholarship that they were trained to do – and that they presumably want to do.

Gardner's desire that PhDs remain "within the professoriate" means, it would seem, that they must all teach at an elite research university with little to no teaching requirements, or else they are "without the professoriate." Changing one's mind about how to spend the course of one's life after accepting an offer of admission doesn't seem to be an option here.

Such a limited description of the professoriate – a binary that excludes just about everyone except a very few tenured and tenure-track professors at R1 research institutions – is the opposite of what we need. Granting Gardner's belief that there should be a social contract ("an agreed-upon bargain") between both PhD-granting institution and the PhDs they produce, we might say that this variant of the bargain restricts PhDs once again to narrow conceptions of how the life of the mind can be lived in the twenty-first century.

Examining language patterns in this area isn't a theoretical exercise. Ideas have legs, and our terminology encourages those legs to take us down certain paths. As George Lakoff and Mark Johnson remind us in *Metaphors We Live By*, metaphors are not usually ornamental. Rather, "human thought processes are largely metaphorical." Thus it is that metaphors like "the mind is machine" are embedded in phrases we use on a daily basis, like "My mind just isn't operating well today," or "I could see the wheels turning in his head." Another metaphor, "time is money," circulates in phrases like "I can't spare the time" and "You need to budget your time" or even "How did you spend your weekend?"[7]

To Lakoff and Johnson's list of metaphors, we might add another that we reinforce every day: "Academia is a place." Or "academia is a container."

But academia isn't a place or a container. It would in almost every instance be better described as a collection of people. The metaphor of academia as container influences us even when we describe the "academic community," because the current version of academic community too often sounds like another class of container that holds certain people and excludes others. The idea of academia as container doesn't capture the interconnected and overlapping relationships that individuals have had with higher education in the past, present and future. (Allow me to pose a quick thought experiment: Was/is Ralph Waldo Emerson "in" academia? Was/is Mikhail Bakhtin?)

To reimagine academia for the twenty-first century, we need new metaphors to describe its variegated nature. Here's a suggestion: let's conceive of the academy and the worlds it intersects with as an ecosystem. Doing so allows us more readily to imagine careers that blend academia and other sectors, and find descriptors worthy of them.

We need to rethink our terms because the language we use closely relates to our personal and collective attitudes toward professional development. In the particular case of graduate education, we need to be more attentive to how we describe what PhDs do.

The metaphors we're looking for can't and should not always be spatially derived. There are plenty of better metaphors. Look to the world of music, in which harmonies can produce overtones, and in which notes can be discrete but also blended.

Each discipline should build a vocabulary around career and professional development that is more capacious. We especially need to stop characterizing careers as in or out, and simply describe them as they are.

Such a change would simply meet reality. All signs point to more blended careers for PhDs, who will hold administrative as well as teaching positions, or move between higher education and other employers. Such

7. George Lakoff and Mark Johnson, *Metaphors We Live By* (Chicago: University of Chicago Press, 2008), 8-29.

careers feature not binaries or barriers, but interwoven communities and overlapping ecosystems, with people and community – not spaces – prioritized.

This is a matter of language, and also of the actual lived experience of graduate students and graduate alumni. Describing academia differently allows graduate students to rethink their approach to their own graduate training, their relationship to the academy, and the ways that preparing for multiple outcomes is not just "professorial preparation, plus other stuff."

A change in language will open our minds toward how we think about graduate training, the skills and competencies graduate students acquire during it, and the ways we think about our careers. If you think about your training differently, you may shape it differently for yourself.

Rethinking (with) Quit-Lit Essays

There is, I propose, a relationship between the genre of quit lit and our habit of thinking of academia as a container. We might even argue that thinking about academia in spatialist ways helps produce the conditions and mindsets that necessitate a genre like quit lit.

Space hasn't permitted me (pun intended, sadly) to look at each of the essays within this volume, but in what follows I reference a few more of them – as well as some not included in this volume – and attempt to outline lessons they teach us, lessons that may help us eventually make quit lit a short-lived genre. After all, when we have all moved past the idea that academia is a container, academia won't be something to leave forever, it'll be a part of a range of options that presents itself to PhDs at a variety of points in their careers.

Be wary of the "just don't go" to graduate school arguments that many quit-lit essays espouse.

One of the best essays on the dangers of blanket "just don't go" essays comes from Tressie McMillan Cottom, who wrote a post on her website entitled "Blanket 'Don't Go to Graduate School!' Advice Ignores Race and Reality?" In the post, she notes with trademarked clarity that "maybe too many people are going to graduate school but not too many of all people are going to graduate school."[8]

Many nuanced arguments can and have been made for those consider-

8. Tressie McMillan Cottom, "Blanket 'Don't Go to Graduate School' Advice Ignores Race and Reality?" *Tressie McMillan Cottom* (personal blog), April 6, 2013, https://tressiemc.com/uncategorized/blanket-dont-go-to-graduate-school-advice-ignores-race-and-reality

ing graduate school. My hope is that, as reforms within scholarly associations, institutions, and individual departments continue to mature, we will move past blanket "just don't go" advice – particularly from those who hold tenure-track jobs, as they are often least suited to making these kinds of declarations. Society needs what PhDs can offer now more than ever, so let's be leery of instinctively steering prospective PhDs away from graduate school. It seems to me that this kind of advice is best given on a personal, one-on-one level, and not en masse.

Give humanities and social science PhDs the same ability to move in and out of professorships as science and engineering PhDs often have.

Matt Welsh's blogpost – "Why I'm leaving Harvard" – written when he announced he was resigning his tenured faculty job at Harvard to take up a post at Google – shows very clearly the ways that for many PhDs in the sciences, academia isn't a space to be in or out of, but rather a career choice that one can leave and occasionally return to with much more ease than in the humanities or social sciences.[9] (Since the essay's publication, Welsh has also worked at the Seattle-based startup Xnor.ai as well as Apple and OctoML.) This type of flexibility is possible in the humanities – I'm thinking of one of my former professors who has taken up the presidency of a foundation. Another example is the career of Ann Kirschner, currently on the faculty at CUNY, whose circuitous path and entrepreneurial deployment of her PhD in English is perhaps the boldest vision of career fluidity.

Terran Lane's essay "On Leaving Academe" gives a litany of reasons one might quit the academy – the essay's sections are "making a difference," "work-life imbalance," "centralization of authority and decrease of autonomy," "budget climate," "hyperspecialization, insularity, and narrowness of vision," "poor incentives," "mass production of education," "salaries," and "anti-intellectualism, anti-education, and attacks on science and academe." Lane's reasons for leaving academe point provide a clear list of areas that need to be improved.[10] One area that doesn't seem as problematic for Lane is the either/or choice often faced by humanists and social scientists as they consider "quitting" academia.

Lane concludes their essay by noting that the choice to leave – it was a

---

9. Matt Welsh, "Why I'm Leaving Harvard," *Matt Welsh* (personal blog), November 15, 2010, http://matt-welsh.blogspot.com/2010/11/why-im-leaving-harvard.html [pp. 19-22 in the present volume].

10. Terran Lane, "On Leaving Academe," *Chronicle of Higher Education*, August 19, 2012, https://www.chronicle.com/article/on-Leaving-Academe/133717 [pp. 29-34 in the present volume].

choice in this case – is neither permanent nor constrained:

> Nor am I necessarily done with academe forever. I'm going to give the industry track a try for a while, but I could well find myself back in higher education in the future. There are certainly many things I still find beautiful and joyful about faculty work. In the interim, I will look for other ways to contribute to society, other ways to help educate the future, and other ways to change the world.

And Lane's essay again reminds us that – at least for now – career flexibility means something different for computer scientists than it does for historians or English PhDs.

Create a flexible model for engaging PhDs beyond the tenure track so that our best minds can teach and research without always moving to locations that don't work for them.

While academia isn't a space, most universities and colleges exist in very real, very fixed locations. One of my favorite pieces of quit lit was written by Alexandra M. Lord. In "Location, Location, Location," she brings together the spatial and attitudinal dispositions that can hamstring careers and warp affections. Lord notes that

> academe is ... a culture in which those who leave are often treated with disdain.... Which is why it rankles now when I hear people urge graduate students to "try the academic job in the place they never dreamed of living" or when I read a piece telling PhDs to "embrace their inner North Dakotan." That is poor advice for most people, especially when it comes couched in an assumption that the failure to be "open-minded" in one's job search is a professional or even moral failing.[11]

Like Lord, Karen Kelsky also left a position in academia. The location dynamic was at work here as well: "my partner and I made a joint decision. If she found a job back in our beloved Pacific Northwest good enough to support the family, I would leave behind academic work entirely."[12]

---

11. Alexandra Lord, "Location, Location, Location," *Chronicle of Higher Education*, September 12, 2012, https://www.chronicle.com/article/Location-Location-Location/134264 [pp. 35-40 in the present volume].

12. Karen Kelsky, "Death of a Soul (On Campus)," *Tech in Translation*, July 18, 2011,

If navigating the pandemic has taught us anything, it is that many jobs can be done remotely, and that includes certain kinds of teaching. This need not mean that we shift entirely to a virtual environment, as short, intensive seminars can be scheduled to allow for PhDs to parachute into an institution to deliver a course in a time frame that allows them to maintain their life elsewhere. And technology certainly allows for us to create palimpsestuous courses and seminars, which would allow for cohorts of graduate students to share lessons and findings with those who follow.

Likewise, we need to use technology to ensure that opportunities, strategies, feedback, and so many other aspects of graduate education that are often shared by word of mouth are now shared in more equitable ways. Opportunities for funding, access to feedback, ratings of PhD advisors – these are all areas in which information can be much more legibly circulated provided we think through the user experience and the technologies that would allow such information to reach those considering graduate school, as well as those navigating the various stages of doctoral training.

Reform careers for PhDs to allow for differing strengths and interests to be accommodated in colleges and universities.

We can do this work by asking PhDs to create career portfolios that would work for them, not by asking them to fit into outmoded categories.

Howard Gardner's essay – quoted at length earlier – notes that Europe has long deployed a dual approach to the job of a professor that he suggests we consider in the US, namely divorcing research and teaching responsibilities. Give research to one group, teaching to another. Neat and tidy.

But such a hewing asunder of teaching and research approaches things from the needs of the institution, and not from the perspective of the twenty-first-century labor market, in which many of us expect more from our employment than did someone in, say, 1843. Here, the American Association of University Professors' (AAUP) report on *Tenure and Teaching-Intensive Appointments* is instructive: their 2010 guidance notes that "*the best practice for institutions of all types is to convert the status of contingent appointments to appointments eligible for tenure with only minor changes in job description*," meaning that those with teaching as the central component of their workload should be tenure-eligible based primarily on their work as teachers.[13] Importantly, the AAUP guidance includes the following coda:

http://techintranslation.com/guest-post-death-of-a-soul-on-campus [pp. 23-28 in the present volume].

13. American Association of University Professors [AAUP], Committee on Contingency and the Profession, *Tenure and Teaching-Intensive Appointments*, 2010, https://www.aaup.

In the long run, however, a balance is desirable. Professional development and research activities support strong teaching, and a robust system of shared governance depends upon the participation of all faculty, so even teaching-intensive tenure-eligible positions should include service and appropriate forms of engagement in research or the scholarship of teaching.

Gardner's suggestion that we reach back to the European model also ignores the fact that higher education in the US has its own history, which shapes what people think of it today. In the US, higher education and teaching are indivisible in the popular imagination. The public often sees universities primarily as spaces for undergraduate training, and funds them with this in mind. What's more, those who would occupy today's teaching and research positions have more diverse needs, interests, and commitments than the professoriate of the past. To hew to a system designed for a largely homogenous group would be simply unjust. We need to resist the desire to approach new kinds of tenured positions in any way that starts with the needs of university systems that are rooted in medieval organizational patterns.

We would do well to flip the ways we think about careers within universities and colleges: *how might the academy get better at accommodating and benefiting from the strengths and interests of PhDs, rather than creating a raft of nearly identical positions – some with security, others mercilessly contingent?*

Here Jessica Collier's realization is particularly instructive. She writes in "Jailbreaking my Academic Career" that

> a year or two ago, I realized that I did not self-identify as a teacher.... When I thought about my occupation, however, my mind reverted to "writer." Working with words is intensely difficult – anyone who tells you otherwise is probably not very good at it – and that difficulty for me is analogous to an endorphin rush. All of which is a complicated way of saying that, while teaching is enjoyable, writing makes me happy.

How might academia create jobs to retain someone like Dr. Collier? How do we create spaces for someone who, not finding academia receptive to her entrepreneurial and leadership skill sets, has gone on instead to be the

org/report/tenure-and-teaching-intensive-appointments; emphasis in original.

CEO of Spot, and to co-found All Turtles, a mission-driven product studio? As Collier notes,

> the world is smarter than academics are trained to believe. In my best moments in private industry so far, the work is stimulating, challenging, intense. It is akin to the best parts of academic life: the moment that you bust through a knotty argument in a chapter or talk, the collegial swelling as strong minds come together at a conference.

How do we create jobs and careers within academia that take the "moments" Collier describes and extend them?

My worry here is that if we keep losing entrepreneurial PhDs (either because they haven't applied in the first place, or because academia isn't accommodating their skill set and inclinations) we will never have the diverse range of faculty and para-faculty university employees to come alongside graduate students to mentor them into this new moment for the PhD.

We won't have real reform until we listen to PhDs who have made it in other careers and industries.

Reimagining humanities and social science PhD programs will be most effective when we center voices like Kelsky, Lord, and many, many others who have quit – but clearly still have a vested interest in academe's overhaul. That's because their perspectives are more nimble, more attuned to circumstances within startup worlds, within government, and within all the various fields that they interact with.

It bears mentioning that most museums, research libraries, and major foundations and nonprofits related to the humanities, social sciences, education, and the arts are led by PhDs. And PhDs in these roles are often faculty, or were for years before – like Elizabeth Alexander, prior to becoming president of the Andrew W. Mellon Foundation, or like Daniel Weiss, prior to taking the helm of the Metropolitan Museum of Art. In 2011 Anthony Marx, a Princeton PhD in politics, professor, and erstwhile president of Amherst College, became the president and CEO of the New York Public Library.

Increasingly, PhDs may turn to para-academic careers without ever going the faculty route. Will Fenton, a 2018 Fordham PhD in English, continues to engage with his dissertation field, early American literature, first as the director of research and public programs at the Library Company of Philadelphia, and now as program officer in the Office of Challenge Programs at the National Endowment for the Humanities. Similarly, John Paul

Christy, a 2010 University of Pennsylvania PhD in classics, remains involved with academic professional development and public scholarship as senior director at the American Council of Learned Societies. And Nathanial Peters, a Boston College PhD in historical theology, continues to engage with students and intellectual life as director of the Morningside Institute in coordination with Columbia University and Riverside Church.

Of course, the fields of publishing, journalism, and media are a natural fit for PhDs who have demonstrated expertise in research, writing, editing, and project management.[14] For example, we might look to Kameron Collins, a Princeton English PhD and current film critic at *Rolling Stone;* Michael Dirda, a Cornell English PhD, Pulitzer-Prize winner, and longtime book reviewer at *The Washington Post*; and David Zurawik, a University of Maryland PhD in media studies and TV and media critic at *The Baltimore Sun* since 1989. In publishing, PhDs of note include Anette Bickmeyer, a University of Hanover (Germany) PhD in English, American studies, and history and program director at Bertelsmann (owner of Penguin Random House). Nicole Gervasio, a Columbia PhD in English, has also found an avenue that runs parallel to the academy as manager of the PEN America Literary Festival and Public Programs.

For examples of PhDs who have found purpose and success beyond the academy, we might also look to private industry and consulting. Maria Bezaitis, a Duke University PhD in French literature and senior principal engineer at Intel, discusses the merits of thinking across disciplinary boundaries in her TED Talk, "Why We Need Strangeness."[15] In the consulting space, Kevin Stevens, a Fordham PhD in English, applies project management skills honed while writing a dissertation to his role as advisory manager at Deloitte. Brendon Reay, a Stanford PhD in classics, is a principal at HarbourHouse Partners, a financial services consultancy.[16]

When you connect with enough PhDs beyond the academy, it becomes

14. PhDs in journalism can transform the organizations they join and help lead. For example, in 2017, Columbia English PhD Radhika Jones became editor-in-chief of *Vanity Fair* and has enhanced the publication's already literary reputation by increasing engagement with con-temporary authors – in particular Black authors like Ta-Nehisi Coates, who guest-edited the September 2020 issue.

15. Maria Bezaitis, "Why We Need Strangeness," TED, 7:47, April 2013, https://www.ted.com/talks/maria_bezaitis_why_we_need_strangeness

16. A particularly intriguing consulting opportunity for academics seeking to apply their research chops is ReD Associates, a boutique firm with offices in New York City and Copenhagen that seeks to bring the perspectives of social scientists to bear on issues in business, branding, and marketing. The majority of ReD Associates employees and leadership have advanced degrees in the humanities and social sciences, including Camillo de Vivanco, an Oxford PhD in comparative literature and a New York City-based manager at ReD.

abundantly clear that there are many ways for PhDs to remain connected to research and scholarship. Just as importantly, there are many ways – most of them currently untapped – for these PhDs to help reimagine graduate education.

How do we harness this collective experience? Let's start by adding a PhD working beyond the professoriate as a supplemental advisor who can advise on extra-academic concerns – ideally in concert with the academic advisor, and, when appropriate, adding them to dissertation committees. Given the numbers of PhDs who currently hold jobs beyond the tenure track, this won't be difficult. Finding ways to recognize the labor of these PhDs will likely prove an issue, but my sense is that re-engaging PhDs beyond the tenure track will have a variety of positive impacts, including but not limited to the donation of time, talent, and in some cases, money.

Let's find more ways for scholars to teach and publish.

We've seen from quit-lit essays in this volume that part-time tenure-track positions do exist. Expanding them, both in number and flexibility (a half-time tenure track, or a quarter-time tenure track), could allow for PhDs to re-engage in the teaching and research life of universities and colleges. Currently, the prestige economy – shaped in part by *U.S. News & World Report* and other rankings – limits the use of these positions at most "elite" institutions, one of many structural barriers that inhibit systemic, sustained change in the academy.

But we also need ways to keep scholars not on the tenure track engaged with the academic community. Hosting guest lectureships for PhDs beyond the academy would add options for PhDs working part time or full time beyond the tenure track to keep their hands in the teaching and research mission of universities and colleges. Make no mistake: PhDs beyond the academy have much to offer. Take the case of Natalie Berkman, a Princeton PhD whose own quit-lit piece ("The Stigma of Silence") outlines her search for multiple kinds of positions post-PhD, and her ultimate choice of a job in Paris, where she works as *directrice pédagogique* (academic manager) at SAE Institute Paris, a leading educator in creative media industries.[17] She continues to produce academic work such as her award-winning monograph *OuLiPo and the Mathematics of Literature*.[18]

PhDs like Natalie Berkman are ideal partners for reimagining and

17. Natalie Berkman, "The Stigma of Silence," Connected Academics, September 11, 2018, https://connect.mla.hcommons.org/the-stigma-of-silence

18. Berkman, *OuLiPo and the Mathematics of Literature* (Oxford, UK: Peter Lang, forthcoming).

retooling the programs and opportunities that will equip PhDs for a range of opportunities, including but not limited to:

- other experiential learning opportunities for PhD students, such as my own institution's (Princeton) GradFUTURES Social Impact Fellowship program, which places fellows at institutions including XPRIZE, New America, and the American Society on Aging;
- exposure to and validation of a range of careers while in PhD programs, including the integration of graduate alumni into the lives of departments and graduate schools via profiles, meetups, and mentorship programs;[19]
- ensuring graduate student fluency with LinkedIn, creating personal websites, navigating job boards, networking, and other professional development essentials.

Increasingly, professional development is bridging the academy and the worlds supposedly divorced from it. One compelling example in the entrepreneurship domain is the Princeton Startup Bootcamp, a recent initiative in which graduate students and postdocs worked on entrepreneurial ventures in very early stages of development. Each participant benefited from mentorship and feedback from seasoned founders, and the experience culminated in a pitch competition, with a $10,000 prize. Lucy Partman, a 2021 Princeton PhD (art and archeology) notes that "one of the key reasons I took part in the bootcamp was to work with people from different disciplines. I believe deeply in the potential of interdisciplinary work, which is something we often talk about conceptually in academia. I think that it really can and does happen in the entrepreneurial space."[20]

Participants in these kinds of programs — whether they land tenure-track jobs or turn to other careers — are poised to be better, more informed advisers for graduate and undergraduate students alike. Because of an experience that stretches them outside of a typical PhD's preparation, they can themselves imagine a greater range of flexible ways to engage with the departments, graduate programs, and institutions they will serve. PhDs who are equipped with a range of experiences in graduate school need to be pro-

19. Princeton's GradFUTURES initiative provides examples of all these kinds of alumni engagement; see https://gradfutures.princeton.edu.

20. Quoted in Wright Señeres, "New Princeton-Techstars Boot Camp Boosts Entrepreneurship for Grad Students and Postdocs," Princeton Innovation, March 10, 2021, https://innovation.princeton.edu/news/2021/new-princeton-techstars-bootcamp-boosts-entrepreneurship-grad-students-and-postdocs

vided with ways – even if only in stretches of their careers – to teach, research, and shape the future of the academy.

Let's reimagine how we circulate the knowledge produced in a PhD.

My advisor and I have remained close, post-PhD. We write together, edit each other's work, and connect regularly for meals and phone calls. We recently had a conversation about who reads dissertations. When I was dissertating, he told me (and wrote in *The Chronicle of Higher Education*) that few people read dissertations. This was supposed to allay my anxieties about the process. And to a certain degree it did. But that was when we both felt that the dissertation would – in a few short years – turn into a book published by a university press. That's not likely to happen for some time now, if it ever does.

The good news is that knowledge produced by PhDs has never been as accessible as it is now. In researching this essay, I found the introduction to Erin Bartram's dissertation on her website. The arguments it outlines are helping me a great deal. I'm also reviewing a book for an academic journal, and the content of Bartram's dissertation deals directly with the book's central arguments. I mentioned Natalie Berkman's monograph earlier: it is by no means the only book published by an academic press that is written by someone who has "quit" academia. As Michael McGandy notes, "PhDs on career tracks beyond the academy, because they are in jobs that connect them to the media, public programming, and policy and outreach professionals who can promote and disseminate their work, are oftentimes more likely to command sizeable readerships."[21]

For these and many other reasons, we need to think less about embargoing the knowledge in dissertations – though in some cases this is of course important – and more about creating openly accessible dissertations that touch a range of audiences while and after the dissertation is being produced. The dissertation, now more than ever, needs to have a public life. So much of what is lost when someone "quits" academia is the knowledge generated in a dissertation. Let's solve that problem.

We need to deal with the emotional aspects of graduate training.

It's tricky to write about quit lit. I see much of myself and my emotions in many of the essays. And those that I disagree with are written by real people,

21. Michael J. McGandy, "Diverse Careers, the Waning of the Prestige Regime, and the Rise of the Influence Economy in Academy Publishing," in *The Reimagined PhD: Navigating 21st Century Humanities Education*, ed. Leanne M. Horinko, Jordan M. Reed, and James M. Van Wyck (New Brunswick, NJ: Rutgers University Press, 2021), 24.

who, when they wrote the essays, were going through an emotionally charged time.

Erin Bartram's essay is so well known in academic circles that she has an entire section of her website dedicated to "Responses to That Piece." And rightfully so. "The Sublimated Grief of the Left Behind" deserves (and will continue to deserve) our attention and respect.

One of the reasons Bartram's essay resonates is its emotion. Leonard Cassuto describes its "beautiful rendering of her sadness" in one of the many responses to the essay. Gardner describes it as a "soul-searching evocative piece."[22] Significantly, even writing that challenges quit lit's propensity for grand gestures does so in language that harnesses, generates, and releases emotion. Katie Roiphe's "Thesis Defense," dubbed an "odious rebuttal" to "Thesis Hatement," describes Schuman's essay as a jeremiad, and then a "polemic."[23] But the essays aren't antithetical, and both Roiphe and Schuman (and Bartram, and many others) have found ways to fashion careers that still intersect with the work of traditional academics on a regular basis.

Those who wrote some of the best quit-lit pieces didn't leave academia, exactly. Or perhaps it's better to say that they've refashioned a place within an ecosystem that we need to recognize as connected to, informing, and compatible with an expanded definition of what "academia" is and can be. For example, as of this writing Bartram works in public history as school programs coordinator at the Mark Twain House and Museum.

| | |

If we resist the tendency to think about the academy using spatial imagery — or at least adapt more fluid language and more expansive metaphors — what can be gained? Non-spatial thinking means jettisoning a lot of what we've inherited and thinking more creatively. It also means connecting this recalibration to other ways we're limiting the PhD.

For example, consider the phrase "going to graduate school," with all of its implications about uprooting your life and committing to a course of full-time study. What would the PhD look like if it were unmoored from time-bound considerations such as semesters? What if the best PhD programs adapted strategies now practiced primarily by for-profit and often predatory institutions, providing working professionals the opportunity to earn a PhD

22. Leonard Cassuto, "The Grief of the Ex-Academic," *Chronicle of Higher Education*, February 25, 2018, https://www.chronicle.com/article/The-Grief-of-the-Ex-Academic/242612 [pp. 149-53 in the present volume]; Gardner, "Two Departures."

23. Katie Roiphe, "Thesis Defense," *Slate*, April 8, 2013, https://slate.com/human-interest/2013/04/a-literature-ph-d-is-not-a-waste-of-time.html

on a schedule that works for them? In my professional development role with the Princeton Graduate School, I've worked with an increasing number of PhD students who begin their programs with prior experience in public historical venues or other jobs that connect directly with the public. How many more PhDs would choose to maintain these jobs if a part-time PhD wasn't something looked at with suspicion? Again, institutions may be inhibited by the current ways we judge and rank PhD programs: any dip in time to degree would hurt a program's rankings. But this needn't sink the idea: adjusting the metrics to include part-time PhDs would take some doing, but it could be done. And this needn't be a one-size-fits-all approach: part-time and flexible ways of doing a PhD will work better for some institutions, not at all for others.

We're right to decry silos and ivory towers, both as metaphors and as reflections of practices we've clung to as academics. Often-rehearsed narratives that build on these metaphors occlude possibilities for us all—for particular institutions, programs, and individuals. Instead of "tracks" let's think about variegated career paths that branch and intersect. Instead of debating whether or not "alt-ac" is a viable way of capturing a slew of career trajectories (it doesn't come close, I'd say) let's use bespoke titles and talk specifics.

Let's create modular experiences and develop the requisite language to describe these experiences. In doing so, we'll honor the trailblazers with PhDs who found careers of all kinds – mostly with little attention from their departments and institutions. And we'll start to unmake the conditions that made quit lit: the conditions that have led so many PhDs whose careers have not followed a single, hyper-specialized trajectory (let's call it the tenure track) to enact a public declaration of their existential separation from the academy.

But they are the academy. And so am I.

References

American Association of University Professors [AAUP], Committee on Contingency and the Profession. *Tenure and Teaching-Intensive Appointments*. 2010. https://www.aaup.org/report/tenure-and-teaching-intensive-appointments

Baker, Kelly J. "My Post-Academic Grace Period." *Chronicle Vitae*, November 5, 2013. https://chroniclevitae.com/news/95-my-post-academic-grace-period

Bartram, Erin. "The Sublimated Grief of the Left Behind." *Erin Bartram* (personal blog), February 11, 2018. http://erinbartram.com/uncategorized/the-sublimated-grief-of-the-left-behind

Berkman, Natalie. *OuLiPo and the Mathematics of Literature*. Oxford, UK: Peter Lang, forthcoming.

———. "The Stigma of Silence." Connected Academics, September 11, 2018, https://connect.mla.hcommons.org/the-stigma-of-silence

Bezaitis, Maria. "Why We Need Strangeness." TED. 7:47. April 2013. https://www.ted.com/talks/maria_bezaitis_why_we_need_strangeness

Cassuto, Leonard. "The Grief of the Ex-Academic." *Chronicle of Higher Education*, February 25, 2018. https://www.chronicle.com/article/The-Grief-of-the-Ex-Academic/ 242612

Collier, Jessica. "Jailbreaking My Academic Career." *Medium*, April 23, 2013. https://medium.com/altac-chronicles/jailbreaking-my-academic-career-3ec7b0fe1671

Community of Inquiry, A. *Keywords; : For Further Consideration and Particularly Relevant to Academic Life, &c.* Princeton, NJ: Princeton University Press, 2018.

Conley, Joseph. "Just Another Piece of Quit Lit." *Chronicle of Higher Education*, March 8, 2018. https://www.chronicle.com/article/Just-Another-Piece-of-Quit-Lit/242756

Fruscione, Joe. "New Game, New Rules." *Chronicle Vitae*, February 12, 2014. https://chroniclevitae.com/news/330-new-game-new-rules

Gardner, Howard. "Two Departures from the Professoriate: A World Apart." *Howard Gardner* (personal blog), March 27, 2018. https://howardgardner.com/2018/03/27/two-departures-from-the-professoriate-a-world-apart

Katsari, Constantina. "Leaving Academia: 'I Can Offer More to the Public Outside University System'." *The Guardian*, November 22, 2013. https://www.theguardian.com/higher-education-network/blog/2013/nov/22/leaving-academia-life-beyond-university

Kelsky, Karen. "Death of a Soul (On Campus)." *Tech in Translation*, July 18, 2011. http://techintranslation.com/guest-post-death-of-a-soul-on-campus

Lakoff, George, and Mark Johnson. *Metaphors We Live By*. Chicago: University of Chicago Press, 2003.

Lane, Terran. "On Leaving Academe." *Chronicle of Higher Education*, August 19, 2012. https://www.chronicle.com/article/on-Leaving-Academe/133717

Lord, Alexandra. "Location, Location, Location." *Chronicle of Higher Education*, September 12, 2012. https://www.chronicle.com/article/Location-Location-Location/134264

McGandy, Michael J. "Diverse Careers, the Waning of the Prestige Regime, and the Rise of the Influence Economy in Academy Publishing," in *The Reimagined PhD: Navigating 21st Century Humanities Education*, edited by Leanne M. Horinko, Jordan M. Reed, and James M. Van Wyck, 24-41. New Brunswick, NJ: Rutgers University Press, 2021.

McMillan Cottom, Tressie. "Blanket 'Don't Go to Graduate School' Advice Ignores Race and Reality." *Tressie McMillan Cottom* (personal blog), April 6, 2013. https://tressiemc.com/uncategorized/blanket-dont-go-to-graduate-school-advice-ignores-race-and-reality

Roiphe, Katie. "Thesis Defense." *Slate*, April 8, 2013. https://slate.com/human-interest/2013/04/a-literature-ph-d-is-not-a-waste-of-time.html

Señeres, Wright. "New Princeton-Techstars Boot Camp Boosts Entrepreneurship for Grad Students and Postdocs." Princeton Innovation. March 10, 2021. https://innovation.princeton.edu/news/2021/new-princeton-techstars-bootcamp-boosts-entrepreneurship-grad-students-and-postdocs

Welsh, Matt. "Why I'm Leaving Harvard." *Matt Welsh* (personal blog), November 15, 2010. http://matt-welsh.blogspot.com/2010/11/why-im-leaving-harvard.html

Wood, L. Maren. "Walking Away from Academia When It Was Your Dream Job." Beyond the Professoriate. N.d. https://beyondprof.com/walking-away-from-academia-when-it-was-your-dream-job

CONTRIBUTORS

Kelly J. Baker received a PhD in religious studies in 2008. She worked as non-tenure-track faculty, both part time and full time, until 2013, when she became a freelance writer covering religion, higher education, gender, labor, and popular culture. She has written for the *New York Times*, *The Atlantic*, *The Rumpus*, the *Washington Post*, *The Chronicle of Higher Education*, and *Killing the Buddha*. She is the author of five books, including a memoir about leaving the academy, *Grace Period* (2017), and a collection of essays about sexism and labor in higher ed, *Sexism Ed* (2018). Since 2016, she has been an editor of *Women in Higher Education*, and picked up another higher-ed publication, the *National Teaching and Learning Forum*, in 2020. She also co-edited (with Joseph Fruscione) *Succeeding Outside of the Academy* (2018), a collection of essays on alt-ac careers.

Erin Bartram is an independent historian and freelance writer. She earned a PhD in nineteenth-century United States history in 2015, and worked as non-tenure-track faculty until 2018. With Joe Fruscione, she co-edits the series "Rethinking Careers, Rethinking Academia" for the University Press of Kansas, and she is a co-founder and editor of *Contingent* magazine. *Contingent* is written primarily by trained historians working off the tenure track, and is funded entirely by small donations from its readers. She also works a part-time job designing and delivering education programs at the Mark Twain House and Museum in Connecticut.

Leonard Cassuto is a professor of English at Fordham University, and an award-winning journalist who writes on subjects ranging from science to sports, in venues from the *New York Times* to salon.com. He is the author or editor of nine books, most recently (with Robert Weisbuch) *The New PhD: How to Build a Better Graduate Education* (2021). His previous book, *The Graduate School Mess: What Caused It and How We Can Fix It* (2015), was inspired by the monthly column, "The Graduate Adviser," that he writes for *The Chronicle of Higher Education*. Other books include *The Cambridge Companion to Baseball* (2011), winner of the Best Anthology Award from the North American Society of Sports Historians, and *Hard-Boiled Sentimentality: The Secret History of American Crime Stories,* nominated for the Edgar and Macavity Awards and named one of the 10 best books of 2008 in the crime and mystery category by the *Los Angeles Times.*

Jessica Collier is the CEO of Spot, a human resources system for employees to confidentially report discrimination and sexual harassment, and for employers to learn more about the incidents. She was also cofounder of All Turtles, a mission-driven product studio. After she received her PhD in English in 2012, she wrangled words for companies such as Medium and Delicious Monster, before moving into roles in user experience content and design at Stellar.org and Evernote.

Joseph Conley is a technical engineer at Blackbaud, a cloud software company focused on nonprofits, foundations, healthcare organizations, and education institutions. His path there from academia was far from direct, taking in positions as a hospital security officer, a freelance writer, an administrator for the archdiocese of Boston, and an English teacher to international students. He now teaches nonprofit professionals the technical and fundraising skills needed for their organizations to communicate their ideas and identity to clients, customers, and the wider world.

Melissa Dalgleish worked in the Faculty of Graduate Studies while completing her PhD at York University. There she supported students with grants and fellowships, and professional development, as well as carrying out research into higher education careers. With Daniel Powell, she edited the MediaCommons #Alt-Academy publication *Graduate Training in the 21st Century.* Dr. Dalgleish went on to design and deliver professional and career development programming for researchers in the Research Institute at the Hospital for Sick Children, and since February 2020 she has been president of the Graduate and Professional Development Network, Canada's professional association for graduate and postgraduate career development professionals.

Sydni Dunn worked as staff reporter at *The Chronicle of Higher Education* from 2013, then moved to the Louisiana Department of Education in 2016, serving as press secretary then director of education. In 2020, she started up her own company, Sydni Dunn Consulting, LLC.

Susan Ferber is executive editor of American and world history at Oxford University Press in New York. Since leaving her PhD course in the mid '90s, she has accumulated over 20 years' experience in the publishing sector, and since 2005 has been a Book Workshop faculty member for Columbia University Libraries' publishing courses.

Christopher Flanagan is a postdoctoral researcher at Syracuse University, a position partly funded by an NEH Next Generation Humanities PhD planning grant. In this role he runs graduate professional development programming and researches new approaches to doctoral education in the humanities. Previous to this, he was a Mellon Fellow at the American Historical Association, working on the organization's Career Diversity initiative. He holds an MA in history from the University of Oxford and a PhD from the University of Notre Dame.

Joe Fruscione has been an independent copyeditor, proofreader, and quality control specialist since 2010. He switched career from professor to editor after eight years adjuncting, setting up his own company, The Consulting Editor, where he helps writers adapt their content to their situations, media, and target audiences. With Kelly Baker, he co-edited *Succeeding Outside the Academy* (2018), and since 2019 he has been a communications and advancement associate at the Siena School in Maryland.

Kristen Galvin is assistant professor of art history and director of the art history program at the University of Colorado. Previously she was assistant director for graduate engagement and lecturer at the University of Florida's Center for the Humanities and the Public Sphere. She is also an advocate for the public humanities, doctoral reform, and fair labor practices in higher education. She has published in the *Journal of Popular Music Studies, Critical Studies in Men's Fashion, Leonardo Electronic Almanac, Art Journal Open, American Book Review* and in edited collections. She received her PhD in visual studies from the University of California, Irvine.

Howard Gardner is Hobbs Research Professor of Cognition and Education at Harvard Graduate School of Education. Among numerous honors, he received a MacArthur Prize and a fellowship from the John S. Guggenheim Memorial Foundation in 1981 and 2000, respectively. The author of 30 books (translated into 32 languages) and several hundred articles, Gardner has since the 1990s directed The Good Project, a group of initiatives that promote excellence and ethics in education.

Malcolm Gaskill is emeritus professor of early modern history at the University of East Anglia. He taught for nearly 30 years in various universities in the UK, and is the author of six books, the most recent of which is *The Ruin of All Witches: Life and Death in the New World* (Penguin, 2021). A regular contributor to the *London Review of Books*, Gaskill has, since leaving academia, become a full-time writer. He remains a fellow of the Royal Historical Society and lives outside Cambridge.

Katie Rose Guest Pryal, JD, PhD, is an IPPY-award-winning author, keynote speaker, and professor of law and creative writing. She is the author of the bestselling *Life of the Mind Interrupted: Essays on Mental Health and Disability in Higher Education* (2017); the Foreword INDIE Gold-winner *The Freelance Academic: Transform Your Creative Life and Career* (2019); and the IPPY Gold-winner *Even If You're Broken: Essays on Sexual Assault and #MeToo* (2019). Pryal writes often about her subjects of expertise for national magazines, including *Catapult, The Toast, Women in Higher Education, The Chronicle of Higher Education, Quartz, The Establishment*, and many more. She lives in Chapel Hill, North Carolina.

Pepita Hesselberth is DFF laureate and assistant professor film and digital media at the Centre for the Arts in Society at Leiden University. She is the author of *Cinematic Chonotopes* (Bloomsbury, 2014), and co-editor of, among other books, *Compact Cinematics* (Bloomsbury, 2016) and *Legibility in the Age of Signs and Machines* (Brill, 2018). She received a fellowship from the Danish Council for Independent Research, was appointed as a research fellow in the Department of Arts and Cultural Studies at the University of Copenhagen (2016-2018), and is the editor-in-chief of a Leiden University Press series.

Constantina Katsari is an internationally acknowledged author, speaker, mentor, and trainer. She received a PhD in economic history from University College London in 2001, followed by a long and successful career in UK academia, including lecturing at the University of Leicester from 2005 to 2013. She has an even longer career as an entrepreneur, and currently specializes in helping high-growth startups and businesses get access to investment and grants, through a large network of investors and mentors eager to inspire businesses and startups in the UK Midlands.

Christine Kelly is assistant dean for student professional development at Fordham University, where she plans and implements new opportunities for graduate student professional development, for both academic and non-academic careers. Previous to this, she directed Fordham Graduate School's Futures program, providing graduate skills training and career resources. She received her PhD in American history from Fordham in 2019.

Karen Kelsky is the founder and CEO of The Professor Is In, which provides advice and consulting services on the academic job search and all elements of the academic and post-academic career. She speaks nationally and internationally on topics related to PhD professionalization, and was a columnist for *Chronicle Vitae*. As the creator of the Sexual Harassment in the Academy Survey and the #MeTooPhD hashtag, Karen speaks nationally on issues of sexual assault in the academy, with a focus on empowering victims and training people in leadership. She is a former tenured professor and department head at the University of Illinois at Urbana-Champaign and the University of Oregon. She is at work on a second edition of her book *The Professor Is In: The Essential Guide to Turning Your Ph.D. Into a Job* (Random House, 2015), and with Kel Weinhold runs the Professor Is In podcast.

Sarah Kendzior is an American journalist, author, anthropologist, researcher, and scholar. Kendzior received a PhD in anthropology from Washington University in St. Louis, and has written for a variety of outlets, including *Al Jazeera*, *The Guardian*, *Foreign Policy*, *Marie Claire*, and the *Boston Globe*. She is the author of *The View from Flyover Country* – a collection of essays first published by *Al Jazeera* – and is co-host of the Gaslit Nation podcast. In 2020, she published her second book, *Hiding in Plain Sight: The Invention of Donald Trump and the Erosion of America*. She lives in St. Louis, Missouri, with her partner and children.

Terran (Heather) Lane is senior architect at athenahealth, a medical administration services provider. After 10 years at the University of New Mexico as a professor of computer science, she joined Google in Cambridge, Massachusetts, working on projects including Knowledge Graph and Google Books. In her current work at athenahealth she deploys the company's immense store of healthcare data to improve healthcare experiences for clinicians and patients.

Oliver Lee Bateman has become a contributing writer to *The Ringer*, *MEL* magazine, and *Splice Today* since leaving academia. He co-hosts the podcast What's Left? and freelances for many other publications. Since 2018, he has worked in various capacities for the real estate company CBRE, first in business operations, then in risk assessment, and currently as a global marketing manager with a specialization in writing and research. In late 2016 he moved back to his hometown of Pittsburgh, where he resides on the city's north side with his wife and daughter.

Alexandra M. Lord received her PhD from the University of Wisconsin. After leaving a tenure-track position at Montana State University in 1998, Dr. Lord held a visiting professorship at SUNY New Paltz. After positions in the Office of the US Public Health Service and the National Park Service, she has overseen the Division of Medicine and Science at the Smithsonian National Museum of American History since 2015. She has frequently written about the historical profession for *The Chronicle of Higher Education.* An active public historian, Dr. Lord served as president of the National Council on Public History between 2016 and 2018. For the past fifteen years, she has run the public history website, Beyond Academe.

Josh Marshall is an American journalist and blogger, and the founder of Talking Points Memo, a leading political news and opinion website. Josh received a PhD in US History from Brown University, but wanted to write for a larger audience, and launched the Talking Points Memo blog at the end of 2000. Twenty years later, the TPM brand has grown into a major part of the political blogosphere, notably winning a Polk Award in 2007 for its coverage of the 2006 US attorneys scandal.

Liz Morrish is an independent scholar and activist for resistance to managerial appropriation of the university. She is a visiting fellow at York St John University. She was principal lecturer and subject leader of linguistics at Nottingham Trent University until speaking out and writing about the mental health of academics brought about her resignation in 2016. She is co-author of a book on managerial discourse in the neoliberal academy, entitled *Academic Irregularities* (Routledge, 2020) and writes a blog with the same name. Having exited the academy, Liz now has more time for other activities, and spends time as a marathon swim observer.

Ian Saxine teaches Early American History at Bridgewater State University, runs the Historian's Forum at the Maine Historical Society, and hosts the podcast Mainely History. His first book, *Properties of Empire: Indians, Colonists, and Land Speculators in New England* (NYU Press, 2019), examines the dynamic relationship between indigenous and English systems of property in early America. The concept and genre of "quit lit" became ubiquitous during his succession of one-year VAP postings, prompting his frustrated outburst in the winter of 2018 and the piece included in this volume.

Rebecca Schuman is a translator, copywriter, consultant, speaker and adjunct professor of literature, German, and creative writing. She is the author of the books *Kafka and Wittgenstein* and *Schadenfreude, A Love Story*, and of a forthcoming English annotated translation of *The Twins*, a play by F. M. Klinger. Her writing appears regularly in *Slate* and *The Chronicle of Higher Education*, and occasionally in numerous other national and international outlets. She lives in Eugene, Oregon, with her daughter.

Grant Shreve is a writer and independent scholar living in Baltimore, Maryland. He spent four years on the academic job market. Between 2013 and 2018 he served in editorial roles at an academic journal and an information services company, and in 2018 he became senior writer for the Office of the President at Johns Hopkins University.

James M. Van Wyck is an assistant dean for professional development with the GradFUTURES team in the Office of the Dean of the Graduate School at Princeton University. Prior to Princeton, he worked for Robert Weisbuch and Associates (RWA), where he served as a senior research fellow and associate. He is co-editor of *The Reimagined PhD: Navigating 21st Century Humanities Education* (Rutgers University Press, 2021).

Jennifer Vannette is an independent public historian who offers a variety of presentations, classes, and workshops to the public. She earned her doctorate from Central Michigan University. Her current projects include helping Anti-Racist Midland with an oral history project that examines the Black experience in Midland, Michigan, from 1960, and research on the 1967 Saginaw Riot. Jennifer occasionally writes history articles for public-facing media, including the *Midland Daily News*, *The Mudsill*, *AHA Today*, *Medium*, and the *Washington Post*.

Matt Welsh is the vice president of engineering at OctoML, a Seattle-based startup developing technology to optimize machine learning models. He left Harvard after getting tenure to join Google, where he became an engineering director on the Chrome team, eventually growing a team of more than 40 engineers to build out Chrome features for emerging markets. After more than eight years at Google, he jumped ship to join the startup world, where he enjoys hacking code again and learning to survive without free food.

L. Maren Wood is the founder and CEO of Beyond the Professoriate, a mission-driven organization dedicated to helping graduate students and PhDs thrive in today's fast-changing economy. She received a PhD from the University of North Carolina at Chapel Hill in 2011, then founded and acted as lead researcher for Lilli Research Group. In 2017 she founded Beyond the

Professoriate, which provides resources for individuals and partners with universities and professional organizations to help PhDs leverage their education wherever smart people are needed.

Glenn Wright is director of graduate school programs at Syracuse University. He has a BA in English from Carleton College in Northfield, Minnesota, and an MA and PhD from the University of Michigan, Ann Arbor. He has worked in academic assessment, publishing, and higher-ed administration, and has taught English at the University of Michigan and the University at Albany, SUNY. He is the editor of *The Mentoring Continuum: From Graduate School through Tenure* (2015).

INDEX